In the Company
—— of a ——
Known Felon

VIC FRIERSON

Fulton Books, Inc.
Meadville, PA

Published by Fulton Books 2019

ISBN 978-1-63338-898-7 (paperback)
ISBN 978-1-63338-899-4 (digital)

Printed in the United States of America

Contents

Prologue

O. J. Simpson. I'm sure you feel, or have felt at one point in time, some combination of disgust and revulsion at the mere mention of Mr. Simpson. He is arguably America's most infamous felon. Historically, the word *felon* meant "a wicked person." Right now, there is a commonly held belief that Mr. Simpson is just that: a wicked person.

Now, if you please, indulge me for a moment and walk to the closest mirror or reflective surface and take a look at yourself. What do you see? I'll tell you what's looking back at you: a felon. Even if you've never been to jail, never been arrested, or never seen the inside of a court room, you are a felon. That is because a *felon* is defined as a person who has committed a grave offense commonly punishable in the United States by imprisonment for one year or more.

Take a moment to think about the implications of what I just said. You do not have to be convicted of a grave offense; you do not have to be on trial for a grave offense; you do not even have to be accused of a grave offense. The act of commission is enough for you to be considered a felon. Downloading music or movies off the Internet illegally? Felony. Cursing and threatening the person who cut you off in traffic? That fits the definition of terroristic threats, assault, and/or harassment. All can be considered felonies. Fudging information on your taxes? That's a big-time felony, the same felony that took down Al Capone, Wesley Snipes, and many other well-known members of American society. Three drinks at the bar followed by a quick drive home—are you sure that your blood/alcohol level is less than .08? DUI can be a dangerous felony in some states.

As sure as you are reading this, I am just as sure that you have committed a felony. Yet I am also willing to bet that, save a minute percentage of people reading this, you do not consider yourself a "wicked person." In fact, you probably feel the exact opposite: you are a tax-paying, law-abiding citizen who may have made a mistake or two in the past but nothing that would warrant jail time. But as a practicing attorney, I promise you this: tell me enough stories about your past, and I'm guaranteed to find a way to fit your adventures, misdeeds, and fun times into the crimes code of whatever jurisdiction you reside in.

America is full of felons; it was even founded by felons. Under the laws of our mother country, Great Britain, every person who signed the Declaration of Independence was guilty of treason, a felony punishable by death. History has been kind to the founding fathers, but in our current society, America is very hard on felons. We don't hire them. We don't want to live next to them. We don't want to be associated with them. And we don't want to help them reintegrate into society. And in some instances, our gut reaction is probably correct. Personally, there's no way to convince me that someone is a reformed child molester. But not every felon is guilty of child molestation. And not every felon is a threat to your personal safety. The difference between the person who is reading this who doesn't have a criminal record and the person reading this who does have a criminal record is some combination of luck, networking and timing. The majority of American citizens simply haven't been caught (yet) in the commission of their felonies. Some have been caught and spent large sums of money to ensure that they were cleared and their record remained clean. The ones who were caught are destined to remain forever labeled as wicked members of society, whether they deserve such treatment or not.

So what should we do with our felons? I mean, what would you want done with you if you couldn't get out of the assault charge for the bar fight in which you beat the guy up for insulting and assaulting a female patron? Or the malicious destruction of property conviction on your record for taking the baseball bat to the headlights of an asshole driver who got mad because you had the audacity to change lanes in front of him while he was speeding and he showed his displeasure by flashing his high beams at you…for almost a mile?

That high school diploma doesn't outweigh your felony conviction. Your college degree won't amount to a pile of beans once an employer runs a background check. The biggest insult to injury is that the two biggest pieces of shit in this equation—the drunk guy picking on the girl at the bar and the reckless driver who thinks everyone on the road should get out of his way—are free to walk the streets without any sort of blight on their printable history.

Of course, we don't view our felons in terms of real-life situations. We see jail as an unnecessary blight on society: *I've never been convicted of a crime. I'm a good person. If everyone were like me, there would be no need for jail.* Problem is that more likely than not, these felons are just like you. When they go to jail, you are told (along with the rest of society) by the state and federal governments that run the prisons that inmates are supposed to be rehabilitated, granted access to treatment programs, allowed to enroll in trade classes, and given every chance and opportunity to change their lives and their future. And every piece of information you have at your fingertips tells you the state and federal governments are lying to your face (again). You see the shows on cable television. You talk to your friends and family members who were incarcerated. You overhear the horror stories. You've seen either *American History X*, *Shawshank Redemption*, and/or any other prison movies. You know that in jail, you do not want to drop the soap!

My point is this: not every felon is Jeffrey Dahmer, nor is every felon a reformed, upstanding member of society. Like people in general, convicted felons cover every part of the spectrum. And in this diverse population of convicted felons, there are a lot of people who have stories to tell and contributions to make if given a voice and half a chance. Unfortunately, the circumstances surrounding their incarceration makes it damn near impossible to do anything other than be a drain on taxpayer dollars.

I personally know plenty of convicted felons: men found guilty of murder, attempted murder, assault, battery, drug distribution, tax evasion, fraud, and other crimes. And I will swear on everything I hold dear that some of these men and women are among the finest people I've ever met.

As well, the opposite could be said about those people who have no criminal records. There are some people who are walking the streets right now who do not have a criminal record who are some of the vilest, most'disgusting human beings you could possibly imagine. You live next door to them. You work with them. You go to/went to school with them. Most importantly, you do not think highly of them at all. For convicted felons, we as a society feel we have the right to judge them, their character, and their entire life *because we have tangible proof of their mistakes*. We won't even waste the time to examine their character. A felon is a felon, no matter how much better of a person they may be than the neighbor who makes your blood boil. Such is life, I guess...

You may think it is right. Even if it may not be fair, life isn't supposed to be fair. You may believe that I am spouting some political agenda to make you feel sorry for the plight of the "poor criminal." Nothing could be further from the truth. Instead, I am asking you to examine why your favorite sports team can employ felons but your job—the common workplace—cannot. I am questioning why it is okay for the movie and music studios to cast and glorify felons, but it is not okay for you to associate with one. I challenge you to admit whether or not you stereotype or assume a person is a felon by their age, race, gender, or national origin. Would I have to call you out if you saw me in court, wearing a suit, and assumed I was the defendant and not the attorney?

I finish my narrative by saying this: The author of this book, Vic Frierson, is one of the finest people I know. I have known him for more than half my life and have found him to be a man of principle, intelligence, faith, and conviction. While in the midst of a gambling addiction, he committed a crime to which he entered a guilty plea. He was convicted. I will not gloss over that fact and make it seem like it is anything other than what it really is: a felony. Mr. Frierson is a felon. However, I refuse to judge him solely for that mistake. I have nearly twenty years of evidence to support my belief in Mr. Frierson as a person, while a large section of society will rely solely on one line from his background check: Conviction—Wire Fraud.

This is the system we have created; this is how we have chosen to mold our society. This system has served us well, right? Overcrowded prisons, high recidivism rates, and a criminal justice system that is somewhere between overburdened and completely broken.

We are a society that values individuality. Yet we are quick to paint with a broad brush when it comes to certain segments of society, including convicted felons. Stereotyping, generalizing, and lazy ideology have become the norm. Certain felons are lifelong criminals who are in and out of jail. But there is a large portion of felons who made a mistake, paid their debt to society, and long to move forward and become productive members of society. Some succeed; many do not. And when they do not succeed, it feeds the narrative we have already created in our mind about criminals being unwilling to change. But did we really give them a realistic chance of success?

As an attorney, I am a part of this legal system and this process many of us bemoan. I am also a part of a profession that is the butt of many jokes. Everyone hates lawyers…until they need one. And if you ever need my services, you wouldn't want me to paint your situation with a broad brush. You would want me to listen to you, as an individual, and hear your story.

It is in that vein that I urge you to read this book. Consider the possibility that the author—despite being a felon, as he surely is—just might have something meaningful to say. I believe in the motto "In the fight for justice, no fight is too small." I fight not only for the good name of Vic Frierson but also, more importantly, for the thousands of other felons whose interests he dares to represent. Because the next time you hear or use the label "convicted felon," your reaction should not be revulsion, disgust, or even sympathy. It should simply be "There, but for the grace of God, go I."

Brandon O. Alexander, Esq.

The Premise and the Promise

The Premise

Before January 3, 2011, on the basis of what I researched about the prison experience, I was of the impression that prisons were bastions of positive change. After all, in the 1980s, many had literally changed their names from "prisons" to "correctional institutions," to reflect not only their role as society's protectors but their *responsibility* for the rehabilitation of the individuals in their care, custody and control.

Before January 3, 2011, I believed that correctional institutions were places where willing inmates could obtain formal educations, learn hard skills, and acquire life skills and abilities—perhaps, trades—that would aid their reentry into society upon release.

Before January 3, 2011, I believed that correctional institutions were staffed by competent, caring individuals who took seriously their vital roles in the rehabilitation process: correctional officers who basically preserved the order and case managers and counselors who helped inmates develop and implement plans for their personal and professional improvement.

In July 2010, I entered a guilty plea to one count of wire fraud. On November 3 of that year, a judge in the United States District Court of Maryland (MD) pronounced my punishment. He sentenced me to serve fifteen months in a federal prison, to be followed by twelve months of home detention. On January 3, 2011, I surrendered into the custody of the Federal Prison Camp in Cumberland, Maryland. Thus began the thirteen-month ordeal in which every notion I ever had about the role of prisons—and the principles and promises asserted by the American Correctional Association (referenced in more detail later)—were summarily shattered.

So astounded was I by what I saw and encountered at FPC Cumberland that I wanted to find a way to make others aware, others who, like I was, are totally misconceived about prisons and prisoners. Admittedly, I wanted to do so for the benefit of inmates—the reservoir of able minds and manpower that is merely being warehoused. The system is failing them, for sure. That was the easy part. That was the challenge that everyone who knows me would expect me to write about.

My bigger—but, by far, more *urgent*—challenge was that I wanted to do so for the benefit of American society. I wanted to reach the people who, heretofore, never gave a second thought about prisons, let alone about the prison systems' impact on *them*. I wanted to expose how unknowing taxpayers—on the premise that they are being "tough on crime"—underwrite the wanton waste, gross incompetence, and corruption that masquerades as federal corrections in this country. The system fails taxpayers and their communities even more egregiously than it does inmates! It's like going to the butcher shop, paying for a roast but only getting the fat. Where's the beef?

What resulted from my ordeal is this book. Be forewarned: I am not a writer. I'm an activist. So I wrote this book for the following reasons:

1. The federal justice system relegates thousands upon thousands of lives to the care, custody and control of the federal correctional system, for *enormous* chunks of time, without the possibility of parole.

2. Correctional facilities, by the ACA's definition, bear the minimum responsibility of trying to effect meaningful rehabilitation of the individuals in their care, custody, and control; I contend that it is the correctional system's *debt to society*.

3. Since the 1990s, despite a *quadrupling* of spending on corrections in this country, the rate of recidivism among released offenders remains at around 40 percent.

4. Significant portions of federal correctional institution's budgets are allocated to provide case management and counseling services as the first lines of support and rehabilitation of the people in their care, custody, and control.
5. Correctional institutions are also budgeted to provide other programming that improves the skills, abilities, education, and life skills of the people in its care, custody, and control.
6. Arguably because federal correctional institutions either forsake or are derelict in the *quality* fulfillment of their case management, counseling, and other programming obligations, recidivism remains high and the cause of rehabilitation is ill-served.

Therefore, this book's simple premise is that the federal prison system—that costs American taxpayers billions upon billions of dollars and yields few of the benefits (to inmates or to society) that the public expects—is rife with inefficiency, indifference, and incompetence that renders it ineffectual. It is my observation—and for good measure, those of eight of my fellow inmates, whom I interviewed for this book—that most of the system's shortcomings, problems, and missed opportunities are entirely fixable, with little-to-no added expense...

The Promise

According to its website, The American Correctional Association (ACA) is "the oldest and largest international correctional association in the world." The ACA establishes and monitors the standards and practices by which correctional institutions operate. Moreover, it formally accredits institutions.

The ACA aspires to facilitate everything, "…from professional development and certification to standards and accreditation, from networking to consulting to research and publications, and from conferences and exhibits to technology and testing" to ensure the excellence, efficacy, and integrity for its individual and institutional members. As it boldly asserts, "ACA is…the leading worldwide authority in corrections."

Since it was first organized in 1870, the ACA has been a vanguard for the effectiveness of both the field of corrections and its practitioners. In an early document that set forth the organization's view of the principles, beliefs, and values that underlie the practice of corrections, the ACA wrote the following:

> The treatment of criminals by society is for the protection of society. But since such treatment is directed to the criminal rather than the crime, its great objective should be his regeneration.

Today, the word *regeneration* would be interchanged with the word *rehabilitation*. Thus, the ACA has, from its inception, embraced the ideal that the field of corrections bears a dual responsibility to (a) protect society from miscreants and (b) make an effort to redevelop miscreants, in order to help them return to society as productive citizens. The same ACA document continues:

> The state has not discharged its whole duty to the criminal when it has punished him, nor even when it has reformed him. Having raised him up, it has further duty to aid in holding him up. In

vain shall we have given the convict an improved mind and heart, in vain shall we have imparted to him the capacity for industrial labor and the desire to advance himself by worthy means, if, on his discharge, he finds the world in arms against him, with none to trust him, none to meet him kindly, none to give him the opportunity of earning honest bread.

There it is. Uncut. The world's leading authority in the field of corrections espouses the philosophy that effective corrections has three essential components: punishment, rehabilitation, and a forgiving public that understands the importance of both.

The preamble to the ACA's "Declaration of Principles" proffers:

We believe that [the] principles of humanity, justice, protection, opportunity, knowledge, competence and accountability are essential to the foundation of sound corrections policy and effective public protection.

The ACA "Declaration of Principles" goes on to list no fewer than seventeen principles, which, if genuinely adhered to, would help assure quality outcomes for both the prisoner and society. They include the following:

- Corrections is responsible for providing programs and constructive activities that promote positive change for responsible citizenship.
- Corrections must demonstrate integrity, respect, dignity, and fairness, and pursue a balanced program of humaneness, restoration, rehabilitation.
- The dignity of individuals, the rights of all people, and the potential for human growth and development must be respected.

I interpret the ACA's principles as more than merely a statement of mission. I interpret it as a promise. It is a promise that those involved in the corrections profession—institutions and individuals—will make an earnest effort to engender rehabilitation...or "regeneration," as it is referred to in the aforementioned excerpt... from which both society and the inmate will benefit.

"I Hate Bullies!"

I was born in Louisville, Kentucky. My birth certificate confirms that I was born of Etta Jean Frierson, on July 20, 1954. My father is documented as "Unknown." That said, Craig Gatewood married my mother when I was three or four and raised and loved me as his own...until his death in 2009. In fact, until I was nineteen, I had no idea that he was not my biological dad. I thought he had sired me, only out of wedlock.

Mine seemed as normal an upbringing as anyone else's in Louisville's Beecher Terrace low-rise housing project. There were single-parent families, like the Mickens, the Wiggins, and the Dudleys as well as two-parent families, like mine, the Andersons, and the Dukes. There were apartments that seemed to have way-y-y too many people living in them—like those of two of my relatives: the Gatewoods and the Millers. And there were apartments in which resided the elderly, like the two Smith couples.

I am the oldest of what would have been seven children, barring the infant deaths of one sister and one brother. I am, and have always been, an intensely protective big brother. I was the seventeen-year-old boy who took odd jobs at the small grocery store on the corner of Sixteenth and Kentucky streets to "earn" scraps of cold cuts to feed my siblings when my mother was in the throes of mental illness. I'm the eighteen-year-old who did the gut-wrenchingly unthinkable—swore out the inquest warrants to have his mother committed to a mental institution—*twice*—when he feared that she had become a danger to her own and his infant brother's life. I'm the one who constantly tried to defend the honor and well-being of his timid younger brother from countless more aggressive denizens of the Cotter Homes

17

housing project; the one who, at nineteen, got his GED so he could get a job and help support his family; the one who—twice—physically wrested his sister from abusive relationships, the latter of which times, moving her from Louisville to Baltimore to live with him; the one who commandeered his floundering baby brother to live with him in New York; and the one who helped facilitate, in one way or another, his siblings' recoveries from a variety of addictions. And I'm the one, as a consequence, whose relationship with his siblings has taken on decidedly parental overtones—perhaps more parent than brother. At the end of the day, I'm a bona fide peace lover; just don't mess with me or mine lest you incur the full extent of my ire.

I was a big child. At nine years old, I was about 5'9", 170 pounds; at twelve, I was six feet, one-half inch tall, 212 pounds; at sixteen, 6'4", 340. Between ages nine and fifteen, my shoe size grew each year to correspond with my age. I literally hulked and towered over my peers. Though I was amply rough and tumble, I was not a ruffian. I could fight—and I *would* fight—but only in defense of mine or myself.

It's funny what one recalls from his childhood: 413 South Eleventh Street—my address in Beecher Terrace from 1958 to 1964; 585-2534—my phone number; 585-5723, 587-7927, 584-7519—my two grandmothers' and my cousins' phone numbers, respectively. Bonita Haines—my first grade schoolmate, who used to call me on the phone and make me sing to her.

I was nine years old on this particular spring Sunday in '63. I went out to play with a couple of friends—brothers of the surname Shield. One was a classmate of mine in Ms. McCall's fourth-grade class at Samuel Coleridge Taylor Elementary School; the other, a year or two older. The Shields lived on the alley behind Jefferson Street, between Twelfth and Thirteenth Streets—just up from the fire station that's at Twelfth and Jefferson Streets, right across from Beecher Terrace's Baxter Park.

We could have played in the park, as we usually did when I played with the Shields, but on this day, we didn't. Instead, we messed around in the street for a while—doing what, I don't especially recall;

I guess nothing in particular. But the Shields introduced me to a neighbor of theirs—a much older boy named Oliver.

Oliver was about as tall as me, though heavier set and very dark-complexioned. He appeared to be in his mid to late teens—I'd guess sixteen to eighteen. He walked as though his feet hurt—more sliding than stepping—in the large but dingy, ragged, badly run-over, used-to-be-white sneakers he wore. His T-shirt and khaki pants were as tattered and filthy as his shoes. His mini-Afro was nappy and full of lint, on an overly large head that sat at about a forty-five-degree angle atop the neck that I could only assume he had. And as if his unkemptness weren't enough, he was loud and boorish…all of which conspired to exacerbate his overall unpleasantness.

Somehow, we all made our way to the front of a crumbling vacant house in their block. Across the street from the house, there sat a forty-something couple on the front steps drinking something neat and brown from mismatched glass tumblers. The man and woman knew all the boys except me, admonishing the entire pack of us to be careful, as we made our way into the empty but open property.

For a while, we played around in the house—up and down the steps, in and out of the ramshackle rooms. Then after a few minutes, the big kid, Oliver, called me into a room where he and the Shields were. The moment I entered the room, Oliver grabbed me from behind, holding my arms together at the elbows. I wrestled with him and struggled as best I could, but I was ultimately overpowered. I fought to no avail, laughing and still thinking it was all part of our horseplay…until I heard the bigger boy tell the Shields, "Here, hold him." As they complied, each grabbing an arm, I wheeled around to see Oliver starting to unzip his pants. Of course, by then, it was finally clear to me what was happening; this big bastard was going to try and rape me!

The first thing I thought about was the two people outside, drinking on their steps. So I started to scream and yell, "*Stop! Let me go! Stop! Let me go!*" And I started fighting again. Not punching anyone, just trying to break free. The Shields tried to hold me, but they were just too small to control the burst of power. Like I said, I was not aggressive, but I was far bigger than my playmates—and, as a consequence, far stronger. And as a byproduct of my docility, I tended not to know my own strength. So I broke away from the much smaller Shields fairly easily, but I still had Oliver to deal with.

As I tried to leave, he grabbed me by the arm. This time, I stomped one of his big bad-ass feet...and I bit him on his arm. Hard—as in latched on! I can almost still taste the saltiness and stench of his sweat and blood. Now, *he* was screaming...and trying to beat me off him, as I maintained a gator's grip on his filthy ass forearm. Nine years old! Laser focused on biting a chunk out of this nasty bastard's arm. Meanwhile, out of the corner of my eye, I saw the Shields skedaddle out of the house...which kind of brought me back to the bigger point; I needed to get the heck out of there. So I released my bite grip on Oliver's arm. Upon my doing so, Oliver's first move was to grab his arm, writhing in pain...at which opening I seized upon to scram!

I ran home straightway—past the Shields, past the unknowing couple across the street. And I never spoke a word of the incident— *ever*. Not to my parents. Not to my siblings. Not to my cousins. Not to my teacher. Not to the authorities—the firemen and the policemen, who were always at the fire station.

I never confronted the Shields, either—nor did they ever mention it to me. We continued as schoolmates, but I never played with them again. Through the years, I've wondered whether they were complicit because they simply didn't know any better or because Oliver had victimized them too. But at the time, I didn't know. I just tucked it away, deep into the recesses of my mind. I was nine. Nine-year-olds can do that. I never spoke a word of the encounter to anyone...until now.

As for Oliver, the next time I saw him was in 1974. I was nineteen, working on my first job, as a salesman at a small men's clothing store in Louisville's East End. He came in one day, as a customer; I helped him. I still remember what he bought: a pair of Levi's flared-bottom jeans—size 38 × 34. I recognized him immediately, while he seemed to not know me at all. And in that very moment— just as I am now—recounting it, I became filled with alternating feelings of anger and shame: (1) at the recollection of what he'd tried to do to me, (2) at the thought that he had attempted such a heinous act and had not even bothered to remember the face of his would-be victim, and (3) that I had done nothing about it.

That incident scarred me deeply because despite never doing anything or telling anyone about it, I never forgot. It's as fresh in my memory today, as if it happened only yesterday. I just swept it under a rug—for damned near fifty years. But two lifelong byproducts of the episode are these: (1) I can sweep almost anything under the rug and just move on, and (2) I *hate* bullies.

I liked school; it was easy for me. I was an excellent student—straight As in elementary and junior high school. After completing eighth grade, I was chosen to attend a state-funded learning experiment called the Lincoln School (www.thelincolnschool.com). Nestled in the woods, about equidistant between Louisville and the state capitol of Frankfort, Lincoln was conceived as a project in which select students from throughout Kentucky could be schooled from an accelerated curriculum but in a sequestered environment. The selection criteria were that students must be high academic performers, but from families that were economically disadvantaged.

I completed one year at Lincoln. Then in the autumn of my second year (1969), I was wrongly accused of misconduct by a racist administrator—and expelled. Rather than fight, I just swept the incident under a rug and moved on.

During my junior year at Louisville's Male High School, my parents separated. My father left the household. My mother sank into a deep abyss of alcohol abuse and clinical depression. Because neither my father nor my mother gave me the money to buy them, I went through the entire school year without the required books… and still managed a B average. More importantly, I became the sixteen-year-old surrogate head of the household.

I entered my senior year at Male needing but one credit to graduate—in English. Meanwhile, the tumult in my immediate family only worsened, and the oppressing stress—the stress of being a seventeen-year-old high schooler feigning normalcy while trying to scrounge enough resources by whatever means necessary to see that my four siblings were fed—that stress intensified. Finally, in April of 1972—on track to pass my English class—I dropped out of high school, a mere two months shy of graduating. Check the '72 yearbook. I'm cited as a graduating senior. I'm named among "Senior Superlatives" as "Best Singer." So close was I to the finish line that many of my classmates think/thought I *did* graduate; so much so that through the years I've been invited to and have attended class reunion after class reunion. But I did not graduate. I dropped out. And I swept the entire episode under a rug and moved on.

In January of 1974, I earned my GED. In September 1975, I enrolled for classes at the University of Louisville, still working at the clothing store. And…and I fell in love for the first time.

In December of 1976, I experienced for the first time the painful but inevitable hazard of falling in love—a broken heart. This time, I fell into my own morass of depression and drug abuse—but I did so quietly, lying on a dormitory room floor, under a constant hail of reefer smoke, listening to Stevie, Marvin, and Earth, Wind, and Fire, and watching *Bugs Bunny* cartoons. Then in October 1977, I quit school and got married to another woman altogether. And thereby, I swept the devastation of my first heartbreak under the rug and moved on.

In 1986, I moved to New York (NY) to pursue my aspirations as a singer—to a town called Newburgh, sixty miles upstate from New York City. In short order, I signed on with a band that was working regularly throughout the northeast United States—mostly New York, New Jersey (NJ), and Connecticut. I was staying busy, musically, doing everything I intended.

In 1987, I even signed a recording contract—with a company called Bon Ami Records. At that time, Bon Ami was the next iteration of the infamous Sugar Hill Records—generally noted as the original purveyors of rap music. I signed a three-year new artist contract that, in retrospect, would have raped me worse than Oliver tried to.

Like many others, music is very much a copycat industry. An act that catches on for one record label is almost always replicated by the others. For instance, if a Michael Jackson worked at Epic or a Madonna at Warner Brothers, then every label had to have its own versions, a copycat. It's an industry that, despite the illusion it perpetrates of being able to "discover the new and the fresh," is always looking for the "next" something or other. I venture to say that the average person would be surprised at just how little genuine originality there is among music industry types.

At any rate, I was signed to be groomed as one of Bon Ami's male "adult contemporary" acts—sort of their Luther Vandross, whose ascension in the biz was in full tilt. Except they never recorded me, not one note. When I called their offices, as I did repeatedly, they neither answered my calls nor returned my messages. Once, in an atypical display of assertiveness, I even drove from Newburgh down to the owner's Inglewood, New Jersey, home. When I knocked at the door, the maid, peeking through a transom window beside the front door, claimed that no one was available to see me. It was comically reminiscent of the scene in *The Wizard of Oz*, where Dorothy, Toto, and company arrived at the door of Emerald City but were dismissed by an attendant peeking through a similar window.

For most of the next three years, I languished on Bon Ami's rolls—no calls, no contact, no nothing. Until one day in late May of 1990, when I got a call from the company's business manager. He said he needed to send me three or four songs that he wanted me to record. The recording sessions, for which he didn't give me a date-certain, would be at George Benson's studio, up near Bear Mountain (New York). And to be clear, in that moment, I longed for *nothing* more fervently than to be a recording artist. But…

Rather than to relate my excitement or rather than to confirm my intention to comply, my response to fast-talking Bob's assignment was—and I will never forget the conversation: "Where the hell y'all been, man? How come you didn't return any of my calls in the past three years?"

"*What?* Are you kidding?"

"Hell no, I'm not kidding. How come, in three years, none of you guys returned any of my calls? It's a simple matter of respect, Bob."

"*Respect?*"

"Yeah, respect!"

Then in almost stereotypical New Jersey-ese, he says, "Look, Vic. Not for nuthin', but do you wanna do this or not?"

My famous last words were, "Well, I guess not!" The next thing I heard was a click and a dial tone.

I had done everything in my power to get exactly the outcome that was now before me. I was thirty-five years old, competing in an industry that covets artists half my age. This opportunity was precisely what, in 1986, I had left all that I knew and loved, in hopes of accomplishing.

But in my mind, they were bullies, and I imagined myself to be standing on the right side of principle. So rather than to call him right back, I decided to wait until the next day and then the next then the next. Until I *never* called back, and neither did he. I swept the episode—right along with, perhaps, the opportunity of a lifetime—under a rug and moved on.

Meanwhile, I was doing a ton of gigs with the band and learning a ton about the sometimes-dirty business of music.

At the same time, I was also honing my community and family-services skills as well as earning a steady income working as parent involvement coordinator for a local Head Start early education program. I was helping impoverished families understand the importance of their meaningful involvement in their children's academic careers, and in the process, I was coming to understand more deeply the barriers they—and by extension, their children—faced. And becoming more aware of the role I could play.

While working in both capacities—simultaneously, enlightened by all that I was learning and doing in the music industry and impassioned by the unfulfilled promise embodied in the young lives in which Head Start enabled me to make an impact—I was inspired to contemplate a program to use both assets. What resulted in 1989 was my first draft of the youth prevention initiative, I would eventually name the PEACE Project. The original program proposed to provide middle school-aged aspiring performing artists with opportunities to perform, while educating them about the business of performing arts—answering questions like "Where do royalties come from?" "What is publishing?" or "What is copyright?" As well, the program proposed to use workshops and other session work to enlighten participants about a narrow array of social issues—chief among them the perils of abusing drugs. Because I was working with Head Starters, my bright idea was to target their older siblings.

My efforts to obtain funding for the drug prevention program were ongoing but unsuccessful. Meanwhile, in 1992, my wife was transferred by her employer to their office in Baltimore. Despite all my developing personal and professional pursuits—the music, the work with Head Start families, the substance abuse initiative—I reluctantly relocated with her. Little did I know that Baltimore is where music careers go to die. So I swept everything—this time, my remaining artistic hopes and aspirations—under a rug and moved on.

In 1994, while working as a community organizer, I was finally successful getting funds for the youth program I'd been nursing since '89. Only, in Baltimore, the program's emphasis was changed. While Baltimore's funding community—foundations and government— was interested in addressing the issue of substance abuse, they had very little interest in substance abuse *prevention* programming. Rather, they opted to virtually pour money into drug programs that emphasized treatment and/or law enforcement.

At the time, in addition to a burgeoning drug addiction problem, Baltimore was losing three hundred people each year to gun violence. So in Baltimore, I altered my proposed prevention program to address the issue of *violence*, rather than drugs. Still targeting middle school-aged kids, I proposed essentially the same programming, but with "violence prevention" as the primary social issue. The director of the office for which I was a community organizer—a woman who, a few years later, was president of the board of directors for the organization that I defrauded—liked the proposal enough to award it $55,000 in 1994.

The project's grand opening was in December. In addition to a bevy of local and regional celebrities like comedian Joe Claire and keyboardist Marcus Johnson, our grand opening panel was headlined by actress Jada Pinkett, a Baltimore native. The project's first class was convened in January '95, with thirty teenagers enrolled for the year-round weekly four-hour sessions that met on Saturdays.

The PEACE Project ran beautifully—even more so than I had envisioned. The kids and their parents loved it, and so did I. Nonetheless, I soon learned firsthand the challenges of sustaining a prevention program.

Generally speaking, benefactors can be persuaded to fund prevention initiatives, albeit nominally—but they are less inclined to provide money to *pay* the people who run them. So for year one of the program, an assistant and I took pittances of $6,000 and $10,000 respectively. After that, it was a volunteer labor of love. I was able to sustain the project at a high level, using almost all volunteer personnel, piecing together grants from a variety of sources. Participation in the PEACE Project was free for the up to thirty kids per year we served—over 350 kids, overall, between 1995 and 2011...with one notable interruption.

In 1997, while in the midst of fundraising, I was robbed at gunpoint outside my apartment building by three teenaged thugs. Three thugs just walked up to me in broad daylight, brandished their pistols, made me hand over my wallet, took the twenty-seven dollars I had in it, handed back the wallet, and brazenly just *walked* away.

I guess I got off pretty easy, as muggings go. But so disheveled was I by the mugging that I immediately ceased and desisted with all of my fundraising efforts—and I decided to let the program dissolve. I allowed this single adverse encounter to cause me to give up on an entire generation. *How dare they?* I thought. *Don't they know what an advocate I am? Don't they know how hard I'm working to make a difference in their lives?* And yes, I realized then as I do now, how convoluted my rationale was. After all, these were three punks that were in no way related to or representative of the young people in the PEACE Project. Yet I swept the PEACE Project's future under a rug and I moved on.

Fortunately, two years later, my head was yanked out of the sand—and out of my ass—both by my lingering passion and by a young man, wise beyond his years, who was at the time a freshman at Johns Hopkins University (JHU). That young man, four years earlier, had been in the inaugural class of the PEACE Project. He had adopted me as his mentor, having permitted me the proximity and privilege of being a part of his most seminal moments: what schools to attend; how to navigate the challenges of being a teenager. I taught him how to drive a car (for as long as my heart could take it; after that, I paid for his lessons). I advised him about everything from girls to job choices and had the privilege of writing a letter supporting his candidacy to receive the coveted Marshall academic scholarship in England—which he won.

Now, as a student at JHU, he had extolled the virtues of his experience in the PEACE Project—and of me, personally—to officials at the university, and he wanted to facilitate a meeting—and a potential partnership—between the project and the university's community outreach office.

Renewed by that young man's ardor, I resumed efforts to obtain funding for the program. And with a grant from a Minneapolis-based foundation, I resurrected the PEACE Project in 1999—this time, with two new features: a tutorial program for PEACE Project kids who needed it and a mentoring component, in which PEACE kids spent time on campus with students of both JHU and Morgan State University (MSU), participating in a range of activities that included observing labs and attending sports events.

It was the same young man—now a professional freelance journalist—who, in July 2010, telephoned me in calm disbelief. He asked me if I was aware of the article in *The Daily Record* newspaper reporting that I had been charged with a count of wire fraud. I was not...aware of the article, that is. But I *was* aware that the day before, I had, indeed, entered a guilty plea in the US District Court of Baltimore to a single count of wire fraud. That charge and the subsequent plea stemmed from what the US attorney's office described in the plea agreement as a "scheme" to bilk a local nonprofit organization out of $233,000. My use of a credit card in the committal of the offense made it punishable under the statutes for wire fraud. A so-called reporter had cobbled together a story by scouring through the documents filed by the court.

I admitted my guilt to him. Then, with a good deal of shame, I explained to him what the newspaper story had not. First of all, I told him that there was no so-called "scheme." I told him that over a period of about three years, I had become so engrossed in a gambling addiction that I had, indeed, used that organization's card to underwrite my habit. I told him that I had grossly abused the unfettered access I had to their funds and that that abuse had spun way out of control. I also told him that neither I nor the prosecutor was sure of the precise amount of my misappropriation, despite the amount to which the published article reported that I pleaded in the agreement. I explained that, according to my attorney, the amount that they knew they could prove was substantially lower—about $120,000. When he asked me why I would plead to a higher amount, I could only respond by describing my "alternative," as it was explained to me. My alternative was to go to trial and try to defend myself against multiple counts, one for each of the more than thirty times I used the credit card.

In a state jurisdiction the great likelihood is that, as a first offender, I would have never gone to prison. I would likely have received some combination of home detention and probation. Frankly, I think that's precisely why the lawyers representing the organization steered my case to federal authorities. I think they wanted me to be prosecuted on a federal violation, because the "right" federal conviction would assure prison time. I think those lawyers wanted to ensure that jail time was a part of my punishment, which to me is the very definition of cutting off one's nose to spite one's face. "I'll get you...I'll hurt me."

What I mean is, my going to prison served no purpose that benefitted the victim—the organization. None. In fact, my going to prison—in conjunction with the ramifications of having a felony conviction—only served to delay or impair the sole avenue of direct redress available to the organization—namely, restitution. For example, in October 2010, I was chosen by the Open Society Institute to receive a $50,000 fellowship to expand the PEACE Project. The fellowship money was not for the program but was solely for me, in lieu of a salary. Without going to prison—being sentenced to, let's say, home detention—I could have accepted the fellowship and begun paying the $500 per month restitution payments ordered by the judge. Immediately. That would have meant payments totaling $6,500 during the thirteen months I was incarcerated, rather than the $0 they received (more on this later).

By contrast, since my release from prison in February 2012, I have experienced firsthand the bitter reality that the employment prospects for a fifty-eight-year-old disabled black man with a fresh felony conviction are severely limited in the Google-informed American workplace. As a consequence, as of February 2013, despite my exhaustive efforts, I remain unemployed. I have no income, with utterly no prospects for employment looming. Therefore, I can only make nominal good faith payments of $50/month—total: $600 for the twelve months since my release. "I'll get you…I'll hurt me."

At any rate, I explained to my young friend that there is no parole in the federal system, that one serves 85 percent of the time to which s/he is sentenced. Plus, for each offense of which one is convicted, there are minimum sentencing guidelines—some mandatory, some advisory. Therefore, if I had opted to go to trial, I would likely have been convicted on multiple counts, with each conviction carrying a separate minimum sentence.

That's because, as I told him, before I lawyered up, I had written a letter to the organization's board of directors, in which I admitted my guilt. Because the organization's board members were community people, unsavvy to the machinations of board function, I sincerely intended the letter as an apology for having violated their trust in me. The prosecutors saw it differently; they deemed it a confession.

So I told him I was sure that I would—rightfully—have been found guilty on multiple counts and that I would have been sentenced to far more prison time than the fifteen months I got. And since I alluded to no specific dollar amount in my letter, the prosecution could construe that it was an admission of guilt to whatever amount they affixed. The amount they came up with was the $233,000 figure, rather than $120,000.

Here's the significance of the two amounts. Consider the federal sentencing guideline range for an offense of the nature that I committed by a first-time offender of my standing and repute. For offenses up to $200,000, the guidelines call for sentences in the range of zero to six months, which means that convicting me of the $120,000 amount might have resulted in my getting no jail time. In that range, the judge could have recommended probation and/or home detention and foregone a prison sentence altogether.

By comparison, federal sentencing guidelines for offenses between $200,001 and $400,000 call for punishments in the range of 27–33 months. The amount I pleaded to was over $233,000. What was my sentence? Fifteen months in federal prison, to be followed by twelve months of home detention—twenty-seven months in total.

It bears mentioning that there was a peripheral outcome from my pleading guilty to the larger dollar amount. That benefit was to the organization. As its executive director, I had enrolled the organization in a line of insurance that insulated them from losses sustained by virtue of employee misconduct. Turns out, that theft by an employee was a covered act of misconduct. So as a result of my plea, the organization filed (and was paid for) an insurance claim in the amount of two hundred thirty-three thousand dollars, rather than for the one hundred twenty thousand dollars loss that I was told they actually sustained.

Extrapolate what you will from the prosecutor's actions. One thing is for sure: prosecutors' careers are built on three factors, for the most part: (1) obtaining convictions that lead to jail time, (2) the dollar amount of the convictions they obtain, and (3) the case's public profile—they covet the public perception that they are being tough on crime. In the final analysis, my case—the case of a nonprofit director who went to prison for "scheming" to defraud a community-based group out of nearly quarter of a million dollars, and whose story was splattered all over the papers and on TV—had it all.

With all that as a backdrop, I offer that this book had to happen. It was destiny, pre-ordained. I now know firsthand of the serious misconception about prisons and prisoners under which I have labored for most of my life. And in so far as I believe that my previous views about prisons and prisoners are typical of those held by the vast majority of Americans, I know firsthand the disservice that is perpetrated by the staff and administrators of the Bureau of Prisons, in general and at the Federal Prison Camp (FPC)—Cumberland in particular, as well as of the enormous cost(s) absorbed by the American public, for which it gets little-to-none of the rehabilitative value the BoP purports is its goal.

The purpose of my book, then, is to use my experiences, observations, and research as a window through which to

1. illuminate the systemic dysfunction, critical shortcomings and missed opportunities of the federal prison system, as I see them; and
2. enlighten the American public about the dire consequences to American society of our failure to fix what is fixable about the dysfunctional prison system.

The good news is that the systemic dysfunction is entirely fixable—and at little to no added expense. Elected officials at every level of government—many of whom are attorneys—are eminently aware of the inefficiencies of the criminal justice and penal systems, and they know implicitly the harm to society that its continued dysfunction portends.

The bad news is that real change requires not money but a commodity that may be in least abundance among both politicians and the administrators of federal prisons, namely, the *will!*

I contend that politicians' overall lack of motivation to take remedial action is in direct proportion to the public's lack of knowledge. In other words, as long as the public remains *un-* or *mis*informed about the role of prisons and/or the monetary and societal costs of its systemic shortcomings, politicians will lack the motivation to fix the problem. Politicians are reactive by nature, not proactive, which is to say, they are reluctant to fix a problem as long as they think Americans either don't know or don't care that that problem exists. Like slavery, for example. Politicians knew that the institution of slavery was morally, ethically, and legally wrong, but they took no action to rectify it for more than two hundred years. In this instance of fixing a broken prison system, perception is all that matters; and politicians don't want to be perceived as being "soft on crime."

On another hand, I believe that prison administrators' lack of will is motivated by an altogether different objective. It is my observation that federal prison is a cottage industry; it's a business. As such, it follows that the objective of federal prisons today isn't rehabilitation; the objective is *profit*. If prisons are businesses, inmates are its life blood. Therefore, I submit in this book that today's federal prisons have almost no interest in actually rehabilitating inmates, only in creating enough of the *illusion* of rehabilitation to keep the money flowing.

In *In the Company of a Known Felon*, I take the added, invaluable step of presenting more than my own perspective. The book is a compilation of interviews—eight conducted by me, with fellow inmates; and one interview *of* me, conducted by Baltimore journalist, Lionel Foster—the aforementioned brilliant young JHU graduate, who was a participant in the PEACE Project's inaugural class.

During my thirteen-month stay at FPC Cumberland from January 3, 2011, to February 3, 2012, I met and was befriended by a bevy of men whose stories and perspectives might have suited the goals I envisioned for this book. There was the former commissioner of New York City police, himself a passionate advocate against mandatory minimum sentencing. There was the Baltimore-based dentist, Kyle, who was convicted of dealing huge quantities of painkillers—and whose encounter with two FPC Cumberland case managers is referenced later in the book. There was the kindly sycophant confidence man, who gave me piano lessons—and who conducted a Ponzi scheme that paled in magnitude only to Bernie Madoff's. And there was my co-favorite cube mate—a forty-year-old from Baltimore, convicted as the kingpin of a drug operation that netted him $20,000 a day.

I add, parenthetically, that in addition to an interview and the right to republish an interesting white paper he authored, the afore-mentioned commish also promised to refer my music CD to his "good friend," television host Gayle King. He eventually reneged on all three promises. So come on, Gayle. Give a brother a listen!

However, I chose for the book the men whose stories best helped me to accomplish my goal of providing the broadest array of perspectives. The interview subjects are from diverse ethnic, educational, experiential, and criminal backgrounds. Indeed, they share their views on the penal and prison systems. They also share the stories of their personal lives and circumstances prior to entering prison—in most cases, from their childhoods. As a consequence, the reader is treated to an array of stories that spans the gamut from fascinating to heartening to maddening to funny to tragic. In particular, they are

1. Marvis Watts—a kindly sixty-year-old African-American software developer, whose suave, gentle comportment belies his nefarious past;
2. Walter "Scribe" Real—an unassuming twenty-three-year-old Puerto Rican counterfeiter, from Philadelphia;
3. Edward "Easy" Lamb—a thirty-six-year-old happy-go-lucky "mighty man of God" from Delaware, whose riveting story I almost didn't get;
4. Matthew Baum—a gangly forty-five-year-old American Jew from Philadelphia;
5. Gregory Bottoms—a thirty-something rapper-turned-family man from the Washington, DC area;
6. Cecile Dwele, PhD—a diminutive fifty-six-year-old Nigerian-born nonprofit administrator;
7. Don Mudd—a thoughtful, soft-spoken thirty-one-year-old African-American muscle man from southern New Jersey; and
8. Mike Pentangelo—a sixty-five-year-old Italian-American retired electrician, who was once mayor of a town in upstate New York.

These are not their real names (although each man signed an affidavit in his real name confirming his consent for me to tell his story). I opted to use pseudonyms in the hope of insulating them and/or their families from further scrutiny.

Some of the men are like me—first-time offenders, serving relatively short sentences—stunned by the depth of his misconceptions about prisons and the criminal justice system. Others are repeat offenders. Still others are "veterans" of the system, serving longer sentences and having served time in several institutions of varying security levels, on his way to FPC Cumberland. Each man's story is dynamite in its own right; each man's perspective on the system, unique.

None of the interviewees alleges that he is innocent. Each of us admits that we earned our way into prison. We all deserved some form of punishment. I know I did. I stole somebody's money. Whether it was $233,000 or $120,000 or one dollar, I deserved punishment. I have no intention of disputing that. Ours is a society whose ability to sustain itself is in direct proportion to its ability to preserve order. There have to be consequences for those who threaten that order. I not only accept that paradigm; I embrace it.

But neither guilt nor innocence is the issue in this book. The issues for me are these:

1. The federal justice system relegates thousands upon thousands of lives—mostly young and mostly black and brown—to the care, custody and control of the federal correctional system, for *enormous* chunks of time, without the possibility of parole.

2. Correctional facilities, by their very definition, bear the minimum responsibility of trying to effect meaningful rehabilitation of the individuals in their care, custody and control; I contend that it is the correctional system's *debt to society*.

3. Significant portions of a federal correctional institution's budget is allocated to provide case management and coun-

seling services as the first lines of support and rehabilitation of the people in its care, custody, and control.

4. Correctional institutions are also budgeted to provide other programming that improves the skills, abilities, education, and life skills of the people in its care, custody, and control.

5. Arguably because federal correctional institutions are either derelict in or forsake altogether the *quality* fulfillment of their case management, counseling, and other programming obligations, recidivism remains high and the cause of rehabilitation is ill-served.

The commonly held misconceptions that I hope to debunk in this book are embodied in the following exchange that occurred during my interview with Easy Lamb:

Vic: These guys should not be allowed to just lie around all day; for three, five, seven...(*leaning in closer, now*) or *nine* years. They should *make* you take some sort of vocational training. Wait until you get out here and try to find a job. It's bad enough that you've got a record. But, when you've got a record and have no transferable skill, the slope is almost insurmountable, E.

Easy: I don't think it's the institution's job to do all that. I'm here for punishment, 12. That's it, that's all.

Vic: "Well then, I guess you're getting what you expect. But the tax-paying public sure is not. They hear, or they read that prisons provide all of this rehabilitation. If they look on the BoP website, they see all of these rehabilitative programs and services that are supposed to be available. They see a list that might include, for example, HVAC class or computer networking class, among others. What they don't know is that the HVAC class is nothing but a useless, informal class, offered for one hour a week for ten weeks, taught by an inmate, in which there are no books, no learning or teaching material, and more importantly, no opportunity to touch so much as a thermostat, let alone a heater or an a/c unit. Or that the computer class is also a farce of a class, wherein you never so much as *see*, let alone touch a computer.

And that neither class leads to any kind of license or certification. It's just a way to kill one hour per week for ten weeks.

"Yet there it is, right on the website, touted as the roster of continuing education opportunities that's available for inmates' enrichment. So the public thinks that when a guy leaves prison, he's had all this opportunity to learn something, to learn a skill. They have no idea that for lack of any meaningful programs at the prison, the guy has sat around for the better part of his time and done absolutely nothing, *learned* absolutely nothing. And when he goes out and does what I personally think the institution *wants* him to do—which is recidivate—the public thinks, *Uh-huh. See, there. He had all of that opportunity to learn something while he was in jail, and look at him. I tell you, he's just no damned good.* The travesty is that the institutions are budgeted to provide this stuff. They *report* that they provide this stuff. That's what makes it almost criminal that they make no legitimate attempt to do it."

Easy: Yeah, that's all well and good, but I ain't trying to help a bunch of niggers who don't want to be helped...

Vic: "What about your ministry, Easy? You trying to help them, aren't you?"

Easy: Yeah, but the difference is, they *want* to be helped.

Vic: "So do some of these inmates, E. *Most* of them want to be helped. They're able-bodied, able-minded men who want to be helped. They deserve it. And so does the taxpaying public..."

So there it is. I'm both saint and sinner. I'm a hero and I'm a villain. I'm brave and I'm a coward. I'm honorable and I'm despicable. I'm a finisher and I'm a quitter, an overachiever and an underachiever. I'm a giver and I'm a thief. I am good and I am flawed, decidedly so. And what's true of a modestly well-educated, resourceful, experienced, fifty-eight-year-old one-time felony offender—who has the advantage of a supportive network of family and friends—is all the more true of the young, under- or uneducated, under- or unskilled twenty- or thirty-something year-old men, of able minds and bodies, who are locked away and merely warehoused for three, five, seven or more years—and who have no effective support network on the outside. We're flawed; we admit it. But even at our reprehensible worst, we are worthy of redemption. We're worth the effort, especially the twenty-three thousand or so who populate federal prison camps because we are coming back to society...sooner than later.

My name is Vic; I'm an addict. (Hi, Vic!) It's been two years and sixteen days since I last gambled—until now, sort of. I'm gambling that the American public will, in an exercise of its better self, "look beyond my faults..." and permit itself to be enlightened by the likes of me, and that once enlightened, it will demand the outcomes from the correctional system that it deserves for the money that it spends.

It's like I'm nine years old all over again! "Laser focused on biting a chunk out of this nasty bastard's arm." But I won't stop and run away...this time. I won't just sweep it under a rug and move on. I can't. I've done it too many times in my life. And there's too much at stake. Because Oliver the bully—in this case, the correctional system—*IS* raping the Shields and me...the American public, unwittingly complicit in its own deception *and* every inmate the system exploits in the process. And I *hate* bullies!

Marvis Watts

"I believe that the media represents black people's best hope for change," he exclaimed. "In my mind, they can be our salvation."

So spoke Marvis Watts at the very top of our interview. I wasn't sure whether he meant it as merely a general observation or as an admonishment to me about how I should treat his specific story. Either way, I confirmed my agreement with him, at least to the extent that I believe that the media has had a substantial hand in shaping the world's view of black people in general and of black men in particular for millennia—to both positive and negative ends.

Marvis Watts, or Mar, is a sixty-year-old software developer from suburban Washington, DC. He is mild-mannered and well-spoken. His dark brown complexion is, for lack of a better descriptor, "dusty," which is only to say that Mar's is not the shiny brown tone of, say, Wesley Snipes. His is softer. More Sidney Poitier than Djimon Hounsou. His hair is mixed but mostly silver, about one-half inch long and brushed neatly back to frame a face that is handsome, even behind his occasional five o'clock shadow. His simple Malcolm X-style eyeglasses make him look scholarly.

Mar's comportment is distinguished, almost regal. One can easily envision his svelte six-foot frame in a gray pinstripe tailored suit, crisp white-on-white dress shirt, adorned with a single-toned necktie, accented with a white silk pocket square, all worn over a pair of immaculately shined black oxfords as he settles into the seat at the head of the table, plops down his leather-bound notebook, crosses his legs, and calls the executive meeting to order.

Or one might see him as the guy next door, in work clothes, piddling around the house and yard. Mar would lend an air of distinction to most any outfit he donned. Even the mismatched green khaki shirt and pants, beige cloth belt, and black faux leather work boots in which he and I were both clad for his interview, that being the required attire at the Federal Prison Camp at Cumberland MD, where we were both inmates at the time...

I was born and raised in one of the poorest neighborhoods in Southeast DC—called Anacostia. My street, Elvans Road,

was unpaved and led to a dead end. We were ensconced amid—I mean literally surrounded on all sides by—housing projects: Berry Farms, Garfield, Knox, Frederick Douglass, and Whitfield. Because we didn't actually live in the projects, the kids who did live there assumed that the kids on my street were soft, that we were wimps. As a consequence, we literally had to fight to get anywhere—to school, to church, to the store—anywhere! So I wasn't a particularly good student, at least not until high school.

I am the oldest of five children. My mother, try though she did, struggled to make a way for us. My father was not around. So while my siblings were raised at home with our mom, I was raised—and I might add, lovingly—by my maternal grandfather and grandmother. I went to Ballou High School in southeast DC, and played football and baseball.

"How about your formal education beyond high school? How did you get into the information technology field?"

After high school, I worked at St. Elizabeth's Mental Hospital, in DC. I worked in the maintenance shop, providing unskilled labor for their carpentry, sheet metal and electrical teams. The 'skilled' labor pool was comprised, to a man, of pickup truck driving rednecks from southern MD, who stole something daily. This was around 1970. I was on no particular career path.

At the urging of my girlfriend at the time, I enrolled in a computer learning center. After I graduated the program later that year, my job search landed me a referral to an apprenticeship in Denver, Colorado. As an employee of Greenwich Data Systems (GDS), I learned how to operate an airline reservation system, called PARS (programmed airlines reservation system). GDS was a contractor with Frontier Airlines. Eventually, GDS brought me back to McLean, VA in the DC area, to implement the system. As far as college, I attended three: University of the District of Columbia, the University of MD, and Northern VA Community College. I did not graduate.

Of course, I was eager to hear about the circumstances that had led to Mar's incarceration, but there was plenty of time for that. Right now, it didn't take a psychoanalyst to see that these were things he hadn't thought about—let alone talked about—in many years. So I was happy to further facilitate his catharsis.

"So the girlfriend who encouraged you to go to the learning center. Tell me you married and lived happily ever after."

No, no, no. We went together for a while, but things never took a serious turn…not that serious, anyway. In 1973, at the age of twenty-one, I married. Her name was—check that—her name *is* Lena. She was only twenty but was light years more mature than me. We were divorced in '75. But believe it or not, we still love and respect each other to this day. Plus, we have a daughter together who's the apple of my eye. Neidra. She's thirty-seven. On the surface, one might think that my incarceration in 1974 caused the demise of Lena's and my marriage. But it did not. I can tell you to a certainty that what caused the demise of our marriage…was me.

Leaning back in his chair and staring pensively into space, Mar continued, **Not only was I immature, but in a way, I was also torn between competing desires. One the one hand, I wanted to be a traditional family man. You know, two and a half kids, white picket fence. The whole nine. But on the other, I was a womanizer and wannabe gangster. I was a chameleon. When I was at home, I was the color of a family man: husband and father. When I was in the streets, I was the color of the 'thug du jour.' You see, all my street friends were into some gangster 'thing' or another. And I did whatever was on the agenda of the one I hung out with that day. If my friend who was a stick-up boy was 'going to work,' then so was I. Same way with my dope-selling friends or the gamblers, the boosters, the loan sharks. In this way, I tried a wide variety of criminal activities…and I liked them all. The only thing I didn't like was pimping. That wasn't for me, for some reason. But anything else, and I was down…**

Mar paused, then leaned in toward me now…his normally fixed smile disappeared. His face steeled, as he continued. **That included bank robbery.**

His eyes turned stone cold. Not gentle now but piercing into mine. It was the first time that I could actually see him…as a criminal.

In '74, I was arrested and convicted of an offense called misprision of a felony. Basically, it meant that I had lied to federal investigators regarding details related to a string of bank robberies that took place over a period of several months. It meant that authorities could place my car there, as well as a gun that was registered to me but that they had no evidence of my active participation in any of the robberies.

He leaned back out again, perhaps to let me absorb what he'd shared. His countenance softened. His half-smile returned. Marvis left. Mar was back.

"So you say that they found no evidence of your active participation in the robberies. That notwithstanding, were you involved—I mean, actively?"

I'd rather not say any more about that. Other than that, I was sentenced to serve eighteen months in prison. I served ten at Allenwood Federal Prison Camp, in Williamsport, Pennsylvania. But that was when I first came face-to-face with my willingness to, I'll say, do the wrong things for the right reasons.

Mar was ready to get right into the account of his next offense, but I deferred. I wanted to know more about his background; his formation; his essence, if you will. As with the others I interviewed for the book, I wanted to walk rather than run through his story.

"When you were a kid, what did you want to be when you grew up?"

I was a product of the sixties…a time of great change. In fact, one of my most vivid memories is of being at the Hecht Company Store on my thirteenth birthday in 1963. I was poised to buy a basketball, but there was no one around to help me. I looked throughout the store but could find no one. Except way-y-y in the back…where they sold televisions. Everyone was there, watching Walter Cronkite's account of the assassination earlier that day— my thirteenth birthday—of President John F. Kennedy.

After that, I became fascinated with shows like *Face the Nation* and *Meet the Press*. On these shows, they talked about things that were foreign to me, things that I was largely uninformed about. I watched these shows because if the need arose,

I wanted to fit in, or at least to understand what was going on around me. And I knew right then and there that even though I wasn't a great student—not yet—I wanted to make a living using words, using my intellect. That passion has served me well in my professional life because I have often been able to 'fit' in two worlds, one black, one white. I've often been the only black in an office, for example.

"Let's get back to your family life. You married Lena in '73, and were divorced in '75. What next?"

I met my current wife, Michelle, in 1980. She had an eight-year-old daughter, Monica, from a previous marriage, and I had Neidra, who was then six. We married in 1985. My job as a software developer with GDS kept us on the road. I had long-term assignments in Denver, Atlanta, Los Angeles, and a couple of towns in Texas. I settled back in McLean, Virginia—a DC sub-urb—in 1987. By '88, we were an otherwise stable, normal family. Michelle, Monica, Neidra, and me, plus our newest addition, our son Raymond, who was born in late 1987. I point out 1988 because an eventful thing occurred that year. My grandfather died.

"Yeah, you mentioned earlier and often how much an integral part of your life your grandmother and grandfather were. It must have been hard for you when he passed away."

Indeed, it was. He was, in effect, the only father I ever knew. Even though I eventually found out who my biological father was, we never had a relationship. Granddaddy was the man in my life. He raised me, we did stuff together. He taught me how to be a man. But that's not the only reason why his passing was so eventful. In a way, it set in motion the events that led to this, my third conviction.

I must have had the word *confused* stamped on my forehead because before I could formulate my next questions, Mar chimed in, **Yeah, this is my third conviction. I actually had another one before this. It was more of an anomaly than anything else. It never should have happened.** Quickly rephrasing, he continued, **Well,** none of them ever should have happened, but the second one just kind of popped up. D'ya wanna hear about that one now or later?

"No, so I can keep everything in sequential order, tell me about that one—the second one." Okay, I'm tripping now. I simply hadn't seen this coming. Mar, this gentleman I had come to know, has not one but three convictions. Anyway, hoping that my normally demonstrative face was concealing my astonishment, at least a little bit, I leaned in to signal an unspoken "Let 'er rip!"

In 1998, on an otherwise ordinary day, I came home from work. I don't recall now the circumstances at work that had caused it, but I was bone tired—drained. Physically and mentally. I wanted nothing more than to eat dinner, catch some news, and turn in for the evening. Soon, though, Michelle's and my typical pre-dinner banter was interrupted when our then ten-year-old son, Raymond, came home—barely! He had been severely beaten by someone. Of course, I was concerned that he needed medical attention. But when Raymond told us what happened, I was also angry. Livid!

It turned out that Raymond had been beaten to within an inch of his life by a pack of neighborhood thugs as a part of some kind of gang initiation ritual. I wasn't clear whether Raymond was just fodder for them or whether he was, himself, being inducted. It didn't matter. I didn't care. As a parent, all I cared about, all I wanted, was retribution. I wanted a pound of flesh. I wanted revenge.

So I went and got out my .32-caliber revolver and went outside to confront the punks, who were brazenly still there. They all knew me. Ol' Mr. Watts. Family man. Computer man. Nerd. Even as I approached the nineteen-year-old I knew to be the ringleader, they were laughing and joking, confident that I represented no threat to them. That is, until I strode up to the punk, pulled out my pistol, and placed the barrel flush against his temple…

Marvis leaned in and glared at me with those eyes again, as before, and chillingly added, **with every intention of killing him, I promise you! Believe me. I was acclimated that you never pull a gun on a man unless you intend to use it. So be clear. I was** going to kill him. The fact that I didn't pull that trigger can only be attributed, I believe, to divine intervention. Of course, many have been the times that I've thanked God that I didn't. I've imagined how different my life might be right now, in the eyes of God, having taken a human life, let alone having a murder conviction on my criminal record. Instead, I was convicted of assault—for which I was sentenced to two years at a southern Maryland prison camp. I served less than a year.

"As opposed to spending, perhaps, the rest of your life in jail. And the spontaneous nature of the episode, the fact that it took place in mere minutes, is why you say that 'It just kind of popped up.'"

Yes.

Rather than judge him, I was strangely inspired by Mar's story. Inspired by his resolve. And yes, by his character. Here's a man who had every reason to kill but didn't. Who had every right to scream, "*Why me?* I'm a decent guy. I treat people the way I wish to be treated. I try to be a good father, a good husband. Neighbor. Co-worker. I don't bother anyone. I mind my own business. *Why me?*" But I'd only heard the stories of Mar's first two convictions. There was more to come, as he continued.

Yeah, it just happened. And, I regretted it on so-o-o many levels. Not the least of which was the fact that my grandmother lived with us ever since Granddaddy died in '88.

"So why are you here now?"

I'm getting to that. Grandma's living with me is central to that story. I settled back as Mar went on. **As I said, Grandma lived with Michelle, the kids, and me since '88. She was never a burden to us, really, in any way. Not physically, and certainly not financially. Grandma received Social Security and money from a retirement annuity. Plus, I was earning over a hundred thousand dollars a year in salary, on my job.**

But eventually, Grandma fell victim to Alzheimer's disease. When she lost the capacity to attend to her own affairs, I became her legal custodian, even for her financial matters—bank accounts, social security, and retirement. Grandma had set up the

accounts in my name and arranged for payment deposits to be made directly to my bank account.

Grandma passed away on New Year's Eve, 1995. I personally notified the Office of Personnel Management (OPM), the Social Security Administration (SSA)—the two government agencies from which Grandma received payments—as well as the Veterans' Administration (VA) of her death. The VA responded appropriately because they helped with her burial expenses. Likewise, payments from SSA stopped immediately. But the retirement payments from OPM continued. And continued. And continued right along. Finally, I didn't mind having the extra money around, just in case, you know? And if they called me on it, I had the money right there to pay it back.

But in 2001, Michelle was diagnosed with both Lupus and fibromyalgia. The costs for her care were substantial. Then my son went to college. This meant tuition. On top of all that, I was released from jail on the assault conviction with no job and no income. First this thing, and then the next. And before I knew it, the money was gone. The lump sum that came when Grandma passed. Gone. The nest egg we amassed from the monthly payments. Gone. All gone. Except the $1,300 per month payments that OPM continued to deposit. Until November 2007.

When I noticed the missed deposit, I called the bank to inquire. All they did—all they could do—was to confirm that the payments had been ordered stopped. I called OPM but only got the promise of a call back. That call never came. Nor did any other contact. Finally, on the Thursday after Ash Wednesday in 2010, federal investigators came to my office to interview me regarding the matter. At that meeting, I wrote and signed a Statement of Responsibility. About a week later, a team of federal agents—including the two that I'd met with before—came to my house, weapons drawn, to arrest me. I was charged with Theft of Government Property, to which I pleaded guilty. I was sentenced to fifteen months plus restitution. I self-surrendered here at Cumberland in August 2010. That's how I got the honor of eventually making your acquaintance.

"That's quite a story, my man. I appreciate your candor in sharing it with me."

No problem. I kind of got a kick out of telling it. I really had never told it as a whole story before.

"Cool. So let me lighten things up a bit."

Cool.

"Who do you miss the most?"

Well, I miss my nuclear family…and their offspring. My wife, first and foremost. I love her so-o-o much. And I really appreciate her. I miss my knuckleheaded son, who's now twenty-three, I miss my daughters [Monica and Neidra], who are thirty-nine and thirty-seven [respectively]. And I really miss my three grandchildren. I miss when they come by the house. I miss wrestling with them. I miss us doing stuff together.

"How do you spend your time in prison?"

Well, my philosophy is that fifteen months is too much time to just let go to waste. I take the ACE (Adult Continuing Education) classes just to stay busy, to keep my mind busy. And I want to develop a closer relationship with God. So I go to bible studies. I used to go to all of them, but some of the study leaders' approaches didn't suit me. Some of the fundamentalists kind of rub me the wrong way.

"So when did your spiritual awakening occur?"

Well, I always attended church. I'm Catholic, by the way. But until my second criminal conviction, God was really just secondary to me. Then while I was being detained at the Maryland DOC (Department of Corrections) awaiting a long-term placement, I met a priest. He gave me a bible. More importantly, he taught me how to read the Bible; to start with the Gospels. That was my epiphany. That's when I began to really see how—and even when—God had intervened in my life. Through no effort of my own, I'd survived being shot. And being stabbed. I had actually cocked the hammer on my pistol, with every intention of taking a life. I had lost a GS-13 job with the government. I was clinically depressed. I turned to psychiatrists for answers. I turned to drugs and alcohol, for escape. Nothing worked. I was guilty—not just

of breaking the law but also of sins and atrocities that men don't prosecute for. Now I can see it as clearly as the nose on my face. God has enlightened me, regarding the things of Him, regarding His way. My attitude had turned from one of guilt, anger, and fear to one of genuine remorse, forgiveness—including for myself. And of enlightenment. That he is alive and with me. And that I have nothing to fear.

"Describe a typical day."

I go out at 6:00 a.m. to raise the flags at the front of the prison. On my way down the hill, I converse with God. After the flags, I go check my emails. Then I go to the chapel to pray. After that, I go back to the dorm to watch news and have a cup of coffee or two. Then I'll read or write letters or read the Bible until midday chow. Afternoons are sort of slow. I might work out or I'll have choir rehearsal or I'll write some more. I'm actually contemplating a website. Most evenings, as I said before, I have ACE classes. And that's it. That's as close as there is to a typical day in the life of Mar Watts.

"Talk about your impressions of the Camp."

To begin with, the food is edible at best. I've heard all kinds of stories through the years from current and past inmates about what they do to the food. I don't know how true any of it is, but I exercise caution, to say the least. They're much stricter here than at, say, Allenwood, another federal camp. There are more rules and regulations here. There is far less recreation and almost no meaningful education or enlightenment. At Allenwood, the camp administrators arranged a lot more interaction with the outside. Many, many volunteers would come in to teach courses and skills. Here, we are completely insulated from the outside. Except for visits. And I really detest the limits they impose on visits: no kissing, don't rest your arm around the back of the person's chair seated next to you, keep your feet and legs pointed forward at all times. Sit in a chair with your back to the wall. It just goes on and on. So I discourage my wife from visiting. As it is, she hasn't been here for three months.

I also think it's a disservice that camp staff—inmate support staff, the counselors, and the case managers—aren't more helpful. Although, as I say that, I have to also say that I'm thankful that when my wife got sick and was hospitalized recently and I couldn't get information regarding her condition, the case manager let me use her phone to call the hospital. That put me at ease.

"But, Mar. That's no more than she should've done. It's her job!"

I know, I know. But I believe that there are inmates here who she wouldn't have done it for—her job or not. And I'm thankful that she did it for me. I believe that things can always be worse.

"What do you miss most about your life?"

Well, my family, obviously. And I miss not being able to physically help Michelle navigate through some pretty tough times. For example, our house may be in jeopardy. Since I lost my job, we've been forced into bankruptcy. My lump sum retirement annuity helped us to forestall it for a while, but we may not be able to sustain after all. We thought we could manage a chapter 13, wherein we repay our debtors in accordance with a court-managed payment plan. But we may have to convert to a chapter 7, which may mean that we'll lose our home. I hate not being there to help her navigate through that stuff.

On a positive note, I love to ski. So I miss my annual trips to places like Ski Liberty. White Tail and Deep Creek—which is its own special torture because it's right down the road from here.

Mar Watts was my first interview subject. I'd taken as much of his time as I was comfortable taking. He had been mostly forthcoming and candid. He had accommodated me more than I could have asked. He'd made me—and, now, you—privy to long-held secrets and to his deepest introspection. So I could only ask one final question. It was a question brought to my mind by a scene in one of my favorite movies, *City Slickers*. At about the midpoint of the film, Billy Crystal's character, Mitch, had been sagely advised by grizzled trail hand, Curly (played by Jack Palance), 'There's only one thing that's truly important in a man's life.'

"Holding up his index finger, he continued, '*Just one thing.*'

"When Mitch asked what the one thing was, Curly lowered his finger to point it at Mitch and replied, *'That's for you to find out.'*"

So my final question to Mar (as I decided it would be for everyone I interviewed) was, "If you could be doing absolutely anything right now, where would you be? What would you be doing?"

Marvis Watts leaned back, looked somewhere over my left shoulder, out into nowhere, and replied, **In bed with my wife!**

Me too, Mar. Me too...

Postlogue

Marvis Watts was released from FPC Cumberland in July 2011. Upon his release, he began efforts to obtain employment that would utilize his expertise in the field of information technology. After an unsuccessful two-year job search, in 2014 Mar studied for and obtained a license to sell life and health insurance. Meanwhile, his house was foreclosed upon in 2012. Mar's wife, Michelle, lost her battle with cancer in 2014. He now resides with his daughter in Prince George's County, Maryland. Mar also volunteers on a speaker's bureau for the local archdiocese.

Edward "Easy" Lamb

It is of no small significance that I once told Edward Lamb that I would welcome the opportunity to be the minister of music for the church that he envisioned starting upon his release from FPC Cumberland. I said that I would not only deem it a privilege but also a spiritual fulfillment to be part of advancing a ministry in which I unequivocally believed. One that I believed would have no ulterior motive, that would exist for no purpose but to save souls.

The gravity of my making such a promise lies in the fact that I count most preachers and politicians as being among the most loathsome of God's creations. So-called leaders who evoke other people's most base emotional attributes—their hopes, their passions, their fears, or even their hatred—and then who parasitically exploit their followers for their own ecclesiastic, political, or even monetary benefit are, in a word, despicable to me. *E'erbody knows that!*

But the one thing I abhor more than corrupt leaders is the one thing upon which every corrupt leader thrives—namely, blind followers. Sheep. Mindless minions, waiting to be told what, when, or even *if* to think or believe. To me, people who blindly pledge allegiance to religious, ethical, behavioral or political doctrine without so much as asking—or even *entertaining*—questions are, perhaps, more dangerous than the ones who lead them. For example, it's not the death-and-damnation pro-life minister that I fear as much as his horde of whack-job devotees, who by virtue of that minister's proselytizing might fire bomb an abortion clinic. Indeed, I believe that if/when the world comes to its demise, it will be because the *many* deferred to the will of the *few* one time too often.

I am not a follower. On the contrary, I am a leader. I am a person whose opinion matters to the people that populate my space. Which is to say, people seem to care what I think—about life or about "the world" or, even more remarkably, about *them*. As importantly, I can get people to do my bidding. One might rightly make the case that it is that same capacity to elicit the trust of others that precipitated the offense for which I was jailed…and that, therefore, I am a hypocrite for expressing my loathing. So be it. After all, anyone who thinks that I am either proud or dismissive of my actions is simply mistaken. It's just that, for purposes of this story, I think it's every bit as important to *acknowledge* one's gift as it is a *shame* to ignore it. *E'erbody knows that!*

Though twenty years my junior, Easy—as I came to call Edward Lamb—was the closest thing I had to a real friend at FPC Cumberland. And, I'm probably one of a battalion of fellow inmates who held him in such esteem. That's because Easy was quite simply the very embodiment of what he called himself: a mighty man of God.

Get it straight. Easy and I saw a lot of things differently. For example, when the leaders of the compound's Christian church ministry expelled a guy named Seth from its choir because he was openly gay, I quit in protest. I did so not as a statement of my affinity for or acceptance of the lifestyle but because I didn't perceive Seth's judgment to be within my purview. Nor was the fact that I counted Seth among my friends on the compound a reason for my outrage. Hell, the guy had not only been in the choir since long before I joined in January, but he was also a favored member, as far as I could tell, at least by the volunteer who coordinated the group.

Seth certainly didn't appear to flaunt his sexuality any more or less, but by October, it had become cause for his discharge—at least in the eyes of the same volunteer leader (who effected the dismissal) and, presumably, the chaplain. My quitting the ministry was on the premise that staying a member of the church body would have been tantamount to tacitly agreeing with the expulsion. I did not. In fact, I thought it was asinine.

On the other hand, Easy deemed the expulsion to be entirely appropriate. To him, it was not a matter of my personal purview—or even his own, for that matter—but of the *church's*. He cited scripture from the Gospel of Matthew that he interpreted as decrying homosexuality as "an abomination." Therefore, it was Easy's view that the church could not abide either homosexuality or homosexuals and that, therefore, the compound's ministry was justified in expelling the gay choir member. To him, it was a simple matter of being obedient to the word of God.

My point is, Easy and I disagreed on many things—from religion to pro football (each of us being ardent fans of the Eagles and Ravens, respectively) to the role of prison—both in society and in the life of prisoners. But we always did so *agreeably*. I respected his views, as did he mine. Each of us was adamant that he was right. Each of us could make passionate, compelling arguments in defense of his position. But each of us was also completely respectful of the other guy's right to disagree.

It was Easy who took the liberty of practically renaming me from "Vic" to the more widely embraced "6-12." It was Easy who helped me put into perspective the myriad occurrences I viewed as injustices that were wantonly perpetrated against inmates by staff and administrators at FPC Cumberland. It was Easy who was so cocksure about his fantasy football prowess that he called himself "the Guru." In fact, it was heading into the 2011 NFL fantasy league he coordinated that Easy coined a phrase that caught on like wildfire throughout the compound.

Starting out as mere bombast, most often during raucous exchanges between him, me, and guys in the league, Easy would punctuate the beef du jour by declaring emphatically, *"I'm the Guru!"* Then, as though I were the Abbott to his Costello, the straight man in a two-man comedy routine, he'd look at me, and in complete synchronicity, we'd raise our arms about waist-high, and with palms turned upward, shrug our shoulders once, cock our heads at about thirty-degree angles, and declare, *"E'erbody knows that!"*

And thus it started. Easy and I would greet each other with the familiar shrug and salutation, *"E'erbody knows that!"* In the chow line. At the barber shop. In the email room. In the gym. From way-y-y across the compound. *Everywhere!* We'd see each other and boldly aver, *"E'erbody knows that!"* After a while, all we'd need to do was to make the gesture. No words. Just the shrug.

But by that time, the phrase had caught on. And everybody was saying it, everywhere. *"E'erbody knows that!"*

It is of Easy that I made record of the following anecdote, drawn for an actual encounter in the FPC Cumberland visiting room:

A fellow inmate—my good friend, Easy, from the Philadelphia area—was visited by his family, whom he had not seen in six (6) months. The family had excitedly made the four-hour trek, in bated anticipation of seeing their son, father, fiancé and uncle. Five people in all.

As a matter of background, Easy was an exemplary inmate—in addition to being a barber, he was generous, courteous, devoutly Christian, and regularly led praise and worship for that faith's Sunday services. He is always compliant with institution rules, as is evidences by his stellar inmate record, having never earned a single sanction in his nine-year stint at a total of four institutions and, ultimately, evidenced by his eventual assignment to a camp.

The visit had been underway for all of thirty minutes when Easy's mom and eleven-year-old niece went to the restroom. While they were in the restroom, Easy's mom realized that her grand-niece had brought a cell phone into the visit with her. The juvenile had not known of the prohibition against said items on federal prison property.

Upon learning of the unwitting breach, Easy's mom—herself a schoolteacher, honest, and devoutly Christian—immediately went to the kiosk where sat the Visiting Room Officer (VRO), who was completely oblivious to what was going on. Easy's mom informed the VRO of the mistake, apologized, and because she was also aware of the Visiting Room's "No Return" policy, asked permission to be permitted back into the room after she took the child's phone to their car. The VRO, without hesitation or apparent compunction, informed her that not only could she not return but that the visit was terminated and that, therefore, the entire party had to leave. Immediately!

The entire episode transpired in front of not only my wife and me but also the handful of other inmates and visitors who were there—my wife and I, seated not more than ten feet away. We could see and hear everything. With absolutely no provocation from Easy or his family, after terminating the visit, the VRO called for backup in the person of two additional Correctional Officers (COs). In fact, until he was summoned to the kiosk by the officers, Easy stayed seated at the visiting station to which they were assigned—at the far end of visiting room, about seventy-five feet away, and out of earshot.

The three officers cited as support for the VRO's decision language in the institution's *Admissions and Orientation (A&O) Handbook*. That language clearly does prohibit cell phones on the premises. However, the same handbook contains the statement that inmates may "wear sneakers in the lunch room," a standard a couple of asshole COs regularly ignored by harassing inmates who wore sneakers to lunch, and they did so with complete impunity. My point is that the *A&O Handbook* is anything but a bible.

But the coup de grace came at the conclusion of the episode. After the family left and after Easy was strip-searched and sent back to his unit, the add-on cops came back to the visiting room kiosk—and slapped each other a triumphant high-five.

A four-hour drive. An exemplary camp resident. A mistake made by an unknowing child. Six months since his last visit. With his mother. His fiancé. His son, daughter, and niece. Thirty minutes into what was planned as a day-long visit. Over. Done. And to a couple of Neanderthal COs, it was cause for celebration.

When I shared my written account of the visiting room episode with Easy a couple of days after it transpired, I presented it as a statement of my sympathy for the injustice implicit in it and of my outrage. To both my surprise and chagrin, Easy's reaction was a hybrid of deference and hope: "The Lord will...*e'erbody knows that!*"

You see, whether in the midst of his own personal adversity or providing counsel to someone else through theirs, Easy's forward and fallback positions were always—*always*—the same. "The Lord will...*e'erbody knows that!*" It was one of the things about him that endeared him to me. And that I oddly envied.

For example, he was told in September 2011—both by FPC Cumberland administrators and his attorney—that he would be granted immediate release on or about November 1, by virtue of what was known as "the crack law." Then in November, when through nothing less than deceit and legal chicanery he was denied release, his attitude—at least, outwardly—was "The Lord will...*e'erbody knows that!*" I *know* he was pissed. Hell, I was pissed *for* him. But Easy never showed a wit of it publicly. He simply shrugged his shoulders and endured the emotional roller coaster.

Shortly thereafter, in December, I learned that my appalling case manager had fucked me out of my early release. Unlike Easy, I was livid. I wanted to do something to this bitch. It was the first time in my whole life that I had actually felt hatred for someone.

The irony, of course, is that my case manager was clueless that I held these feelings, and thus, my hatred of her affected no one but me. My hatred of *her* was eating *me* alive.

Because I knew he could empathize, I sought Easy's counsel to get me through, to gain some perspective. And he did not disappoint.

Easy calmly said, **12, if you think I wasn't disappointed, you're wrong. Shucks, I was mad as heck! I mean, c'mon. I was told to be ready to go on November 1. I walked around for two months thinking that I was out of here. I gave away all of my stuff. Heck,**

I had made arrangements for you to take over as commissioner of the fantasy league. I was ready to go. My family was ready for me to come home. Oh, I was disappointed, all right.

But I've seen so much bull crap since I've been in this place that nothing surprises me. Nothing! Not when it happens to other people, and not when it happens to me.

From behind his huge, ever-present, disarming, almost childlike smile, Easy added, So I choose to trust in God. I have to. I have to trust that He's in control of this thing. I'm at the finish line, either way. I get out in May, no matter what. Ain't nothing they can do about that. And that's what I recommend for you, 12. You're out of here in February, man. Okay, she took forty-five days from you. But so what? Let it go. I know you would've enjoyed being out of here for Christmas. I get it. But like you said, harboring all that hate is eating *you* alive, and [the case manager] don't know a thing about it. So what good does it do you? Trust that God is in control, 12, because He is.

And so it was, the turn of events that enabled this, my eighth and final interview. The interview with the gangster, the gentleman, the poet, the minister that was my spiritual advisor, my barber, my debate partner, and my friend. It was lying there, right under my nose all along. And the truth is, if I had not been duped out of my early release, it likely would not have happened. I would have left FPC Cumberland on December 21. My interview with Easy started in late December. "The Lord will...*e'erbody knows that!*"

Edward "Easy" Lamb is, at once, a man child and a manly man. His boyish disposition completely belies his imposing physical figure. That's not to say that Easy was, in any way, immature. He was not. It's just that he was so upbeat and positive about things that I thought him able to paint a smiley face on a freaking murder/suicide, much like an innocent child might. As thoughtful as he could be at times, when he made up his mind about something, he sometimes possessed an almost maddening lack of nuance. To Easy, things were either black or white. They were rarely gray.

There isn't an ounce of noticeable fat on his chiseled six-foot, three-inch brown-skinned frame. Tipping the scales at about 240 pounds, with a massive chest, broad shoulders, sleek waist, and long muscular arms, he looks like he should be playing outside linebacker for one of our beloved NFL squads...regardless of the sobering fact that, at thirty-six years old, he'd likely be too old.

He is indisputably handsome, made all the more so by his wide, toothy, confident, ever-present smile. While it would be a stretch to say that they "look alike," Easy's complexion and facial features were vaguely similar to actor Dennis Haysbert's (of television's *The Unit*, *24*, and Allstate insurance commercials) but with a rounder nose. He wears his hair closely shorn, perhaps to blunt the visual impact of his modestly graying temples. But any notion that he is "old" is debunked by his quick, bouncy bop of a walk, his energetic comportment, and robust, ready handshake.

Easy was articulate and intelligent but never far removed from his urban vernacular. Just like me. Paraphrasing the 1970s-era consciousness rappers known as The Last Poets, "You can take niggers out of the hood, but you can't take the hood out of niggers!" And he was effusive; his nature, effervescent. More than talked, Easy brought words to life! He certainly required neither coaxing nor coaching. I needed only to ask a question...and then *try* to write fast enough to keep up...

"Tell me about your upbringing, Easy."

I was born in 1974, in Wilmington, Delaware, the youngest of thirteen kids. I was raised in a lower class, poor neighborhood, in an atmosphere of abuse, hate, deception, and rape. I'm mainly talking about my father, Big Ed. See, to the world, my father was the most loving man in the world. To the community, he was Mr. Nice Guy.

He was a hustler. He sold crack, he sold 'works,' he sold coke, he sold everything. Women. There was nothing he wouldn't sell. So his means would fluctuate, depending on how the hustling went. I remember a time when we had no fridge, we'd have to put food outside to refrigerate it. I remember other times when Big Ed would feed the homeless on Thanksgiving Day.

But at home, he was a tyrant. He demanded excellence, all right! I played football in high school, and if I had a good

game, I might get $100. If not, I might have a fight on my hands. Literally punches. The man was abusive. My mom was a school-teacher, and I remember her having to take off work for days at a time because she looked like Elephant Man from bruises he had inflicted.

Big Ed ruled his house more out of fear than out of love. I was too small to do anything about it, so I just accepted it. He had nine kids with six different women before my mom, and he had me with my mom—who also had two boys and a girl of her own.

But here's the thing. Big Ed raped my sister, my mom's daughter. My sister got pregnant and had the baby, a boy. So I have a nephew...who's also my brother.

I paused briefly so we could both absorb the gravity of Easy's disclosure before diving back into the interview.

"Does the family know all of this? Its appearing in my book won't be a revelation to them, will it?"

My family knows. My nephew just recently found out. He's in prison.

"Talk about your school days. Were you a good student?"

I was an average student, I guess. I didn't get into any trouble. I guess I feared the consequences at home more than the consequences at school. But, as I got bigger, I started fighting back. And, eventually, the abuse stopped.

Like I said, I played football. I was a wide receiver. I was pretty good too, 12. When I was a junior, I was getting [recruitment] letters from schools like Penn State and Clemson. Then in my senior year, I tore my [anterior cruciate ligament], and that was the end of that!

I wound up enrolling at Widener University, about fifteen miles outside of Philly. It was my first time away from home, and I was buck wild, man. Different women, partying. It was also when I started hustling.

One day, I went into my dorm room, and my roommate was there. He had been beaten up. I said, you know, 'What's up?'

He said, 'I got beat up. Sometimes I drive into Chester [PA] to buy drugs. Sometimes I get em, sometimes I get beat up.'

Asking to see the drugs, I said, 'Let me see that sack. How much you pay for this?'

He told me, and I said I could get it for $20 less per gram. That's how it started. That was my lightbulb moment.

I'd seen it a million times before, right in my own household. I saw the bags and knew how much they were worth. My father's oldest boy, Junior, had a guy my age that worked for him. His name was Tiny. He drove my brother around. We were good friends too, so I paged him to ask about getting some drugs that I could sell to my roommate and his friends. He said, 'Are you crazy? Junior would kill me *and* you.'

But after some persuading, Tiny finally gave in. He said he'd get me an eight-ball [one-eighth of an ounce], which he did. I went into Philly with him. I remember the street—Arramingo Avenue. I was very watchful of my surroundings because I planned to go back...by myself. Which I did.

Like many other college students, I had been given a couple of credit cards. I would get cash advances from those two credit cards and I'd go buy an eight-ball or a quarter. Tiny showed me how to bag it up for profit. And almost right away, it was like *chiching!* I was slinging coke on campus and making money hand-over-fist. That was it. I didn't want to do nothing else but sell drugs. No more football.

In the meantime, Junior still don't know what's going on. He got some money from me about four months earlier, which he called me about. It scared me when he called because I thought he was calling because he had found out what I was doing. But he was calling about the other money. So I go to see Junior. Tiny was with him. He gives me $300.

Meanwhile, I'm turning $400 into a grand, then into two, then three. It was crazy, 12. Minus shorts [bargain packs], I was clearing about $3,200–$3,500 a week off my college student crowd. I called them 'Rudolph and his red-nosed white boys.' With Tiny's help—and without my brother, Junior, ever finding out," said Easy, behind a triumphant grin. "This all started around October. I stayed on campus through Christmas, spring break. Shucks, I didn't go back home until, like, May sometime. The whole time flipping and burning.

Around April, Junior calls me for some money again. This time, though, he's clearly on to me. He said he'd heard something about 'me and some white dudes from Chester.' I had managed to put away about $11,300, but I told Junior it was $4,000. Of course, he goes off, talking about, 'Boy, you lost your mind?' See, 12, to them—my brothers and sisters—I was supposed to be the one who didn't go down that path. I was supposed to be the one to go to college, get a degree, and live a life that *they* could be proud of. I wasn't supposed to be selling no darned drugs, that's for sure.

What seemed to me to be equal parts pride and shame crept across Easy's face. It was as if he was, at once, pondering how his life was supposed to go and lamenting the way it had actually turned out. He continued, **I didn't know it immediately, but Junior was trying to hustle up enough money to make a big coke buy in New York (NY). He came to my spot and demanded to know, 'Where da money at?' So I gave him the four grand.**

Next thing I know, we're going to New York. Four grand would get you eight ounces. Junior got the drugs and took me back to Delaware, declaring, 'You ain't doing no more drugs. You can't get in trouble. I need you to stay in college. You s'posed to be my lawyer. You the one!' He gave me back $6,000 and made me promise that I wouldn't sell no more drugs.

So I did go back to Widener. But I didn't go to class. I didn't play football. I was just selling drugs…and eventually, I flunk out.

After I flunked out, another of my brothers intervened. They sent me to live with *another* brother in Atlantic City, which was cool. I worked for about eight months at Trump's Castle, as a valet. Now, mind you, I still have about seven grand left from the money I had saved up, plus the six grand that Junior gave me. But I didn't have to touch it because I was living with my brother and making pretty good money as a valet—about $2.50/hour, but the tips were real good.

After a little while, though, I decided it was time to go back to school, back to college. This time, I decided to go to Cheney [University, PA]. I took eight grand and bought a Nissan Pathfinder. That leaves me with about six.

Now I'm at this HBCU [historically black college/university], I'm nineteen, I'm partying and having a good time. But I still manage a 3.79 GPA. That summer break, my brother, Jock, comes back into the picture. He's selling drugs out of Brookmont Farms [a neighborhood in Wilmington, DE], so he don't really care nothing 'bout me selling drugs.

I told Jock I got some money and I know a spot in New York where we can get some *excellent* coke at a great price and come back and move it in Delaware. Jock jumped all over it. We put together about eleven thousand bucks, and in the summer of "94, we bought our first half kilo of rock cocaine. My man Tiny was with us the whole time, hustling for Jock.

Now we bugging, yo, selling eight balls and quarters of crack. We selling weight in Wilmington—at Fourth and Rodney. I remember the first person I saw was a guy I grew up with named Daryl. He was a twin. Anyway, he wants to know who got the weight. I say I do. My spot was a short distance away, up the hill at Seventh and Franklin, so I went and got the drugs for Daryl.

Man, all of a sudden, my pager was blowing up. Within about half an hour after talking to Daryl, I moved nine ounces. Half hour later, I moved nine *more*. I barely had time to get back up the hill. Jock is absolutely *pumped*, talking about we got to get back to New York—to buy a whole key. People are starting to know me—Little E, not Jock. I'm getting a rep.

At that moment, I just wished I had a camera! Easy was becoming more animated, more blissful, his smile hitting high beam. We go to New York and get the key—me, Jock, and Tiny. But we're gone for twenty-four hours, which meant we weren't doing any business for twenty-four hours! We needed a plan because it was just the right time, man. We had the good quality drugs and the right price. There were some guys from Baltimore who had built up a little business in Wilmington, but they got locked up. There were some other guys that came down from New York every now and then, but we really had no competition.

We were hustling full blast by '95, when Jock and me got a plan together. We would get three keys at a time. When we sold two, we would re-up. That way, we would never run out. We put a little team together. We started sending two females to New York to get the product. We made Tiny a 'captain,' so to speak. His job was to move the product. He had three guys under him: Truck, Spooky, and Trey.

Tiny would bring back all the money, and at the end of the week, he got 5 percent; the other three got 3 percent. In a typical week, we made a minimum of $50,000. Up to about a hundred grand. This one summer—from June to about September—we were *rolling!* And we were living the life, man. Buying Lexuses, 929s. 12, I bought a ten-thousand-dollar chess board. I had a coffee table with fish in it. I went to Atlantic City and blew $30,000 at a crap table. Whatever stupid thing you could do with money, we did it.

Then about a millisecond after Easy's face was aglow with euphoria from his recollection of the high life, his expression grew starkly grim. His smile was gone, his jaws tightened, and he slunk back in his seat. Clearly, of whatever thoughts he had suddenly become possessed, they were not pleasant.

There was a bad side though. If there is such a thing as an alter ego, mine was emerging. And it evolved completely after we were robbed.

Jock sent a guy named Deuce to go with one of the girls to New York to make the buys. What we didn't know is that they were sleeping together. One night, they were getting ready to make a run. When they had to make a run, we always made them leave from my spot. They stayed with us until they left. I was the money man. Nobody touched the money but me. We were going to get two keys of 'hard'—about $36,000.

I get up to go out and warm up the car. Deuce says, 'I'm going with you.' It's about 3:45 in the morning. I put the money in the trunk. Then, out of the corner of my eye, I notice two black figures...jumping out of the Dumpster. Immediately, I knew what it was. So I hollered to Deuce, 'Run!' They're coming to rob us!' I turn and run, but Deuce stays in the car...with the money.

They start shooting. Lucky for me, they shoot like a couple of white girls in the movies. Bullets flying everywhere, but as far as I could tell, they never get close to hitting me. I run back into the building. I make it to the apartment and bang on the door. 'Jock! Jock! Open the door! They tryin' to rob us! Open the door! They tryin' to rob us!'

Jock opens the door, and I fall in. *'Get the guns!'*

Now we haven't figured out yet that Deuce was in on the robbery. So a minute later, he comes banging on the door, and we snatch him inside. Deuce says, 'They got the money, man.' Nobody—*nobody* but us—knew when we were going to make a move, a run.

'They got the money?' Whop! I slap Deuce upside the head with the gun. 'How they know about the money, huh?! How they know about the money?'

The cops are coming, so we gotta wrap it up. We make Deuce strip and put him out. But we lost $36,000. That was the beginning of my transition. That's when I realized that this thing was for real!

"For real," Easy said.

I was certainly eager to hear more.

I went back to Cheney, but I was a different person. One thing I did do was pledge [a fraternity]. I pledged in the spring of '96. I went through weeks of grueling pledge activities—I did everything but go over.

"How come you didn't go over?"

One of my [fellow pledges'] moms had filed a complaint with the national because of his being hazed, and the chapter was suspended. By the time they went over the next semester, I was not in school. I had dropped out. I did everything but get initiated. To this day, I'm what's called a *yard dog*.

"What was next?"

The summer of '96, I went back home. Still hustling, and like I said, a different person. I had acquired a rep...and a name.

"So the transition to Little E was complete?"

Actually, they started calling me ER—for Emergency Room. But here's what happened. I had my own spot, but Jock and I decided to get our moms a dog—for company and for protection. We got her a mean little pit bull named Capone. He was an absolute terror, 12.

"Sounds like it."

One day, some dudes came by Mom's house. They knocked on the door. They asked for Jock. Now, my moms always put Capone away when she had company, which she did now. When she opened the door to tell the guys that Jock didn't live there, they ran up in the house. *Boom!* They immediately started ransacking the house and beating up my moms, throwing her around, tearing up the place. They were looking for money. They thought Jock and me had some loot up in there. Or some drugs.

Hearing the commotion, Capone was in the other room, going crazy. He started slamming his head into the door, trying to break out and get at 'em. He butted his way through the door just as one of the guys had grabbed a pillow and put it to my mom's head. They were gonna kill her, man. But here came Capone. One of 'em hollered, '*Kill 'im!*' But he was out the door and headed for them too fast, so they took off running.

Then looking at me with fire in his eyes, Easy said, **"They were gonna kill my mom, 12! They were gonna kill her."**

Easy stopped the story in its tracks. With neither of us realizing it, he had stood and was acting out the scene and had now, just as suddenly, succumbed to the emotion of his next recollection. Losing his battle to hold back the tears that were now trickling from the corners of his eyes, Easy sat back down and more calmly related, **"I was in Newark [DE]. Everybody was at my grandmom's house. And, 12, when I saw my mother's face..."**

He shook his head, lightly massaged his brow, and said in a near whisper, **"When I saw my mother's face, it took me back. It reminded me of all the times I'd seen her look like that when my dad would knock her around. Only now, this was because of *me!* This was because I was in the drug game!"**

Of course, I backed off and let Easy decide when, where—and even *if*—to resume. He did. **"Around the same time, my man Tiny got into a beef one night—at a club called Safari. He was drunk and got into a fight with this super rock-hard Negro—named Abdullah. We called him Dullah. Dullah was like the boy Debo in the movie *Friday*—big, strong and stone cold. He was a vicious known stick-up dude.**

Anyway, Tiny got drunk—Dullah don't drink—and he pulled a gun on Dullah. *My* gun. Dullah knocked Tiny's butt cold out! Of course, he beat Tiny down. And he took my pistol. Then he was just leaning over top of him, slapping him in his face, saying, 'Wake up, nigger, wake up!'

Tiny called me at about 2:00 a.m., saying, 'Man, we got a beef. With Dullah!'"

Half-laughing, Easy said, **"I'm like, 'How the heck *I* got a beef with Dullah?'**

Tiny tells me what happened, and I'm like, 'Aw, shucks! I know what this means, because this boy Dullah is straight crazy!'

But at about nine the next morning, I got a call. Easy looks at me, as though he's awaiting a response.

So I ask, "Dullah?"

Dullah, he confirms. He says, 'I got something that belongs to you. I need you to meet me.' I don't quite know what to make of it, but I say okay. We make the arrangements, and we hook up.

The first thing Dullah says is, 'Look, man, I like you. I like what you doing out here. But an organization is only as strong as its workers. Check it out.' He goes behind his back. 'Your boy Tiny is weak.' Then he hands me the .357...and nine ounces of rock.

I say, 'What's up?'

Dullah says, 'Nothing. That's for you.' Turns out, he wants to be on my team!

I'm like, 'Okay, okay, I can work with that.' So we hook up.

Man, when we'd go to the clubs, the people be, like, 'Oh, snap! What's up with this? ER and Dullah?' Like we the Wyatt Earp and Doc Holliday or something. Treacherous! After a while, even he and Tiny become best of friends.

"Sounds like a match made in hell."

Nah, 12, it worked out pretty well. Dullah was sho' nuff muscle and e'erbody knew it...which was good.

About three months later, Dullah tells me about this dude he's been casing. A kid in Jersey, who's making mad loot. According to Dullah, the kid kept *thousands* of dollars in a safe at his house. And it would be an easy hit.

I'm thinking, '*Hit?*'"

Sh-h-it, me too! Anyway...

Man, other than the boy that messed up my moms, I ain't never robbed nobody. But I say okay. We gonna do it. I don't know what I'm doing—or how or *why*—but we gonna do it. I'm in! I'm gonna use the money to get three more kilos. Dullah had told me how it was gonna go down. Almost like a script. He had been crystal clear that I needed to do *exactly* as he said, every step of the way!

So we go to the kid's spot in Jersey. It was a big, beautiful spot in..."—then thinking better of providing more detail—"in the suburbs. We crept around to the backyard. The dude had a couple of broads coming over, just like Dullah had said. So when the broads got there and went in, me and Dullah followed them in. Everything Dullah said would happen was happening.

Dullah hit one of the girls upside the head. *Whop!* She starts screaming. We got masks on. The dude comes toward the commotion, and I put my gun on him. Dullah smashes the girl right in the face, smacked her with his gun, so she's on the ground, woozy. I'm still holding the gun on the dude. My adrenaline is pumping!

We go to the room where the dude's safe is, and we tie everybody up. Dullah takes the boy's Rolex and jewelry, and starts slapping him around a little bit. Then Dullah starts poking him over and over again with this needle. '*What's the combination?*' Poking him again and again. '*What's the combination?*' The dude is swearing that he don't know the combination.

Then Dullah takes some duct tape, and he duct-tapes the dude's head. He tapes his whole darned head, face and all. '*You 'bout to die tonight!*' I'm scared to death, 12. I'm thinking we getting ready to commit a multiple murder! I'm actually contemplating killing Dullah, and I'm thinking that he's thinking the same thing about me.

Then Dullah takes an ink pin and punches holes where the dude's nostrils are so he can breathe. '*You 'bout to die tonight, nigger! If I don't get that combo, you dead. And I mean right muhfuckin' now!*'

12, when Dullah cut a slit where the dude's mouth was, *immediately*, the dude yells, '*45-22-31! 45-22-31!*' I still remember the numbers," he says, over a belly laugh.

Me? I'm thinking, *What the—*

We open the safe, and man, there's *stacks* of cash in there! So Dullah re-duct tapes the boy's mouth. We stuff the duffel bags we had brought with us, and head back to the stash spot. *260 thousand dollars, man.* 260 grand. I got a hundred grand. But just as importantly, now, it wasn't enough for me to just sell drugs. Now the greed is kicking in. Now I see how easy it is to take other people's money. Now, I'm thinking, 'Damn! I can just let other niggers make money and then take it from them.'

"Is that what you did?"

Yeah, for the most part. I mean, we still sold drugs, but between '96 and '98, we did about seven robberies. All of them except one was clean as a whistle. That one was one where we had done our usual casing. But when we got to the place, right before we were going to make our move, we noticed some figures moving around in the darkness. Next thing we know, there's fifteen or twenty cops deploying around the house, about to raid the place!

If they would've waited another two minutes, they would have busted in on a robbery in progress.

"Damn, Easy. That would have been messy. Hey, by the way. Did you and Jock ever get payback with Deuce and the girl?"

Yeah, Easy said devilishly. With Deuce, but not the girl.

"Want to talk about it?"

C'mon, 12. You know better than that!

"I had to ask, bro. So how'd you get busted?"

Well, the first time I was arrested, a guy wore a wire on me. He got locked up on a state case and gave me up to 'em. When the state turned the case over to the feds, they said that I must have been the Invisible Man because they had never heard of me.

Anyway, in the summer of '98, they try to get me on a controlled buy. Now this guy had always been an eight-ball and quarter kind of guy. He ain't never been for no onion before, not with me. So I played him off when he, all of a sudden, approaches me about getting not one ounce but *two*. But, eventually, the greed kicked in, and when he called again, I said okay. I arranged to meet him, which we did.

Where we met was a place in the hood we called 'Down the Hill,' where there was always about fifteen guys hanging out—all wearing white tees and Tim[berland]s. The dude shows up, and unbeknownst to me, he was wearing a wire. What I also didn't know is that the feds were in a van a short distance away—filming.

So he leans into the window of my BMW and asks for the stuff. I tell him to get in. I tell him to look between the console and the passenger seat. He tries to hand me the money, but I tell him to leave the money on the seat. So the feds never get me and him exchanging anything...and I never say anything that was incriminating. The deal was done, just like that.

A couple weeks later, the same guy calls again and says that he wants some more product. This time, he wants a big eight—an eighth of a kilo. I said okay, and we arranged to meet again. Down the Hill. I don't recall why, but this time, instead of driving my BMW, I was in my girl's Saab. I planned to park out back of

my grandmom's house and walk down. You could see everything Down the Hill from my grandmom's house.

It just so happened that my uncle was sitting in his van behind my grandmom's house, so after I park, I ask him to drive me Down the Hill. He agrees. When we drive back up the hill, who do I see but the feds? They're parked in front of my grandmom's house, looking for the BMW.

So I scrunch down in the van and tell my uncle to keep going. My uncle sees them but don't know what's up. He says, 'Is that car following me?' It was.

And after a second, they stop us. They rush the van, with guns drawn, shouting, 'Hands up!'

I say, '658-8980. That's my lawyer's number.'

They say, 'You're under arrest!' I ask what I'm being arrested for.

They say, 'Distribution of fifty grams or more of crack cocaine.'

That was on November 13. My bail hearing was on November 16. They brought me into the courtroom in shackles. Between my family and folks from the hood, there must have been a hundred people there. It was so packed that some of my family couldn't get in. The judge denied me bail, saying that I was a flight risk.

On November 21, I'm sent to Fairton Medium/High-Security Prison to await trial or to take a plea. In the meantime, my lawyer said he believed he could get the charge cooked down to under fifty grams and that I could take a plea for a mandatory five years. I asked him what my chances were. He said that their prime witness—the guy who set me up—had recently been arrested for murder, so we could eat him up on cross [examination]. But he said that even with that, the odds were about 70/30, their way.

Meanwhile, while I was in jail, I meet this guy, 12. I had never seen this man before in my life. Nor had he ever seen me. But he said that he had these visions every now and then—premonitions, like. He told me that at that moment he'd had a vision about me, a prophesy. He said, 'With all you've done in your life, you should be dead, and you know it. But you're not. Now they want you to take a plea. Don't do it! Go to trial. You gonna win. You gonna beat it. I've seen it. You gonna go home and become a mighty man of God!'

Sure enough, as the credibility of their star witness dwindled, so did the severity of the plea agreements they offered. First it was ten years, then it was eight, at Lewisburg. Then they dropped it to five, then to boot camp, with five years' probation.

But, 12, I'll tell you what. That man's words kept ringing in my ear. 'You gonna win. You gonna beat it. I've seen it.' Call me crazy, but I told my lawyer, 'We're going to trial!' And that's what I did.

In March of '99, the trial started: *The United States versus Edward Lamb*. They got their video, they got their wire. Man, my lawyer comes into the courtroom wearing a black suit, a pink shirt, and a purple polka-dot bowtie. I swear! He looked like a darned clown, 12. He said he did it to take the jurors' attention off of the evidence and put it on him. It was brilliant!

But here's the big thing. Do you remember how I said that the day they got me on video, there were all these dudes Down the Hill wearing white tees and Tims? And they shot the video from pretty far away? Well, at trial, the prosecution could not prove conclusively from the video that it was me that their guy was talking to. They couldn't prove it. So I was found not guilty on all charges due to lack of evidence.

Easy was *clearly* getting a kick out doing this interview. Like the others before him, he admitted that telling the story was a sort of therapy for him. It was cathartic, strangely liberating. Even had he not said it, the satisfaction was all over his face. What a terrific storyteller.

"So the guy's prophesy was fulfilled!"

Then I offered, as much as a question as a statement, "But you're here."

Well, the prophesy was only *partially* fulfilled. The prophesy was that I would go home and become a mighty man of God.

I went home, and within four months, I went right back to selling drugs.

"So how did you get here?"

I still had a lot of money. I had been dabbling into dogs. Fighting them, I mean. I used to go to fights all the time, and I was amazed at how much money was in it. You know, dudes spend $20,000 or more on a good fighting dog. So you know me. Always trying to see the big picture, as far as making money. Back then, anyway.

So I rented some land. I started calling kennels and buying dogs. And I opened my own kennel, Sic 'Em Boy Kennels, in Delaware. Now I'm hosting dog shows and confirmations... and of course, dog fights. I'm going to Maryland, Virginia, Texas. Man, I *stayed* in New Orleans, gambling on dogs, betting with bookies, hitting the casinos. Losing a lot of money, really, mostly on sports betting.

Then a fight comes up. Sic 'Em Boy had a dog named Mandy. She was a beast! Everybody in the circuit knew of her. She killed everything she touched. Literally killed them all. An absolute beast. So this guy called, trying to get a fight for Mandy. Remember, dogs that fight each other have to be the same gender and weight. He says he's got a dog he wants put against her. He wants to promote it. In Biloxi, Mississippi.

"I had no idea that dog-fighting was that organized, or that far-flung."

Shoot, this thing is something, 12. We had referees, judges, vets, dentists. You name it, we had it. And *everybody* was gonna want to see this fight.

So I fly into New Orleans. We flew into New Orleans, but the fight was in Mississippi, where we had to drive. After a while, we got off the highway and were driving on this dirt road. Next thing I know, these police lights come on. Flashing behind us. I'm scared to death—my heart's pounding like crazy. But we pull over!

The cop walks up to the driver's side window, leans in and says, 'Y'all them Sic 'Em Boys?'

Yeah.

'Follow me.'

After I get my heart back in my chest, we follow him back into some woods then into a clearing. 12, they had all these generators, bleachers, lights. Man, this was like Pacquiao-Mayweather! The excitement was thick. Everybody was there! The cops were there. Local bigwigs were there. It was crazy."

On that note, I yielded to the curiosity that had overtaken me. "You know I have to ask, right? Did you ever have occasion to run across the most infamous alleged dog fighter of them all? Of course, I'm talking about Michael Vick."

Bad News Kennels was a small operation by our standards. They had a few dogs, but we had eighty animals, man. We were the real deal. Bad News was kind of a local yokel outfit. Of course, we knew of them, and we had heard of Vick's financial involvement. But it wasn't like he was ever in the pit or anything. I never saw him.

"All right. So what happens next, out in the woods in Mississippi?"

Yeah, right. Well, Mandy kills the other dog—in nineteen minutes! I win $50,000, plus some side bets. After the fight, I meet a guy from Galveston [TX]. He says he's got powder for twelve grand a key. That's the price I need to hear. We exchange information, and two weeks later, I fly to Houston to get three keys. I turn those three keys into 6½ keys of crack and make $130,000 off the $36,000 I invested. Now I'm trying to go back. I'm talking 'bout getting a U-Haul. I want to tie it back to my New York connect. We'll take it all, at that price!

Before I can put all of that together, though, I go back to Houston to get some more. This time, I take a dude and two girls with me to get three more keys. We get the girls naked and stuff the three kilos into their body suits. Then at the airport, one of the girls has a house key that sets off the darned metal detector. It might have been cool, but her behavior was so peculiar they decided to wand her and then search her stuff. And they got her.

That made them search the other girl, and they got her, too. They locked both of them up.

Me and my man actually got through and got back to Delaware. When I got back, I had my lawyer to call and try to find a lawyer for the girls in Houston. But one of the girls was *gone!* The first one they caught with the drugs. She had told on us. The other one was trying to stand strong, but she also had a federal felony credit card case. It took a while, but she finally gave me up.

So of course, they arrest me. The feds. One of the things she told them was that she saw me cook up the crack. They try to use that as evidence to establish what they call 'relevant conduct,' so they can hit me with a four-point *ringleader* enhancement. There is a two-point enhancement for merely having a leadership role and the four-point bump for being a ringleader.

They also add two points for obstruction. I'd asked my lawyer what was the best-case scenario. He said ten years and advised me to take the plea, which I did. Then I wrote a letter to one of my co-d[efendant]s, telling him to take the plea too. I gave the letter to this third dude, who was headed back to where my co-d was, for him to deliver it to him. Instead, he gave the letter to the feds, and they deemed that as me obstructing.

At sentencing, the judge said, 'Mr. Lamb, you appear to be quite intelligent. You've been to college. You should have known better. Let me do this formally. The United States sentences you to serve 180 months [15 years] in prison.' Then he looks at me and says, 'Just from sitting here watching and listening to you, I can tell you have the power of persuasion. You almost had me swayed. So he said that's why he bought into the ring leadership enhancement.

For months, Easy had known of my book project. I'd talked about it ad nauseum during my biweekly visits to the barber shop. He said he'd thought about volunteering his story on several occasions but decided against it. Then after I let him read the draft of Marvis Watts's interview, he decided that he wanted to tell his story.

Conversely, I never asked Easy for an interview because of my impressions about him and on the basis of those impressions because of my preconceptions that his story might be uneventful. Meanwhile, I conducted seven formal interviews and garnered feedback from countless other sources that ran the gamut between chats with individual inmates to visual observations to group discussions, convened under the guise of being an ACE class. While each of the alternative sources were of benefit, my discussion now with Easy was proving to be more enlightening and interesting than all the others—*combined.*

"Okay, Easy, those are some hellified stories, my man. I have long since said that nothing I learned about any of my fellow detainees would surprise me. But I have to admit. You got me. At almost every turn. Now let's turn the corner. Tell me something else about you. You have kids?"

I have three kids by two mothers—two boys and a girl. They're eleven, eleven, and nine (years old). I had lived with the mother who had two kids by me for five years. But that relationship is pretty much over now...since '04.

"How's your mom and the rest of your family?"

My moms is fine. As far as my siblings, I had a sister that died of cancer in 2003 and a brother that was murdered in '05. Plus I've had two aunts to pass since I've been in.

"Were you able to attend any of their services?"

No. None of them. Oh, by the way, I have two nephews in prison, including the one that's my brother.

"How have you spent your time?"

Well, I finished my degree since I've been in.

"Did the institution pay for it?"

Shucks, no. I paid for it. I got a Bachelor of Arts degree in 2009, from the Christian Bible College and Seminary (CBC). My degree is in Divinity. I'm just twelve credits from getting my master's.

"Explain that process to me."

Sure. There's really not that much to it. You send them the money, and they send you the books. There is no teacher or no classes. And no deadlines. You work at your own pace. When

you're ready, you notify the [FPC Cumberland] education director, and he arranges a time to proctor the tests.

"You've been to a few different institutions during your bit. Tell me about them."

Well, as I said, I was held over at the Fairton [NJ] Medium-High awaiting trial. That was before the Federal Detention Center (FDC) in Philly. While I was at Fairton, I was subject to the same rules and treatment as all the other inmates of that institution—ten-minute moves, metal detectors, two-man cells, nine o'clock lock-ins. At chow, you sat at certain tables, depending on where you were from. The New York boys, Philly boys, Delaware boys all sat together. And there was none of this cutting-in-line business that they try to pull here.

FDC Philly was just a holdover. I was there for a year. I was at Fort Dix for 3½ years. I started in the medium for a few months before I was switched to the low. In the medium, the respect level was higher. I'm talking 'bout the inmates. That's where I learned how to act—learned the expectations between inmates.

At the low, they had six- or twelve-man rooms, no locks. The bathroom was in the hallway. They had ten-minute moves but no metal detectors. The inmates and the staff at the low are a little louder and a little harsher, a little less respectful. The inmates tend to have lesser sentences, which gives you more to think about before you decide to retaliate.

I've also been in the Lee County (VA) camp and finally to Cumberland. They transferred me here for the [Residential Drug & Alcohol Program] R-DAP program.

"I want to discuss things here at Cumberland. As you know, I am adamant that they are perpetrating a colossal fraud on the tax-paying public by not making any sort of serious attempt at rehabilitation. No vocational training. No occupational training. No educational opportunities…none that are counselor-led, anyway. And none that lead to any licensing or real certification that translates to jobs on the outside. What are your thoughts about it?"

Well, you've told me your views many times, so you're probably going to be disappointed with my response, but here goes.

The best way I can say it is I'm tired of niggers, 12. You know I love my people, but I'm not talking about the average black person. I'm talking 'bout niggers. And I know you know the difference. These niggers don't want nothing, and I'm done with them.

Needless to say, Easy was exactly right. I *was* disappointed with his response. Very much so. "Wait a minute. You've been in the system for nine years. In that time, other than the Divinity degree that you afforded yourself, have you ever received any kind of programming that will be useful to you when you leave in May? Any class? Any training?"

No. But I've seen some good programs here and there. Heck, I even taught GED myself. And all 'em Negroes did was bitched about it.

"Did anybody get their GED?

Yeah, some of them did.

"Well, it was good for those guys. Fuck the ones who didn't take advantage of it. But here's the thing. *Nobody* would have benefited from it if it wasn't here. Plus don't get it twisted. They don't offer the GED program because it benefits the inmates, any more than they do R-DAP. They *only* offer it because the institution gets $2,500 for everybody that gets his GED. In fact, they make it *mandatory* for people who don't have a diploma."

Yeah, that reminds me. There's R-DAP. That's a good program. At least it knocks a year off my sentence.

"*R-DAP!* Are you kidding me? Give me a break, Easy. The year off is the only benefit it is to you…or to anyone else in it. And what do you learn in the program that helps you on the outside? Hell, from what I understand, drug programs that pick up guys from here for aftercare are astonished at how unprepared they are when they get them, compared to people they get from other institutions. How can you defend that, Easy?"

I'm saying these Negroes don't want nothing else. The year off is all anybody wants. Besides, you ever been in R-DAP? he asked, knowing full well the answer.

"No, I haven't," I relented, "but not because they didn't try."

What you talking 'bout, 12?

"A few days after I arrived here, they called me to R-DAP. I was interviewed by the psychologist. Now the judge had ordered me to receive mental health services for my gambling addiction, so I thought this was it. At the time, I didn't know shit about the R-DAP. But all she did for the whole time I was interviewed was ask me about my drug and alcohol consumption. Talkin' about 'You sure you don't have a drink or two in the evening? Maybe after dinner or when you go out?' When she learned that I didn't drink or do drugs, that was the end of the interview—and the end of my usefulness to R-DAP, Easy. Hell, they don't even give a shit if you get your year off because in my case, with a fifteen-month sentence, completing the program would have saved me the grand total of two weeks. Did they give a shit? Hell, no! They would have gotten their $25,000, and that's all they cared about. They take in twenty-five or twenty-seven grand for each of y'all being in the program and spend practically nothing on you that I can see, other than the staff's salaries."

But if you ain't been in it, how do you know whether it's good or not?

"I've never been to Japan, either, but I know it's there! I've had the good sense to ask about the program, Easy. And don't get me wrong. In the beginning, I was naïve enough to actually hope that R-DAP took its mission seriously."

Look, 12. I'm just saying you can't help nobody that doesn't want to be helped. These Negroes lay around all day and do nothing. Oh, they'll go work out or go play basketball. But anything meaningful? No, sir.

"They can't do anything meaningful if there's nothing meaningful here to do, E. These kids are a captive audience. Literally. The institution has an opportunity and the obligation to do all kinds of good for these kids!"

***Kids?* 12, some of these Negroes are over forty! Sitting around watching *106 & Park* and videos all day. What the hell is the institution supposed to do for them? They grown men!**

"Yeah, but what about the kids? What about the ones in their twenties and thirties? What about them sitting around watching *106 & Park*? One thing about it. At a camp, you are *going* to be back in society sooner than later. The institution could start some kind of training programs. Auto mechanics. Food service. HVAC. Landscaping. Even drug counseling. They've got the capacity to do that right here and now. Hell, you've got a college right up the road. I'm sure they would be willing to offer some meaningful classes in, say, computers or small business.

"Or the institution could arrange apprenticeships, for certain inmates. You will never convince me that some of the businesses in Cumberland wouldn't be glad to host apprentice programs; interested in getting free labor for their electrical or plumbing companies or for their public works. All anyone from the prison has to do is act like they give a fuck and get off their indifferent asses and approach them. They *make* you take GED. They *make* you take R-DAP. These guys should not be allowed to lie around all day. For three, five, seven…"—leaning in closer now—"or *nine* years. They should *make* you take some sort of vocational training. Wait 'til you get out there and try to find a job. It's bad enough that you've got a record. But when you've got a record and have no transferable skill, the slope is almost insurmountable."

I don't think it's the institution's job to do all that. I'm here for punishment, 12. That's it, that's all.

"Well then, I guess you're getting what you expect. But the taxpaying public sure is not. They hear, or they read, that prisons provide all of this rehabilitation. If they look on the BoP website, they see all of these rehabilitative programs and services that are supposed to be available. They see a list that might include, for example, HVAC class or computer networking class, among others. What they don't know is that the HVAC class is nothing but a useless, informal class, offered for one hour a week for ten weeks, taught by an inmate, in which there are no books, no learning or teaching material, and more importantly, no opportunity to so much as touch a thermostat, let alone a heater or a/c unit. Or that the computer class is also a farce of a class, wherein you never so much as *see*, let alone touch a computer. And that neither class leads to any kind of license or certification. It's just a way to kill one hour per week for ten weeks.

"And the public thinks that when a guy leaves prison, he's had all this opportunity to learn something; to learn a skill. They have no idea that for lack of any meaningful programs at the prison, the guy has sat around for the better part of his time and done absolutely nothing; *learned* absolutely nothing. And, when he goes out and does what I personally think the institution *wants* him to do—which is— the public thinks, 'Uh-huh. See, there. He had all of that opportunity to learn something while he was in jail, and look at him. I tell you, he's just no damned good.' The travesty is that the institutions are budgeted to provide this stuff. They *report* that they provide this stuff. That's what makes it almost criminal that they make no legitimate attempt to do it."

Yeah, that's all well and good, but I ain't trying to help a bunch of niggers who don't want to be helped. You know who I'm about trying to help? Those eleven-, eleven-, and nine-year-olds of mine. That's it!

"What about your ministry, Easy? You trying to help them, aren't you?"

Yeah, but the difference is, they *want* to be helped.

"So do some of these inmates, E. They deserve it. And so does the taxpaying public. Frankly, I think the whole camp should be R-DAP."

R-DAP? I thought you said R-DAP is such a sham.

"It is a sham, as it's presently done. But if they did it the way it was supposed to be done—which is to say, the way that T/C [therapeutic community treatment model] is supposed to be implemented—it would be a good program. No, I think the whole camp should be R-DAP, but with the inmate placed on two programming tracks: one track for drug treatment, the other track for vocational training. Or some kind of career development.

"And I think participation in *both* should be mandatory. Lying around the damned unit all day for seven years should not be an option! That way, it's a win-win. The institution gets its precious $25,000 nut for all three hundred people at the camp, rather than for just half. Plus the inmates get both the treatment and the training they need to help prepare them for successful reentry into their homes and communities—who would also benefit."

Man, you can't make grown men do anything.

"Bullshit! You *make* grown men come here. You *make* grown men work at some meaningless job, making twelve cents an hour; virtual slavery. You *tell* grown men when to eat, when to sleep. Don't tell me you can't *make* grown men do something that's for their own good, Easy. Or if you're not going to do that—if your sole objective is punishment—then stop lying to the taxpayers. Quit taking the taxpayers' money for doing something more than punishment. And quit lying to the whole damned world that what you're doing is 'corrections,' as opposed to punishment. Quit saying that it's rehabilitation!"

Wow! What an exchange. Like I said. Easy and I disagreed all the time, and about a lot of things. This was clearly no different. But also no different was our willingness to each respect the other man's viewpoint.

If Easy thinks that punishment is all anyone has a right to expect from his prison experience and that, therefore, anything one receives above and beyond said punishment is icing on the proverbial cake, then that is certainly his prerogative. It seems to me that after spending nine years, at five institutions, he's earned it.

If I, on the other hand, think that the rehabilitation of inmates is the *responsibility* of the system—especially a system that insists on referring to itself as "correctional" rather than merely penal—then that too is my option.

Easy thinks that gays have no place in the Christian church. I think that such a position is patently hypocritical—at least in those congregations that are predominantly African-American, whose membership, choirs, usher boards, and even pulpits would be decimated by the exclusion of gays. Hell, Easy even likes the Philadelphia Eagles, while I love me some Baltimore Ravens.

So there is always room for reasonable people to disagree. Whether either of us was swayed is irrelevant to the larger point that we respected each other's right to an opinion.

"Easy, what's a typical day for you?"

Well, I get up pretty early. [R-DAP participants] have to meet for group every morning at 7:30. Then we meet for t/c at 12:30. That can last anywhere from a half hour to three hours. Then after four o'clock count and dinner, I work out. Some evenings I attend bible study, depending on who's leading it. Or I might work out. The rest of the evening, I read. The bible or sports magazines. And I'm still enrolled in CBC, so I make time to read my work materials. I'm still trying to get those twelve hours to finish my master's by May.

"Easy, you're one of the most spiritual people I know. Would you say that your—let's call it, spiritual *awakening*—occurred while you were in? Or was the seed planted when you were a kid, and it kicked back in after you got sidetracked?"

I think I know what you're asking, 12, and you know what? I don't think I *have* yet. Don't get me wrong. I love the Lord. But I still have impure thoughts.

"You mean, like, you still look at women, and stuff like that?"

Yeah, but it's more than that. Like, I'm not sure that I wouldn't still play football tickets. Heck, look at me playing fantasy. Does that mean that I might still go gambling?

I could certainly appreciate his concern. He had just articulated the very reason why I decided *not* to participate in the fantasy league after all. Even though it would cost only two dollars per week, when it occurred to me that it was still gambling, I opted out...but still offered to take over as commissioner if it turned out that Easy was to leave in November.

"But no one's perfect, Easy, you know that. And doesn't your God forgive the manifestations of that imperfection?"

Absolutely. But I'm talking about my own heart. Don't get me wrong. I believe, intensely. I know that I am called to preach, no question. Look at [fellow inmate] Vega. To me, that man not only loves the Lord but he's also *in* love with the Lord. It's summed up in the scripture Matthew 22:37–40. It says, 'You shall love the Lord your God with all your heart and with all your soul and with all your mind.' That's the way Vega is, man. That's the way I want to be.

Easy's face is now growing stern, and in almost desperation, he continues, **I am so sick of phony churches, phony religious folk. I'm sick of so-called *church people*, man.** That passage in Matthew goes on to say, 'Love your neighbor as you love yourself.' **That does not mean that the pastor should be sleeping with his parishioners. Or that the deacon should be sneaking around with the choir member. Or stealing. Imagine what it would be like if we so-called Christians were not judgmental but loved each other as we claim to love the Lord. Or if we didn't backbite. Vega, man, he's got it right. A pure heart. I'm just acknowledging that in my heart, I don't feel like I'm there yet, 12. And how can I preach to these people, knowing that I despise them?**

Actually, in that moment, I found myself thinking that "those people"—the sinners, backbiters, and the "niggers"—were precisely the people to whom Easy was called to minister. It had sure worked for me. But, hey, what do I know?

"Talk about your relationship with the institution's staff."

I'll give you a perfect example. Every month, [The Counselor] calls me to sign my pay sheet. Every month. This is my counselor—one of the people who're supposed to help me through this madness. And every single month, he asks me the same questions: 'What unit you live in?' and 'What's your job?' Every! Darned! Month!" Then chuckling behind that massive grin, he says, **"12, his office is not only in my unit but on my *wing*. But you know what? That's just how I want it. I *like* being invisible to him. I like being off their radar. I live right down the hall from his office, and he don't know me from Adam! Guess we all look alike.**

Alluding now to R-DAP, I asked, "What do you think about the so-called *programming*? Is there anything you'd change?"

Like you said, it's all about the money. They just run people in and out to get the money. I'd rather see it for people who really need it.

"What do you mean?"

Well, take me, for instance. I've never taken drugs in my life. I don't need no drug treatment. My lawyer just told me to make sure it got on my jacket [case file]. That way, I would qualify for

the program and get the year off. A lot of guys in R-DAP did that. They either stretched the truth or twisted it...or just flat lied, outright. That's not to say that I haven't learned anything, because I have. But the program should be for people who really need it, not just so dudes can get the time off...or so the institution can get the money.

Or even if they just grab the money, at least they should do the program right. If I could change anything, I'd change that. I'd make everyone on the R-DAP staff like DTS Williams. He plays it straight by the book. You can tell that he genuinely wants you to go home and not use drugs again. He'll get you up at, like, six o'clock. Ain't gonna be no staying in bed until twelve. Not with Williams. He says one thing that I love: 'You've got to have somebody out there that you love more than you love yourself. And you've got to tell yourself that you don't want to hurt them.' For me, that's my children. I don't ever want to be away from them again.

"What are your plans for when you leave?"

Well, I'm going to preach, of course. And I'll probably do some motivational speaking. I think I've got a story to tell—about my exploits in the streets and with Sic 'Em Boy. At the very least, it would make for a darned good urban novel. Of course, I've got my spoken word and poetry. I've written a screenplay. My brother and I are going to start a nonprofit wherein we expose inner city youths—especially black youths—to black men who are successful in the traditional way. Men who have succeeded by virtue of their education or their business savvy...which, in a lot of ways, is the same savvy that it takes to sell drugs.

I enjoyed every one of my interviews immensely, Easy's chief among them. He was insightful, forthright, and flawlessly authentic. But as delighted as I am to have gotten his story, I am doubly so to have earned his friendship. I concede that I wonder whether some of the guys I interviewed will succeed in their reform attempts. In a couple of instances, I flatly doubt it.

Not with Easy. As I said earlier, once he makes up his mind, he is among the most immovable objects I have ever encountered.

It's irritating to me, at times, but it's also reassuring. It's reassuring because I know that he will be resolute. I suspect that he's always been a very decent guy at heart. Decency of the nature as he exudes cannot be feigned. He, like so many others—both inside and outside these walls—simply became sidetracked. As his brother said those many years ago, I think Easy is, "The One."

All that bravado. All that charisma. And all that honesty. The latter of which made him comfortable enough to assert, at the beginning of each of our two interview sessions, **Full disclosure, 12. If I see a mouse, I'm gone.**

"Okay, Easy. Last question. Same as I've asked everyone else. If you could be anywhere, doing anything, with anyone, where would you be?"

Oh, shucks, that's easy, 12. I'd be home on the couch, with my three children around me, eating popcorn and watching TV.

I hear you, my friend. *E'erbody knows that...*

Postlogue

Easy was released from FPC Cumberland in May 2012, taking up residence in Raleigh, North Carolina. After months of futility in his job search, he started what has become a very successful moving and hauling business. In the meantime, he evangelizes in churches from Raleigh to Wilmington, Delaware, *a mighty man of God.*

"I did it..."

So how did it happen? How did my American dream evolve into an American nightmare? How does a man who devoted his entire adult life to the betterment and uplifting of countless others cause the devastation and near destruction of his own life and those of the ones he holds nearest and dearest?

As cliché as it seems, I can honestly say that *I don't know.* I don't know how it happened. I never saw it coming. For me, it was a bit like aging—one holds a certain youthful image of oneself, and then in a flash, everyone's calling you "sir" and "mister." The infant you only yesterday cradled in your arms is graduating from high school, then college. You're attending your own class reunion—your fortieth—consorting with a collection of gray-haired, thick-waisted, snaggle-toothed people you scarcely recognize as your classmates. I seemed to go to bed one night as a vibrant young buck and wake up the next day as a creaky old man. Likewise, it seemed that I went to bed a well-respected, responsible nonprofit executive and woke up as a disgraced, gambling-addicted convicted felon.

All I know is that I *loved* everything about casinos in general—and about Atlantic City's Borgata/Water Club in particular. The grandeur of its lobbies; the splendor and comfort of its hotel rooms; the complimentary perks, like rooms, meals, and shows; the shows themselves; the array of excellent eateries; the always congenial, accommodating staff; the lovely, scantily clad servers who kept the free Coronas coming; the repartee between the players and dealers at the blackjack tables; the constant buzz from the hordes of people on the playing floor; the almost hypnotic chorus of bell tones from the always busy slot machines; the disparate and all-too-occasional sound of a hit jackpot and the accompanying yelps of elation by a lucky patron. It all turned me on like a light.

Before it was banned, I even got off on the sometimes overwhelming stench and cloudy haze of the cigarette and cigar smoke that permeated the casino floor. The smell met me at the elevator door and seemed to flex an alluring come-hither finger, ushering me to my seat at the playing table. It brought to mind for me the countless poker games that, as a child of the 1960s, I saw depicted on TV shows like *Gunsmoke*, in Miss Kitty's Long Branch saloon. It was all so Dodge City…

It certainly wasn't the winning that motivated me. I remember one Friday night, taking my seat at a blackjack table at about eight o'clock. As I typically did, I bought into the game with $300, and played two hands, wagering $25 on each, for starters. By nine o'clock, I had parlayed my way to nearly $6,000 in chips in front of me. "Black action," the dealer yelled to the pit boss, signifying that I was now wagering the black $100 chips on each hand. That was at nine o'clock…

At ten o'clock, I was standing in the cashier's line, making a cash withdrawal on one or another of my credit cards. Just like that, I had lost every dime of the $6,000. And scenes like that one must have played out a hundred times during my ill-fated gambling career. I simply cannot count the number of times. Because, I loved it…

That is, until the next mornings…when the reality of what I had done the nights before inevitably sat in. At those moments, there was a sullen sense of depression, hopelessness. Intellectually, I could certainly comprehend the sheer absurdity of it. I *knew* that I was consumed with it. I *knew* that, other than attending Baltimore Ravens football games, everything I did: every trip I took, every activity I participated in, every waking thought, and even my *dreams*—my whole *life*—revolved around gambling. I *knew* that I was completely ransacking my own and eventually my organization's fiscal resources. I *knew* that. I *knew* that I couldn't continue to sustain losses that ran literally into the thousands. I *knew* that given both the frequency and the abandon with which I gambled, I was never going to break even, let alone win. I was like the person with cirrhosis who couldn't stop drinking, or the one with emphysema who couldn't quit smoking. I *knew* that what I was doing was not only destructive but it was completely foreign to who I am, as a person. Yet I felt utterly helpless to stop.

The emotional turning point for me occurred one night, after a particularly grueling loss. That night, I sat at the foot of my bed, quietly undressing and staring into space, when I whispered to myself but loud enough for my wife to overhear, "When did I become a loser?"

"Testing. Test. Okay, we are live in the home of Vic Frierson, on May 15, 2012. Okay, Mr. Vic, let's just jump right in. How'd you end up in prison?"

Okay, that's fair enough. Let's see. The short version is that while I was executive director of a community-based nonprofit organization, I used the organization's credit card and other resources in manners that were not authorized. Which is to say, I used it at casinos—to get cash to gamble with, which made me subject to prosecution under the federal statutes for wire fraud. But that's not really how it all started nor is that nearly the whole story.

"How'd it start?"

Well, it all started innocently enough. There were a couple of bars I frequented down in [Baltimore's] Federal Hill that had these video poker machines. I'd seen them for years and had actually been naïve enough to believe that they were "for amusement only", as the sign on the front of every one of them says. That was until my wife hipped me to the fact that the club owners actually pay off certain people for certain jackpots.

I started out putting in five bucks here and there. That was about the extent of it for a good, long while...until one Saturday night, I hit a $400 jackpot. After that happened, man, I was *in*!

Five dollars, then twenty, then fifty. Over the course of about six months, I evolved from being an occasional player to a guy who played every single day and who was putting untold amounts of money into these stupid bar-side machines.

"That was a problem? Was that illegal?"

Well, in and of itself, it was not illegal for me to play the machines. Like I said, they all have these stickers on them that read 'for amusement only.' What *was* illegal was the bars paying off on them. That was definitely illegal. On the books, it was a prosecutable offense. But for whatever reasons, the local authorities rarely, if ever, enforce the prohibition. But that wasn't the problem for me.

My problem was that, as I said, I was director of a community-based nonprofit organization, albeit one that I had built—for the most part, singlehandedly—into a viable organization. I raised a ton of money for them, I got them into the then brand-spanking-newly constructed building that they occupied—without a mortgage! I situated them as partners in a whole host of projects with a whole host of high-functioning, high-profile organizations—hospitals, schools, colleges, churches, other community service providers—as well as brought in a number of programs in which we were the principals. Generally, I shepherded their evolution from being a mere *concept* into being a viable organization. I did some wonderful work for them, even if I'm the only one who'll say so now. All of which was no more than I should have done, as executive director. And none of which gave me license to do what I did.

But for the most part, I took little to no hand—on purpose—in the effort to build or develop the capacity of the organization's board of directors. And what for a while was the most appealing part of my tenure turned into the most detrimental.

"What do you mean by that?"

I mean that the board was populated by a bunch of people to whom I used to jokingly refer as 'little old ladies, wearing baseball caps on top of wigs.' I mean they were wonderful, nice people, certainly imbued of genuine passion...but they were totally inept as board members, administratively speaking. And that ineptitude afforded me a great deal of freedom. I came and went as I pleased. I did what I pleased. Through it all, the board's attitude—regarding any- and everything—was basically, 'Vic'll handle it.' If it was money they needed, 'Vic'll handle it.' If it was a new program or a new idea they wanted to develop, 'Vic'll handle it.'" A problem with the building, pre- and post-construction, 'Vic'll handle it.' Staffing, fundraising, community relations, partnership building. On any issue of any nature, 'Vic'll handle it.'

The end result was that, at times, I felt accountable to no one. I literally felt like I could do anything I chose. And I felt like I could spend their money as I saw fit…which is also why I opened the credit card accounts that turned out to be the keys to Pandora's box.

For a long, long while, it was great that they entrusted me with so much freedom and access. But if my story is nothing else, it is a testament to the fact that that kind of freedom—coupled with that degree of unfettered access—in the face of an addiction, can be a deadly mix. The board's ineptitude bred their trust in me. Their trust in me bred my complete and total freedom. My freedom afforded me enough rope to violate their trust and to hang myself.

"How old were you at that time?"

I was about fifty-three or fifty-four when the gambling started…fifty-six when I was prosecuted. At any rate, years earlier, back in the organization's formative years, I had opened a few credit accounts in their name—including a couple of credit cards. Although the credit card accounts were opened with my social security number and other information, they were always solely intended for the organization's use. I knew that and have no reason now to try and skirt that fact. Only my administrative assistant and I had cards. Most relevantly, all bills incurred by the use of those accounts were paid from the organization's coffers—including when I frequently used those credit cards to get cash to play the machines, and later, even worse than that.

"Worse?"

Oh, yeah. Like I said, in relatively short order, my thirst for gambling grew from five bucks here and there to where I was dumping hundreds of dollars into those machines...at two bars, in particular, which I will not name. I was addicted...which is so 'me.'

"Meaning?"

Meaning that I am an all-or-nothing type of guy—I either do a thing to excess or I don't do it at all. Which, on the one hand, makes me rife with potential for falling into addictions—as I have throughout my life. But which also gives me the capacity to quit stuff fairly readily—which I've also done, over and over again. If the addiction didn't lead me to oblivion, it was very likely that I would divorce it, sooner or later, and then never revisit it. Whether it was cigarettes or alcohol or cocaine...or gambling, I would get involved to the point of excess, and then, as quickly as I'd started it, I'd stop. *Whoomp!* Just cut it off. But the point is, there soon came a time when those bar-side video poker machines were insufficient to satisfy my lust for action. They simply weren't enough.

Pretty soon, I started making the drive up to AC [Atlantic City]. At first, about once every other month or so. Back then, the worst I was doing with the organization's cards was using them to reserve my rooms. Getting perks. However, in pretty short order, I was going up there every weekend and losing tons of money, interrupted by the occasional blip of good fortune.

I distinctly recall the first time I used their card at a casino. I was at a blackjack table—that was my obsession—blackjack. I had lost all the cash I'd brought with me and was rifling through my wallet for a credit card to take to the cashier's window for some more cash. Card after card of my own was tapped out. Then I stumbled across the organization's card. My thought was that I'd go get a couple thousand dollars, which I did, then pay it back from my next paycheck, which I did not.

See, in that very same moment, I thought, 'Hey, who's gonna know?' Other than my assistant, it was very unlikely that anyone from the organization would ever know. Ever. Fact is, I believe to this very day that, had I not been fucked out of my job by [the administrators of the hospital that underwrote my salary], I could have kept up the deception indefinitely. I could have just kept covering my tracks, just as I did for the better part of three years."

"Really? What did the hospital do? I thought you lost your job because of what you did."

No. Absolutely not. That's what everybody thought, but that wasn't the case. One thing had nothing to do with the other. I'd love to tell you about the horseshit move the hospital president orchestrated to get me out, but it really has nothing to do with why I'm writing the book. But if you want me to tell it, let me come back to it, okay?

"Well, yeah, I want to hear it, I guess. But go ahead. We'll come back."

Cool. So I went to the cashier's window and made a cash withdrawal of two thousand dollars. It was all just too, too easy. I did it over and over. Get the cash, then when the bill came in, pay it...but paying it with the organization's money. I'd even set up online the organization's bank account as the payer account. After a while, I started making online purchases with the card—shoes, clothes, whatever. I even made the monthly payments on my car. I was completely out of control. And like I said, the only one who knew, other than me, was [my assistant]. But I didn't worry about her snitching because she was my best friend. Hell, she used to make unauthorized use of the card too. Nowhere near as bad I did, but she certainly did it. We used to even joke about it. I would say to her shit like, 'You know we're gonna have adjoining cells one day, don'tcha?'

"Did she tell on you?"

No, I don't think so. What I did didn't come to light until long after she had gone on to another job...which too is all part of the hospital story. Of course, I knew from the very first day I was notified of my impending lay-off that it was only a matter of time before they found out.

The way I actually found out that the gig was up was that the board president called me in July 2009, about two weeks after my last day on the job. She said that after I was laid off, at the behest of my so-called successor [hereinafter referred to as the Weasel], the board had commissioned an audit of 'the books,' such as they were...just a cursory audit, at first, that she said had revealed about nineteen thousand dollars' worth of misappropriation. It seemed to me that she was actually trying to give me a chance to come up with an explanation—*any* plausible explanation for the discrepancy—when I stopped her midsentence, saying nothing more than, 'I did it.'

"*I did it*. I don't think I ever felt lower in my life, to that point, than I did in that moment. You see, the board president was a close personal friend of mine. In the wake of my admission, I could almost hear in her stunned silence the feelings of betrayal, disappointment, and anger that my words had elicited. 'I did it' seemed like the last thing she wanted to hear me say. But there was nothing else to say. I told her that I had abused the funds. And I told her about the gambling addiction—certainly not expecting absolution but empathy, given that she was, herself, a recovering addict, who was about to earn her doctorate in some discipline related to addiction treatment. I also told her that I would cooperate fully with whatever remedial action she and the board pursued, up to and including prosecution—to which her response was emphatically, 'Oh no, no, that ain't gonna happen.'

I also suggested that she didn't want word of this to go public, that I thought it was in the best interest of the organization that we resolve the matter privately and avoid media exposure. Yes, I admit that I was concerned about how it would affect my own job search. But I also thought that an organization such as ours—that subsisted largely on grant monies it raised from foundations and other private and public benefactors—did itself no favors by letting the word get out to potential funders that they were such poor stewards of the monies they raised. She said that the Weasel had said as much as well. As importantly, I told her that I had amassed some funds for my retirement that I was willing to liquidate and surrender to the organization as a settlement, once we negotiated a fair amount.

I felt terrible on so many levels. She had been an ardent supporter of my professional undertakings from as far back as 1993, when she hired me as a community organizer for a program she headed up for the City. She had facilitated the endowment of the first grant monies I'd obtained to start up the PEACE Project, then later, as executive director of a national philanthropic foundation, she awarded thousands of dollars to the same project and, for that matter, to the organization that I defrauded.

But not only had she been a professional supporter of mine through the years, like I said, she was a good personal friend as well. We had laughed together to the point of tears, on more occasions than I can recall. She even steered me in the direction of the woman I would eventually marry.

So we ended that conversation with her saying that she'd call me the next day—to discuss a plan of action. My original, naïve thought was that she was as genuinely concerned about my personal plight as she was about how to resolve this unfortunate dilemma. That's what I thought at first. Maybe she was. I don't know…

"What do you mean 'at first'?"

Well, the next day came and went without me hearing from her. So on the third day, I called her. When she answered the phone, I immediately sensed her distance. The contrived aloofness. The measured responses. I reminded her that we'd agreed to touch base. Her response was that she was just *so* overwrought with anxiety after we talked that she tossed and turned and couldn't sleep, all that first night…so much so that the next day, all she could think to do was call the organization's lawyer to get his advice about what to do. "Don't you think that was the right thing to do?"

Without her saying another word, I figured out what was going on. She had called the lawyer, who had, in turn, advised her to not speak to me any further, to sever ties with me altogether. That's also when the thought recurred to me that in addition to her being a friend—and in addition to her being a powerful professional advocate of mine—my dear friend had repeatedly through the years demonstrated another tendency, a downright proclivity for covering her ass. And believe it or not, I understood. In a way, it was what appealed to her about me, professionally...the fact that I did not require constant oversight and that she could always rely on me to thoroughly and competently complete a task...and to, thereby, do no harm to her reputation.

"So that was your undoing?"

No. My undoing was that I misappropriated—or stole, as you insist—their money. I hold no one accountable for that but me. But I knew in that moment—once the lawyers had gotten involved—that she was no longer in control of the situation.

"Are you still friends with her?"

No. That was about the last time that we ever talked. It was 2009. I sent her an electronic birthday card on November 16, as I always did. Plus I sent her a copy of the music CD I released the next summer. She was always a fan of my singing. Other than that, the only correspondence I had with her was when I wrote a letter—not just to her but to the entire board—in which I expressed my regrets and accepted sole and full responsibility for what transpired. As I saw it, my offense was against the entire board, not just her.

So when I agreed to meet on November 18 with their lawyers, I wrote the letter. I emailed a draft of the letter to her, to which she emailed me back, 'I love you, Big Fella.' Actually, I assumed that at least some members of the board would be present at the meeting, and I wanted them to literally hear me say from my mouth, 'I'm sorry.' Whether they accepted it or not—and regardless of ramifications—my objective was to apologize.

As it turned out, none of the board members was present at the meeting. In fact, I haven't seen any of them—including her—since the entire episode began. Well, that's not quite true. I bumped into one of my phony-ass frat brothers at Morgan State's homecoming. He was a board member. But I never saw or spoke with any of them throughout the entire formal legal process.

At the meeting with their lawyers, I read my statement into the record, anyway. And, I promise you that, as I wrote in the statement itself, it was neither a request for sympathy nor a plea for leniency. For me, it was purely a statement of apology, for whatever that's worth. To everyone else, though—especially, to the lawyers—it was a *confession*, one that both the organization and the lawyers would later use to their respective advantage.

But was I disappointed that it went down the way it did with me and [the board president]? Sure. I couldn't see how my incarceration served any good purpose. I still don't, all the more now! Don't get me wrong. I'm okay with society's need for rules, and for punishment, when those rules are broken. Seems to me that it's essential to the preservation of order…lest we end up with the opposite of order—chaos! And I get that the criminal justice system, flawed as it is, is one of society's attempts at achieving order—it's one of our tools. I understand that, and I wouldn't have it any other way, really.

But in my mind, my *issue*, so to speak, was the addiction, not the theft. In my mind, although I stole, I wasn't a thief; I was an *addict*. In my mind, if I were Hawthorne-ized, I'd be condemned to wear a scarlet letter *A* for addict, not a *T* for thief. And I thought that she, of all people, should understand that. And after a while, after I actually went to prison, I became angry. Yeah, I suppose I've got a lot of nerve to say that. But it's the truth. The fact is, there came a time when I was utterly consumed with the thought that if some dire fate had befallen either her or the Weasel or [my assistant], that my regret wouldn't be that harm had befallen them…but that I hadn't caused it!

"Wow, Mr. Vic. That's pretty deep."

It is what it is. Fuck 'em. Be clear. I feel nothing, necessarily, for the Weasel. He doesn't exist to me. He's a caricature, a pint-sized wannabe big shot. He's a joke. But he was never purported to be my friend. And in that regard, I had no expectations that he should act like one. No, my animus toward the Weasel is solely rooted in my strong suspicion that he had a hand in the plan to fuck me out of my job.

On the other hand, [my assistant] and [my board president] were my *friends*. Friendship, to me, is a powerful but burdensome thing. It has rewards and it has responsibilities. Don't get me wrong. I know that what I did wasn't exactly the greatest display of friendship either. I get how my actions compromised both relationships. Hell, one of them had an organization to run. The other had four kids and a grandchild to feed. My actions had put all of that at risk. I really do get that.

But to me, that's no different than when a brother or a sister or a parent or a child falls into an addiction. What do they do? They fuck up. They do things that they wouldn't ordinarily do. They do things that are out of character for them. Things you don't expect...like, say, *steal!* And it causes disruption. It causes frayed feelings. You start hiding shit when they come around. Or maybe you don't even let them come around at all for a while. I get all of that.

But even if you're the type who subscribes to the theory of so-called tough love, you still *love* them. You let them fall, you let them hit their so-called rock bottom. But you still love them. And when you sense that they are sincerely trying to get better... trying to atone...trying to heal, you help them. You help them through it.

I expected better from both of them. They were among my very closest friends. Plus, in addition to being a friend, I expected better from [the board president] because she...let's just say she was someone who knew firsthand about addiction. She was surrounded by it throughout her life, and according to stories she shared with me through the years, was affected by it in the most personal ways. I guess the least I expected was that she'd be as compassionate with my addiction as I suspect others were when she was in the throes of her own. And as I said before, the last time we were in touch, she was about to get her doctorate from Morgan in something related to substance abuse addiction.

As for [my assistant], she was in my wedding party—among my groomsmen! I am godfather to her son...and I was an active mentor to all of her kids. We had been through a ton of stuff together: relationships, divorces, triumphs, challenges, travels. You name it, we did it.

So do I think they owed me something? I guess I do—certainly more than to just cut me off when the shit hit the fan. *Whoomp*—as if I never even existed. I can tell you that there is no way that anyone—under any circumstances—could cause me to turn away from a friend in the way that they did me, on a dime. It couldn't happen. The very least I would do is call you, my friend, and say something like, 'Hey, you know you're my boy and everything, but these folks are giving me a ton of grief about being in touch with you. They're threatening me with all kinds of shit. Now you know how much I have to lose. So for a while, I'm not gonna be able to holler atcha, not while you're going through this. But know that I love you. And know that when you come out on the other side, I'll be there. Count on it.' That's the very least I would have done.

I spoke with [my assistant] one day in early January of 2010…right after the New Year. We talked damned near every day. On this particular day, I knew that she was scheduled to meet later with the lawyers. I don't know whether it was the lawyers for the organization or the US attorneys—or both. At any rate, when we concluded our phone call, we said we'd talk the next day. Like I said, we talked almost every single day.

But I didn't hear from her the next day, or the next, or the next. Then, on January 16, I called her on her cell phone, to speak to her son—my godchild—on his birthday, as I did every year. She didn't answer, but the boy's dad—another friend and former employee of mine—did. When I was done talking to the boy, I spoke to the dad and I asked him about [my assistant]… you know, how was she doing? He said, *"She's fine. She's right here."* They were all in the car together. That's when I found out that she hadn't shared any of this with him…or at least, not of her role.

"What do you mean, 'her role'?"

Well, first of all, I mean that she was now cooperating with the folks who were prosecuting me. In fact, he told me later that she hadn't told him about any of this...I guess, because to do so would require that she tell him about her having been co-opted, the very thought of which would have stunned him.

And I also mean this: there was rarely a grant that I got for the organization in which I didn't throw a few bucks her way. In every grant I went after, I included a line item for someone to manage the administrative/clerical functions—money which I paid her. We used to joke that she had to be among the highest paid assistants of any working at a community-based nonprofit. I hooked her ass up! I was paying her extra money on top of what she was earning from the hospital payroll. She did the work all right, but she did 99 percent of the work while she was on her regular time. It rarely, if ever, required any extra commitment of time, outside of her normal nine-to-five day. The problem is that, technically, it put her in the position of what's called *double-dipping*. I don't know if it's necessarily illegal, but there are those who would certainly allege that it's unethical. And its potential illegality was possibly enough for a team of sleazy lawyers to use as leverage to gain her cooperation.

But I also mean this: she was the one who opened, filed, and sometimes paid the bills when they came in...for years. So I suspect that the prosecutors scared the shit out of her, possibly alleging that her not ever reporting my improprieties to anyone made her complicit in the so-called 'scheme.'

Also, like I said before, she too had made unauthorized use of the credit card, which I'm certain was unearthed during the more extensive audit that ensued. Her abuse was nowhere near as bad as mine, but abuse is abuse, right? Hell, her daughter even stole her card from her and used it—in which case, I intervened to avert a fraud charge against her that the credit card company was threatening to pursue.

"I got you. Go ahead with the phone call."

Yeah, he gave her the phone, but she hung it up straightway. After a few minutes, I called back. [He] answered again, and I asked him to give her the phone again. When she took it, I told her to not speak, to just listen. I went on to say that I got it! I understood what was going on with her. I told her how hurt and disappointed I was at how she was handling it…and I said goodbye. She mousily said one word. One. *Okay*. That was it. With that, I hung up and we haven't spoken since…

Walter "Scribe" Real

Among the first things that I came to understand about inmates is that few go by their real names. Typically, names are chosen to reflect one's initial(s), hometown or state, or a physical attribute. Thus, the five guys with whom I shared cube #30 in the Camp's General Unit were known as D, Tex, Squash, T, and Memphis. Indeed, although I greatly preferred my lifelong nickname, Vic, in no time at all, I'd adopted the moniker 6-12—whether I liked it or not.

At 6'8" tall, I was the tallest inmate at Camp Cumberland. In reference to my height, one of the guys, named Easy, with whom I became friends early on started calling me—at first, just to me—6-12. Soon, Easy started using the name—*loudly*—in the presence of others: at chow, in the email room, in the library, in the gym, everywhere. More importantly, I started answering to it. Everywhere. Before long, everyone—including complete strangers—was calling me 6-12. To Easy, I am affectionately known, in perpetuity, as simply 12.

The point is, few inmates actually use their real names. Perhaps, then, it follows that few are what they appear to be at first glance or encounter. Like Scriber—or Scribe, as I called him. His real name was Walter Real—a name which, on the basis of what I learned in his interview, was as ironic as any—like if, at 6'8", my name were Victor Short.

At the time of our interview in 2011, Scribe was a twenty-three-year-old second semester sophomore at Temple University, in his home town of Philadelphia, Pennsylvania. He was affable, personable and outgoing…always willing to chat about the variety of topics on which he was knowledgeably conversant beyond his twenty-three years.

A number of adjectives described his look and carriage, some flattering, some not so much. At five feet, eight inches tall and 140 pounds or so, his look evoked descriptors like *soft* or *gentle*. Boyish. He looked neither hard nor hardened. I'd describe his features as noncommittal—not quite white, not quite black. In fact, on the basis of his looks, I could easily believe it if Scribe said he was black or white or neither. I'd buy Latino, Middle Eastern, Eskimo, or Native American. They all fit his features: milky, light-skin complexion, with a hint of freckling; lips of medium thickness and reddish hue; bushy brown hair, worn short, but with sideburns; moustache and the thin, spotty beard of a twenty-three-year-old. He had a thick nose and heavy eyebrows. And his walk lacked either the arrogant pomposity of the white-collar inmates or the leaned over, shoulder-rolling, side-to-side, dick-grabbing, wannabe-tough-guy mack of the urban guys. His was more a bounce, a lilt. A dance, up on his toes. So much so that I spent more than a couple of occasions debating with my cubies whether or not Scribe was gay, with mine being the lone dissenting opinion. Plus, in his coming and going about the yard, Scribe did not eschew the company of the known gay guys on the compound, which, in the narrow minds of my cubies, seemed to lend further credence to their Neanderthal allegations. Frankly, I would probably fear for Scribe's safety at another facility. But here, it was unlikely to cause him any serious challenges. Of course, to me, the matter of his sexuality was moot. I didn't give shit either way. The man had a hell of a story to tell, and I wanted to hear it…

"Okay, Scribe, tell me about yourself—where you're from, talk about your upbringing, your family."

Well, I was born, raised, and still live in a rough part of north Philly called the Badlands. The neighborhood is heavily populated by working class and/or poor Hispanics and African-Americans. My family includes my mom, four brothers, one sister, and two dads. I—

"Whoa, whoa. You know I gotta stop you. *Two* dads?"

Yeah. My biological dad and my stepdad. Actually, for years, my stepdad thought he was my real dad—because that's what my mom told him, knowing full well that it wasn't true. My biological dad was convicted of murder around the time I was born, and was serving seventeen years in prison. He served ten years. He's out now, but while he was down, he got an associate's degree and a barber's license and now owns his own barbershop in Philly. But my stepdad raised me from a newborn—even after he found out that he wasn't my dad.

We were poor. We were not the kind of family that took vacations or went away for weekends. We didn't even have car. But we always had a roof over our heads and food to eat. Then when I was fourteen, Dad—my stepdad—lost his job. Within weeks, he suffered a stroke and completely lost the ability to walk or talk.

"Damn. Sorry to hear that. Is he still alive?" I asked cautiously.

Yeah, but he still can't walk or talk. He's lived in assisted living ever since the stroke. I still visit him often…well, I did before [coming here]. I go by on Sundays and we watch movies on my laptop.

"Cool. I'm sorry for interrupting. You were talking about your family. Why was your dad in assisted living? He had a wife."

Yeah, well, after my dad's stroke, my mom turned to alcohol and drugs as a means to deal with her depression. It was her, me, my sister, and one of my brothers. She just fell deeper and deeper into depression.

Eventually, it became more than my brother could take, so he just up and left. At the same time, my sister was regularly truant. As a result, the state took her away from my mom and placed her in foster homes. That left just me and Mom. One day—the precise timing is fuzzy, but I know I was still fourteen—one day she just left me. My mother left me.

She was afraid that she'd be prosecuted for neglecting my sister, so she just left. Leaving just me to fend for myself. I was probably headed into foster care myself. But I escaped foster care because my grandmother got custody of me—formal custody, anyway. The problem was that my grandma lived in a two-room hovel that barely accommodated her. So when I was fifteen, I lived by myself. I rented a room over top of a bar at the corner of Fourth and Norris. I paid $175 a month to rent one of seven rooms that the owner rented out. All the tenants shared one bathroom.

"Damn. That's a hell of a story, Scribe."

Yeah. Try living it.

"What about your mom? I assume you guys worked it out."

Oh yeah? Look. The next time I saw her was a few years later. I was home on leave from the army. Some friends and I were at a bar, having drinks. I looked down the bar…and I saw my mom. Just leisurely having a drink.

"Did you say something to her?"

I sent her drink—a double Bacardi, her favorite.

"You mean to say that no conversation ensued?"

Yeah, 'conversation ensued,' as you say. The sum total of it was that we exchanged numbers. And we've sort of kept in touch. But there is no real mother/son connection.

"Okay, go back to after your mom left. You're fifteen, living by yourself. What then? Were you in school?"

Well, technically, yes. I was enrolled, but remember, I'm fifteen. I've got a little bullshit job. I've got my own place and a handful of debts, my dad's in assisted living, and my mom is gone. I had what I call a 'grown man syndrome.' And school was just not a priority for me.

With the need to eat and pay bills, I started printing money. It was just that simple. That's how it all got started. On a very low level. I'd copy four or five $20 bills on a copy machine, turn the bills over, copy the other sides, cut them out, then peddle them at the darkest night club or the busiest 7-Eleven I could find.

Meanwhile, I stayed enrolled in school. But I never—*ever*—went to class. When I finally dropped out, I was seventeen, but only in the tenth grade. Not for a lack of aptitude…

I interrupted, "You just didn't go to class."

I just didn't go to class. Anyway, I dropped out of school in '04, got my GED in '05, and joined the army.

"You were in the service? Talk about that."

I went to basic training at Fort Banning, in Georgia. I completed four months of infantry training and one month of airborne school. I was a paratrooper. After basic, I transferred to my duty station at Fort Bragg, in North Carolina. By that time, my brigade had already been deployed in Afghanistan for six months. After two months at Fort Bragg, I joined them.

"How long were you in Afghanistan? When were you discharged from the army?"

I was there for a year. I was honorably discharged in 2007.

Damn! At twenty-three, this kid had done more living and seen more of life than many people twice his age. On this day, Scribe and I would talk for a couple of hours. We'd had other protracted conversations, during which he'd told me enough for me to know that I wanted to include his story in the book. As I said before, he was an affable kid. Able and willing to go on for hours. But I had to draw him back on point. So I asked, "So far, I can't see how your operation grew. How'd you go from personally exchanging crude copies of $20 bills at 7-Eleven stores to having a cadre of regular customers, who purchased large quantities of your product?"

Smiling coyly, he replied, **Practice, practice, practice! I found out that the product was pretty good...**looking more intently at me, adding, **but not perfect—at, of all places, my high school.**

One day early in the school year, I caught the eye of this bea-u-u-tiful Asian girl in the lunch room. I had just used one of my $20 bills in the cafeteria line about twenty minutes earlier. I mucked over to where she was sitting and just started flowing. Out of the corner of my eye, I saw a school cop approaching me. By the time he came over and tapped me on the shoulder, I had removed about $600 of the funny money from my pocket. The school cop said he needed to see me. Because I knew what he wanted, as he turned to lead me upstairs to the office, I dropped the bills in the girl's lap, somebody I'd known for all of ten minutes.

They take me upstairs and call the city cops. They search me but find nothing. Still, the city cops take me to the station. They put me in a holding cell and hold me there for two days, until my parents came. Problem was, as I said before, I ain't got no damned parents! Finally, they got a hold of my grandma, but she had no way to come get me. So they drove me to her house and dropped me off. No charges were ever filed.

"You're a lucky son of a bitch, Scribe."

That ain't the half of it. Check this out. Three days had passed, right? I'm in a holding cell.

"Okay."

I go back to the school after three days. After school, I saw Lynn—the girl from the other day. Who also saw my ass...and she was heading toward me with a purpose!

"Oh, shit!"

Yeah, right. But check it. She walked up to me...and smiled. And she handed me all of the money rolled in a knot, bound in a rubber band, and said, 'This is yours.' I took her to lunch, and her we are, seven years later, still together.

"Quite a story."

Yeah, but it also opened my eyes to the need to improve the quality of my product. If a damned school cafeteria could catch it, then I had work to do. I bought a better cutter, started using a high-grade resume paper, downloaded photo editing software that enabled me to get clearer resolution. I worked to perfect the process. Well, two processes, actually.

"What do you mean?"

The product I sold was not the same as the product I used myself. It was excellent, but it couldn't pass the scrutiny of a counterfeit pen—the markers they use at cash registers. The product that I used for myself did pass the pen test, but the process for making it was far more tedious and time-consuming.

"Can you explain the difference?"

Sure. If I was selling the money, I scanned the bills, used PhotoShop to clarify the images, and then printed four to five bills per sheet on high-resolution resume paper. I'd cut it with my laser cutter, and that was that. I defy anyone to tell the difference just by looking at it. I could sit at my computer and print about $5,000 in no time. I'd set it up to print one side, leave the room for an hour, come back, flip it over, and print the other side. The total print time for $5,000 was about two hours plus another half-hour to cut it out.

"That's what you sold. What about the other?"

The money I used—like, say, for Christmas shopping or for clothes or whatever—I made in a different way. Art supply stores sell a chemical that will delete the ink from money. To make a much, much longer story short, let me just say that I'd use the chemical to delete the print off a $1 bill and through careful, meticulous measurement, superimpose onto the cleaned bill the printing and images from a twenty and thereby convert a $1 bill into $20 bill. It was tedious. It took about half an hour to make one twenty. So you can imagine how long it took to make five grand. But the thing is, it was printed on actual mint paper, so it passed the marker test.

I'd hit a 7-Eleven here and there. Or a night club with multiple bartenders. I'd hit the boardwalk at Atlantic City, never the casinos. Too much surveillance. No toll booths, either, because they've got cameras. But my favorite place to use the money was at Rita's Water Ice stands. There are about twenty-seven stands that I would hit on the regular, because I knew I'd never get caught.

"What did your customers use the money for?"

Well, one guy was a drug dealer. I know he used it some of his transactions. Another owned a furniture store and peddled it there. My favorite was a sweet elderly couple who used the disguise of their senior citizenship to wash bills from store to store.

"At your high point, how much money were you making? I mean real money."

At my highest period—a period of about twelve months—three major customers were buying $16,000 per month total. I sold $1,000 blocks of counterfeit cash for $350…netting me a little under six grand a month. I wasn't greedy. I just wanted stability.

"So how'd you get caught?"

When I got caught, I was just starting back up after an eleven-month hiatus. I made the mistake of selling to a new customer—a friend of a friend. He got caught with a few hundred bucks—after buying a mattress and having the fucking thing delivered to his house. The bastard gave me up as his supplier. Next thing I knew, I woke up one Monday morning and got dressed for work.

I was working at Bank of America at the time. At 7:30 or so, as I left my apartment building, six cars—all Dodge Chargers—pulled up from both ends of my one-way street. They exited their cars with shotguns drawn. They didn't restrain me, but they made me sit on the sidewalk, while they executed a search warrant. In my apartment, they found $1,000 in uncut bills.

"Damn. You had a hell of a run. From age fifteen to twenty-three, you—"

Cutting me off midsentence, he said, **Yeah, but the thing is, they had no knowledge of the scope of my operation or of how long I did it. Because all they found was the uncut $1,000, they thought I was just playing around. They didn't know that I'd been doing it since I was fifteen or sixteen...including while I was in the service.**

"So what are you saying?"

Leaning back, smiling a guilty smile, not gloating, he said, **I'm saying that I'm luckier than you know. I feel like I'm truly getting a do-over. The charges I pleaded to are one count of passing counterfeit money, which is using the money yourself; one count of dealing, which is providing it to someone else to distribute; and one count of forgery. Each charge carried a maximum possible sentence of twenty years. So you can imagine my reaction when my court-appointed lawyer informed me that I could face up to sixty years in jail. But since they only found the small amount of uncut bills and only confiscated a laser cutter, a printer and a computer...**" He looked at me now, adding, "**That they gave back, by the way.**

Incredulous, I marveled, "They gave it back?"

Yeah, there was nothing incriminating on it. My operating templates for both products were on a thumb drive that they never found.

I was still mildly dumbfounded as Scribe continued, **So since they had so little on me, really, at my sentencing the judge literally called me to the bench, and said, 'What is a military man and college student—a bright young man like you—doing messing around with this stuff? And for what? A thousand dollars? Listen.**

The sentencing guidelines in this case call for ten to fifteen months. The Prosecution wants fifteen months. Your defense is asking for home confinement. But I've got to give you a smack on the head, so go back to your seat."

He sentenced me to serve three months, with three years' probation, and to pay a $300 fine. After passing the sentence, he looked at me and sternly said, 'Don't let me see you again.'

I'm a convicted felon. This is my first and only foray into prison life—prison culture, if you will. And I get it. While I have to admit that if one has to serve time in prison, this is probably among the better circumstances under which to do so. In many real ways, Camps provide a better overall environment, as compared to higher-security facilities. One has more freedoms. The food is better, as are the overall conditions. But all of that notwithstanding, one's chagrin while imprisoned—if one has built any semblance of a normal life—is not the quality of one's life inside these walls—but what one misses of his life on the outside. The missing breeds a yearning, the yearning breeds introspection, and the introspection invariably engenders a commitment—a pledge to oneself, no matter how fleeting it may turn out to be—to never come back.

With that in mind, I asked Scribe whether he intended to heed the judge's admonishment.

Yeah, I think so. But, 6, I have to say this—and as a gambler, you can appreciate it. The thing that kept me doing it…is that I *liked* it! It was thrilling, man. You know what I'm sayin'? I got a rush that was indescribable. Not like robbing a bank or selling drugs. This was more like riding a fucking roller coaster. It was exhilarating. I took on a persona. I played a role. Every time. And I had to improvise on the fly. It was exciting…

I have to say that there was palpable ardor in his expression and his tone—perhaps even a glint in his eyes, as he relayed to me the depth of his enthrall. Still, I ceded to him the benefit of the doubt when he offered in conclusion. **But I'm done. I have too much to lose now. Remember, all I ever wanted was stability. That's what we never had as a family. And I got a do-over.**

"Who do you miss the most?"

I miss Lynn. We've been together all these years, and I really love her. And I really miss our four-year-old daughter, Alexa. I used to take her to school every—pre k. Then I'd go to school myself. I'd also pick her up and take her to the babysitter before I went to work.

"What are your plans for when you're released?"

Over the summer, I'm going to make up the classes I missed being in here. By the fall, I'll be a junior. I plan to graduate in a couple of years. After that, I want to work in a foreign country—preferably somewhere in South America. I want to teach English in a Spanish-speaking country. My purpose is twofold: (1) it will give me the opportunity to travel, to broaden my horizons, and (2) it's hard to jump straight into a college teaching job with no experience. So I'll teach for eight to ten years, gain valuable experience, and come back stateside to teach.

"What's a typical day for you, Scribe?"

Well, I sleep until ten—every day! I go to lunch at eleven then shoot pool or read books. I also participate in the Camp's volleyball league and recently played on the winning team in the All-Star game. That's really about it. There's not a lot else to do. I'd love to learn something while I'm here. Maybe brush up on my Spanish. To that end, one of my first times in the library I asked for some literature that would educate me in the Spanish language. I was told that all of the literature was strictly for entertainment. Novels. Nothing academic.

I couldn't help but wonder by what definition the Camp library fell under the purview of the so-called Education Department. At any rate, I continued with the interview. "Is prison different from what you imagined?"

Yes. TV and society depict prison as being on one level, no matter what your crime. But different crimes get different levels—of security, I mean. At the lower security joints, like this camp, we're permitted to roam around the compound somewhat freely, which I didn't anticipate. The staff, however, is a much different story. Some of the staff—far too few, I might add—are cool. They get along with you as long as you try to go along with them. Others are purposely spiteful—based on their own pre-dispositions about your character, based on where you are—as though there are no decent people in prison, especially people of color. Like I said, some of them are cool. They treat you like human beings. Others are just assholes, just because they can be.

I sat quietly. Scribe pondered and then continued, **There is no privacy. Ever. I miss being able to do the things I want to do, when I want to do them. Here you're never alone. Not in the rack. Not in the bathroom. Nowhere.**

Then, too, there are the cliques. Cliques form on the basis of damn near anything folks might have in common. Where you're from. What crime you committed. How long or how many times you've been locked up. Your race, your age, your ethnicity, what language you speak. There are dudes from DC or Baltimore who run together. The white-collar guys, who think they really don't belong here, hang together in the library. There's the chess playing crew or the basketball playing crew, the rummy crew. It just goes on and on. Me, I don't attach to any of the groups. Hell, I'm a twenty-three-year-old Puerto Rican who doesn't speak fluent Spanish. So I don't attach to any particular group.

"Okay, Scribe. I appreciate your cooperation, my man."

No problemo, *mi amigo grande*!

"One last question. Same as I'm asking everyone I interview. If you could snap your fingers and be anyplace, doing absolutely anything right now, where would you be?"

Shit, that's easy. I'd be at home, eating a good meal with Lynn and Alexa.

Postlogue

Scribe was released from FPC Cumberland in March 2011 and returned to his family in Philadelphia. As of this printing, I have been unable to get details regarding his progress.

The "Circumstances"
(I'll Get You, I'll Hurt Me)

"Mr. Vic, in your book, you talk about the shortcomings of the system. You talk about what should happen next, who should benefit, and how. But one big thing the book has working for it is that you get other people to speak out honestly and from their own perspectives. It's not just like, 'What? So Vic has this story, this point of view, but what about the other guys?' And you capture that. It isn't just you telling your story—you talk to other people…people who are older than you, younger than you, some from completely different backgrounds and with a variety of experiences within the system… and I think that's great.

"But hold on to that for a minute. My question is this: go back to sentencing. Pretend for a moment that the judge would listen. Pretend that he wouldn't come in with any preconceived notions. What would you want him to do? What would your argument be for what should happen next, who should benefit, how the next two to three years should go?"

"That's a very fair question because my response may make me sound as though I am bitching and whining a little bit. You're asking me to set aside the feedback I got from eight—well, actually a plethora of other inmates, eight of whose comments I actually documented. And you're also asking me to overlook what I deem to be the prosecutorial bullying that I believe took place in my case that practically forced me to accept a plea that ensured jail time versus probation. You're asking me to forget that part too…"

"Maybe I'm not asking the right question, but what I'm trying to get at is, if you could go back to before the law said, 'Vic, this is what's going to happen to you,' but still hold on to everything you know about the [criminal justice] system, go back and say, this is what should have happened…"

Okay. You're asking me to be the judge. Fine. Here's the crux. *Somebody*—which is to say *anybody* other than the Bureau of Prisons and the prosecutor, who got a notch on his gun belt—somebody should have benefited from the penalty that was set forth! So with that, ultimately, my question becomes: 'Who got helped?' Because the objective of criminal justice is supposed to be twofold: punishment *and* rehabilitation. So as the judge, I would have to look beyond the punishment aspect of sentencing, which pretty much establishes whom to hurt and how much, and I'd have to ask myself, 'Who gets helped by the sentence I'm about to impose?' In my case, no one got helped.

So you might ask, who's supposed to be helped? Certainly not me, right? One could make the case, as many have—behind my back, of course—that the people around me who were impacted by the consequences of my actions deserved it. You know, my wife deserved to lose the roof over her head, that she deserved to be forced into bankruptcy or foreclosure, that despite the fact that she didn't know anything about what was going on—and she didn't—she should've known and, thus, deserves whatever happens. I expected that kind of—let's say—*narrow* judgment from the general public and from casual observers. Hell, just recently, one of my classmates from the 2006 class of the [Greater Baltimore Committee's (GBC)] Leadership—a person that my wife and I had gone out with on several occasions in the years that ensued and a person at whose wedding I'd sung—said to the Leadership's director something to the effect of 'and he sang at my wedding,' as though my presence at her wedding *six years ago* had somehow retroactively sullied the sanctity of it.

That kind of judgment, as asinine and unreasoned as I think it is, is almost to be expected from a public that, it seems to me, grows more mean-spirited by the day. But in my opinion, judges are supposed to exercise a broader standard of evaluation. In my opinion, judges should employ a higher level of objectivity than the general public. Hell, at my sentencing hearing, the judge in my case made a statement to the effect that he was appalled by my actions because he'd been personal friends with the namesakes of one of our larger benefactors...a benefactor, by the way, whose resources were completely unaffected by what I did, 100 percent accounted for.

But even if you believe that my wife, my family and my friends deserve to be punished—just for committing the heinous crime of knowing me—what about the victims? What about the organization I victimized? As you know, I'd just won a $50,000 fellowship—money paid directly to me to expand the PEACE Project—and I could have immediately begun paying the restitution I was ordered to pay. What about the children I worked with in that project? What about the community and the city? What about the local and national economies that would be hurt by another unemployed person; yet another home in foreclosure? What about the society that I'm coming back into, let alone what about the man who's coming back into that society? Do you think for one second that I'm not going to do whatever it takes to provide the basics for myself and my family...*by any means necessary?*

I contend that in my case, the system not only did nothing to help me but that it did actual *harm* to all of the aforementioned. Moreover, I contend that that's the case in many, many instances—especially at the federal level. I contend that within the federal criminal justice system, the mind-set toward mass incarceration, the imposing of sentences that are entirely too long for the crime(s) committed—with no possibility of parole— and the abject indifference among prison administrators toward effecting meaningful rehabilitation of inmates all conspire to serve but one interest: to feed the so-called *prison industrial com-*

plex. The federal prison system is an industry, and inmates are both its product and its life blood. The system thrives on inmates, so it does nothing but create more and more of them!

"Okay, Mr. Vic, I understand all of that. But you still didn't answer the question. You were found guilty of stealing more than $230,000. Forget for a moment, whether the amount is real or contrived. You pleaded guilty to it, so you did it! What do you think the judge should have done? You didn't tell me what you think the judge should've sentenced you to, under those circumstances."

Well, that's my point! Those *circumstances*, as you call it, included that I was, at the time, a fifty-six-year-old, first-time, nonviolent offender. I was from a stable background—long time married, a long-time homeowner. For the whole of my life I had been—I'd *earned* for myself—a sterling reputation, personally and professionally. My commitments to family and community were exemplary. And as I said before, after more than a year unemployed, I had just won a fellowship that would have let me start making restitution payments to the offended party—immediately. I posed no flight risk. I posed no danger to myself or others. Those circumstances also include that there was an addiction at play, for which treatment would have been in order—treatment that the judge did order but that the penal system completely ignored. All of that is inextricably part of what you call *the circumstances.*

Given all of that—and given all who would be impacted by the sentence—if I were the judge, I would have sentenced me to home detention. That way, I could have worked my fellowship, I could've made restitution payments, I could've kept my house, I could've addressed the addiction by getting treatment and going to [Gamblers Anonymous].

No, when you're black or brown, your ass goes to jail. And when you go to jail and you have half a brain, you see it for the useless waste of humanity that it is. And when you see it for the useless waste of humanity that it is, you *think*! And when you think and have a pencil and paper, you write. I spent twenty-eight days in the Hole for no other reason than having the audacity to

think…and to write a book! Even though it was at a camp, even though it was only for thirteen months, I maintain that, given my circumstances, no good purpose was served by the sentence that was imposed in my case—none, that is, but those of the prosecutor and the prison industry.

"Yeah, but, Mr. Vic, isn't it possible that some of what happened to you was because of your combativeness? Or even your comportment? You have a very imposing presence. And on top of it, you're not exactly a shrinking violet, you know. I mean, why wouldn't you just say, 'Look, America. I know I'm right. And if this was coming from somebody else, you'd say I was right too. If I was anyone else but an outspoken 6'8", 280-pound black man with dreadlocks…and a felon, you'd listen. But because it's coming from me, you're gonna dismiss it as self-serving. You're gonna say that I'm just bitching and moaning. You're gonna say, "You did the crime, so why don't you just shut up and do the time?" I know all of that.'

"Why wouldn't you just say, 'So here's the deal, America. I have some idea what you might think about me. So why don't I, right up front, just stipulate that all of your notions about me are true? I *am* Black. I *am* 6'8" and hefty and dreadlocked and outspoken. I *did* commit a crime. And for good measure, let's throw in *angry*… because I am that too.'

"'But can you, America, just set all that aside for one minute… and just consider—just *consider*—that what I'm saying has merit? That just maybe, this is something that you—*we*—need to know… and act upon. Because, America, before now, I, too, was imbued of the same ideas…about prisons and about prisoners. I had no idea how misconceived I was about the criminal justice system—its purpose, its aims, its missed opportunities, or its shortcomings…until I went there and I saw what I saw.'"

"See, I think you're on to something here, Mr. Vic. I think your book says something that needs to be said. But I'm not sure that the casual reader will get past their preconceived notions if you come off merely as just another whining inmate who got caught with his hand in the cookie jar."

Well, some folks are gonna think that, regardless. But your point is well-taken, and I don't want to do that, that's for sure. Because, as I said to you from day one, *I did it.* I *did* get caught with my hand in the cookie jar. And I was—and I *remain*—willing to accept that punishment was warranted.

But as you also said, I *am* angry. Not about the punishment—or at least not about the *concept* of punishment. Be clear. The sentences in the federal system are too damned long, that's for sure. But that's not the travesty, that's not the worst of it. The travesty is that having committed a crime is merely a sliver of a prisoner's so-called *circumstances.* There are mitigating circumstances that are worthy of consideration—that is, if redemption and not merely punishment is, to any degree, the true goal of corrections. Committing the crime is a sliver of the circumstances, so punishment only addresses a sliver of the problem.

The fact that the federal system puts men away for huge chunks of time but then does next to nothing to make them better participants in their homes and their families and their communities, in society, is abominable. "I'll get you. I'll hurt me.' Said differently, 'I'll see that you get the punishment you deserve, but in the process I'll pay the tab for a system that virtually assures that you'll reenter my community as an even bigger threat to me and mine than you were when you went in."

Prisons are budgeted to provide rehabilitative services, but they either underperform or forsake those services altogether. It's an absolute scam that does disservice to the inmates, yes, but more importantly, to the public it exists to protect and serve. And nobody ever takes them to task for it. They get away with it scot-free. That's what makes me angry…

Matthew "Matt" Baum

"You can't judge a book by its cover!" To me, these words never rang truer than when applied to my first impressions of Matthew "Matt" Baum. Matt arrived on the FPC Cumberland compound in August 2011. He was assigned to the same unit as was I, though to a different wing.

The first thing I noticed was Matt's curious gait. He lopes more than walks; glides more than strides. To see him walk, one thinks him barely moving. He is not. He's actually moving at a fairly brisk clip.

His slow, easy gait; his gangling, backward-leaning, six-foot, three-inch frame; his too-short pants, and his clown-like big feet conspire to give one the impression that Matt's a Clem Kadiddlehopper—a rube, a bumpkin. He is not. He is actually among the most urbane people I've ever encountered.

Matt's mild manner, creamy pallor, round boyishly handsome bespectacled face, under a full head of medium-length, stubbornly coarse, would-be-curly hair give him the scholarly comportment of, well, a nerd. He is not.

In fact, Matt Baum is nothing that he appears to be. He is a paradox, a walking, talking contradiction. A push-me-pull-you. Moreover, the one thing that Matt Baum decidedly is, is the last thing that I'd have thought him to be…despite our environs. Matt Baum is a cold, calculating career criminal. He has the "look" of a man who might own a jewelry store but is far more likely to be the man who robs it.

Matt and I hit it off right away. In hindsight, as much could probably be said—about both Matt and me—regarding everyone we encountered on the compound. Like me, Matt could just as easily be found in the company of the hardest thugs as in that of the openly gay crowd. Each of us was as comfortable with the erudite, the educated, the elite, as we were with the un- or undereducated, as with rednecks, as with rude boys, as with Muslims, gentiles, or Jews, of which Matt is one. Each of us is a *people person*. So that Matt and I hit it off is, in and of itself, no more than either of us should have expected.

We played cards together. We talked about politics and religion. We talked about the Bureau of Prisons (BoP). And we talked about the so-called justice system. In fact, more than anything else, it was an initial difference of opinion about the latter that precipitated this interview. Here's the story.

One evening, when we were each awaiting our turn on an email terminal, Matt overheard me describing to another inmate the context of my book—this book. I described it as a book that was intended to relay my views about (1) how the BoP miserably and willfully shirks its responsibility to effect meaningful "rehabilitation," and (2) the Department of Justice's imposition of sentencing guidelines that, in my view, are the reason that individuals convicted of federal offenses serve sentences that are too, too long.

I added that I was taking the extra step of garnering the views of my fellow inmates on the matter, as well as telling their individual stories along the way. I went on to say to the other inmate that I had not met a single inmate whose sentence was not significantly longer than the circumstances of his offense warranted. The punishment, in my observation, rarely fit the crime.

Hearing that, Matt invited himself into the conversation, proclaiming, "**Not me. I got much *less* time than I deserved!**"

Understand. To me, inmates are a fraternity, of sorts. In this microcosm of larger society, there are inmates of diverse races, religions, ethnicities, cultures, educational backgrounds, and beliefs from various parts of the country and the world. There are Democrats, Republicans, communists, socialists, capitalists, doves, hawks, Klansmen, Panthers, bullies, wimps, he-men, gays, merchants, thieves, addicts, hustlers, back-biters, snitches, teachers, and law-and-order guys. You name it, it's here. The only thing missing is women.

But while the inmates at FPC Cumberland come from wildly divergent backgrounds, at the end of the day, we are all each other have. Not the staff. Not our families and friends, though we relish their support. Certainly not the administration, which uses both subtle and blatant tactics to discourage anything akin to a unified prisoner population, which I believe is among the things that the administration fears most. That and an informed taxpayer public.

It is my belief that on any given day, the inmate population is only as strong as the weakest among us. So I flinched with a note of disdain at Matt's comment and asked him, "How much time do you have?"

Forty months

"What did you do?"

Well, I pleaded guilty to nine offenses that included mail fraud, wire fraud, and theft of government property.

"How much money did your offense involve?"

About $780 thousand.

My first thought was, *Damn! Maybe Matt was right. Maybe he had, indeed, received a lesser sentence than his offense warranted. Forty months for a 780-grand offense? Whose ass did you kiss?*

That's what I *thought.* But what I *said* was, "What about your family? Did they deserve forty months?"

I should have thought about my family before I did what I did.

Wow! This guy should be working for the BoP. He's swallowed too big a dose of the tough-on-crime swill that the bureau serves to the public, the notion that if you're in jail, then you're getting no more than you deserve. So I concluded that it was of little use for me to argue with the guy, and I bailed on the debate. After all, he was new to the compound and to the experience, and I, among many others, was of the same misconception before I came in.

It could not have been scripted any better by a Hollywood writer that on the very next day, Matt was visited by his wife and daughter for the first time since his surrender—while my wife and I were seated directly across from them.

On several occasions throughout the duration of their emotional daylong visit, all three of them wept and bawled uncontrollably—Matt, worst of all. Of course, I had pointed him out to my wife, telling her of our previous night's conversation. And honesty dictates that I confess thinking, initially, "How's that forty months look to you now, big guy?"

But there's no way that I could hold on to such a sentiment in the face of Matt's and his family's abject grief. Like I said, we're all each other have.

So my wife and I sympathized with them from afar…as did several others appeared to.

I'd resolved to not mention a word of it to Matt. So you can imagine my surprise when he came to *me* a couple days later, saying, **I want to apologize for what I said the other night.**

"Yeah, I saw you guys going through the other day, Matt. No apologies necessary. But, tell me this. Were the feelings you expressed based on your knowledge of *all* the wrong you've done through the years? Were you saying that forty months was little enough price to pay—not for what you were convicted of but for all the wrong you've done through the years?"

Yes…

And so it was. The turn of events that landed me this, my seventh interview. In late November 2011, Matt and I sat down to talk. For what it's worth, Warden, I told you the truth when I replied "no" to your question whether I had conducted anymore interviews. You asked on November 22. I didn't interview Matt until the 28th…

"Matt, talk about your early background. Your upbringing, so to speak. Education, aspirations, etcetera."

I was born in Philadelphia, Pennsylvania (PA) in 1967. I got a GED in '86 then enrolled at the Philadelphia Community College. I dropped out after three weeks so I could get a 75 percent refund of my tuition. I took the money and went to Atlantic City and lost it all. The next semester, I did the exact same thing.

I grew up around crime. When I was three years-old, my mother was busted for shoplifting, with me on her side. All my uncles were criminals, always doing insurance scams and the like. Other kids wanted to be firemen or police. Not me. I wanted to be a criminal.

I was—and am—a product of my environment. When you're raised around people doing good stuff, you do good stuff. When you're raised around people doing bad stuff, you do bad stuff.

"When did your 'career' in crime actually start?"

I'd say when I was seventeen. My mom would give me a credit card, and I'd buy a bunch of stuff, max the card out, and then report it stolen. Mom and I would buy stuff—pricey stuff—and

then say it was stolen from the car at the time of the purchase. Insurance would pay for it. It *always* worked!

As time progressed, a couple of friends and I paid a mailman to divert credit cards to us. We paid him $500 a card. We never got caught. Later, in like '86, we ran a telemarketing scam, where we would call people—usually businesses—and solicit donations on the behalf of the AIDS Association of Greater Philadelphia. Of course, it was a bogus organization, and we spent the money.

Matt seemed always to have a big, all-out smile on his face, as was the case as he continued, **Well, I finally got caught, sort of. I was approached by an investigator for the Pennsylvania AG's [Attorney General's] office, saying that he had the authority to arrest me but that what he really wanted was information that I could provide him on other people. He basically wanted me to break into their offices, steal their files, and turn the information over to him. We met many times to formulate plans for me to rob the offices and turn over incriminating information to the AG's office. And as long as I did what I was told—even if I got caught—the AG's office would keep me out of trouble, right?**

But my stupid ass decides to sell some of the information— viable leads—to another telemarketing scam firm.

So I was arrested by cops from the Philadelphia Police Department's Second District. The AG's investigator comes to the station and says that they can't help me because I did exactly what I was told *not* to do. The case was prosecuted, and I got two years' probation.

I was arrested in '87 for check fraud. I made restitution then turned around in '88 and started opening up 'shell' corporations." Looking at me more directly, Matt asked, **"You know what a shell corporation is?**

"Do you mean a gas station?"

No, a shell corporation is a corporation is name only. Basically, you use the corporation's name to get a line of credit, you run up the credit, and then you dissolve the company. I did it for years.

"Damn…" I said, as I thought, *Who's the Kadiddlehopper now?*
"How many times did you do it?"

I've probably had fifty shell companies. My actual crimes probably total around $10 million.

"So are you here for activities related to a shell company?"

Yes, but I'll get to that.

Matt leaned back and appeared to ponder his next words. **I opened a legitimate printing company in Florida in 1993. It grossed about three and a half million dollars a year. But it started losing money—about a quarter million a year. We fell behind about $147,000 on taxes. We needed money, and a lot of it. Fast!**

So I decided to infuse the operation with some capital—by setting the company office on fire. I mean, I really did. I set the building on fire.

There was a lot of smoke damage, which actually turned out to be better than fire damage. Smoke left more of the kind of investigative evidence I needed to file a successful insurance claim—without actually ruining the machinery.

See, unlike the average person, I told the investigators that I *did it.* **I have a friend who's an MIT grad, who helped me put together my insurance statements. Plus, he rigged everything— the equipment and stuff—so it wouldn't work.**

So I just made it look like I made a mistake. I threw an ash-tray in a paper bin, so it looked like someone had simply been careless with a cigarette. I got a report that declared the fire an accident, and I filed an insurance claim for the smoke-damaged, non-operational printing equipment. Within thirty days, the insurance company settled for over $600,000.

"When did you move back to Philly?"

I moved back to PA in 2000. I opened a small printing company, along with a shell company, to funnel bad money into the good company, to keep it going for free. I'd bury one company and keep one good. I'd buy stuff on the bad company's credit and sell it. I got about half a million bucks from the printing company as well as lived off the money.

Okay, you've got to know that my head is spinning, by now. Matt's was such a dizzying array of stories. Back to back to back. It would be an impressive résumé for anyone—even for someone more suited to type. But it was all the more intriguing coming from a man who is physically as miscast as a bandit as would be Mike Tyson as Gandhi!

After a year or so, I ended the printing company and decided to steal full-time. And from 2000–2004, I set up a string of shell companies. In '03, I was arrested for setting up a shell printing company; setting up merchant accounts so that the company could accept credit card transactions—for no other intention but to steal money. I got in trouble when I hit [a high-profile credit card company] for about $75 thousand.

I hired the best attorney in Philly—a guy named Jack McMahon. The case dragged on for four years and through three judges. It was determined that there was no solid evidence, and I was found 'not guilty.'

In the interim, in '04, I joined a legitimate printing company that I put about $125 thousand of my own—albeit stolen—money into. My interest in the company was bought and financed with absolutely legitimate intentions.

That company was going okay, until I was thrown out of the company by my partners. One partner, in particular, said that I was 'using the company as my personal ATM.' In a way, he was right, because I was kiting checks between three different bank accounts. But in his accusation, my partner talked about the entire amount I had taken out—about $85 thousand. In reality, maybe $10,000 of that money was for my personal use. The rest was for verifiable business-related expenses.

At any rate, I was voted out of the company in June of '07. As a measure of revenge, I called to have the printing equipment repossessed, since it was financed in my name.

"So I'm still not clear. Why are you here today?"

After I left the printing company in '07, I really had nothing to do. So I went back to stealing. In a building that a friend owned, I opened three shell companies at one time, plus about twelve to fifteen bank accounts. By that time, I also had about a $400-a-day coke habit. Things were beginning to spin out of control.

For the next year and a half, between the bank accounts and a check-cashing company, I was kiting literally *millions* of dollars—about $275,000 a month. I was $50,000 in the hole with the check-cashing company but paid him back with the money from some of the stuff I stole and sold. That included $89,000 worth of US postage stamps that I sold on EBay. I stole and sold about $1.5 million in goods and I gambled constantly. In fact, from the age of thirteen, when my dad got me into my first casino, I was hooked on gambling. I could lose all concept of time at a craps or blackjack table.

By the way, I used to rob hotel rooms in the [Atlantic City] casinos. Matter of fact, I was one of the reasons they switched from keys to swipe cards. When I checked in, I would get extra keys and not turn them all in at check-out. A couple of weeks later, I'd come back and use the key to reenter and rob the rooms.

One time, I went back to Caesar's and went to this room. While my accomplice and I were in the room, we heard the door open. People were coming into the room. We hurried out to the balcony, but there was no fire escape. So I shimmied across to the next window, grabbed a brick, and threw it at the window, trying to break it. Know what it did? It bounced back! The window was unbreakable.

We had no escape. We were trapped. So I told my buddy to not say a word...to just follow my lead. Then we belligerently barged back into the room and threatened to harm the startled group of six or seven people if anyone so much as moved! We walked right out the door.

"Well, you know I can identify with that, Matt. The part about how enrapt you became when you were gambling. But, let's get back to the shell companies. Did any of the people you opened those businesses with know that they were fraudulent?"

Absolutely. *Everybody* knew! Everybody went in with their eyes open. And everybody made a lot of money.

"But, Matt. Get me to the reason why you're wearing FPC green."

I decided that I was going to open another legitimate printing company. But to do so, I needed one last big score. I set up a shell company and stole two state-of-the-art printing presses, worth about $400,000, as well as all the other equipment. It all totaled about a half a million dollars, for the legitimate company. I stole another million dollars and change worth of stuff from [a prominent electronics store] and [a copier company], among other companies. I got about $97,000 worth of stuff from [the copier company]—mostly toner—and sold it on EBay.

It turned out that they had a retired FBI agent working in its Fraud Department. He started a case but turned it over initially to the local police. In November 2009, I was arrested by the Penn Salem Police Department, with a bail set at $100,000. I was out the next morning.

"How did the case go federal?"

Well, I hired McMahon again to represent me. After saying that I had to be among the dumbest people he knew, he said he could make it all go away if I repaid [the company] the 97k. They claimed to be contemplating the deal, but all the while they knew it would go federal. They were already in touch with the feds.

So in January 2010, about twenty-five federal agents raided my house. I was actually arrested by a postal inspector and the FBI.

Matt was immediately and noticeably stunted. As though hit by a boulder. His countenance grew sullen, pensive. He continued softly, **At that moment, I realized…my child realized that her dad, my wife learned that her husband…** He looked down at first, then dead at me with cold eyes, over a guilty half-smile,… **That I'm this criminal**.

Speaking softly now, almost in a monotone and rubbing his brow, **When she picked me up from the Center City Detention Center, I told my wife that I realized our marriage was over.** Then with a smile that bespoke the contrary, Matt added, **Vic, all she said was, *"I'm not happy, Matt, but I'll stand by you. But this is the last*** *time I'll go through this."* Now she realizes that everything I'd said or done before…was *bullshit.*

At any rate, I told my lawyer that I was just a nice guy that does bad things. He quickly disputed that, saying, "Don't get it mixed up. You are not a nice guy. But you haven't raped or murdered anyone, so you can still turn your life around."

"What then?"

For the next twenty months—until I came here—I was a 'regular guy.' I sold cars. I kept getting fired whenever my story aired on the news or hit the papers. And those scum bags in the media sensationalized everything. Without giving me so much as an interview.

In fact, I was due to report [to FPC Cumberland] on August 1, but on July 16, I drove a rental car into a bridge. I woke up in the hospital with a shattered hip. The headline in the paper read something like 'Baum Attempts Suicide to Avoid Prison.' Can you imagine how my daughter felt reading that?

Anyway, my family—including my in-laws—has been wonderful. Being away from them all kills me every day.

"Describe your current circumstances—your marriage, the status of your businesses, your financial situation."

Well, I'm broke. After all the money I had, the cars, the gambling, the high rolling, I came here flat broke. My daughter turns seventeen in a few days. She's doing okay. My wife is getting by. We've been together for twenty-seven years—since ninth grade. We're married nineteen years. We have a 4,200-square-foot house in suburban Philly, Bucks County. She's really something. She pared down our living expenses from $11,000 a month to about $45 hundred. She's got a job that keeps everything going.

Looking as serious as he had at any time during our talk, he said, I love my wife as much as the day I married her. I'm lucky to have her and my daughter in my life.

"Let's talk about your impression of prison—specifically or in general. Talk about any differences between what you expected and what you found."

First of all, my attorney had told me that the camp was populated by a majority of white-collar offenders. Mostly middle-aged, mostly white. Guys like me, so to speak. So when I get here, and there are so many guys who are nothing like me, well, I was like Goldie Hawn in the movie *Private Benjamin*. When she first got to boot camp and found it to be different from what the army touted in the brochures, she said, 'I must be in the wrong army.' That's how I felt. Like I must be in the wrong jail.

But in pretty short order, I was glad to be around people who are different from me.

Plus, I had Googled life at Cumberland. All I got was sales pitches. Sharks, trying to sell me information about prison. That's why one of the things I'm definitely going to do is set up some kind of service where people can get useful information about the FPC, for *free*! I want to answer the questions of people who are about to come in.

At any rate, it has been enriching getting to know people that I seemingly have nothing in common with. Turns out that we actually have lots in common.

I will say this. Anyone who says they're not racist is probably lying. I think we all have at least a little bit in us. That being said, it is my observation that the staff here don't like blacks. They don't like Jews either, but it's easier to tell that you're black than it is to tell that I'm Jewish..."

At this point, I note to Matt that when I was in the Hole, an FPC lieutenant had haughtily confirmed for me that around 80 percent of the 1,800 inmates housed at Cumberland's medium-security and camp facilities are black or brown and urban, while upward of 90 percent of the staff is white and non-urban.

I also noted that Matt's and my case manager, among others, had willfully denied me the early release to which I was entitled—the last 10 percent of *every* prisoner's sentence, in which s/he is entitled to be released to either halfway house or, in my case, home detention.

I told Matt that she did so to me, while letting another man with whom I self-surrendered on January 3 of 2011 walk out in accordance with our shared 10 percent date—a man with an identical fifteen-month jail sentence; a man who, like me, had a court ordered of home detention to follow his imprisonment; a man with an identical release date, identical BoP calculated 10 percent date, identical first offender status, identically spotless institutional record and sterling personal repute as me. She facilitated his release so that he got out forty-five days earlier than did I—precisely, 10 percent of a fifteen-month sentence on December 21, 2011, while for no comprehensible reason, opting *not* to process my timely release. And she did so in blatant contradiction of BoP standards that say, in effect, that similarly situated prisoners *must* receive like treatment.

The only difference between the other inmate and me is that he is white—as is the case manager.

I also told Matt the story of how my former cubie, J-Boy, who stole $480 thousand worth of US government property that he sold on EBay, versus my $230 thousand plea. The judge in my case sentenced me to the twenty-seven months recommended in the advisory guidelines (fifteen months behind bars and twelve months of home detention). The judge in my cubie's case "pointed him down"— which is to say, she took into consideration mitigating factors (i.e., military service and childhood irregularities)—so that he was sentenced to a mere eighteen months, despite the fact that his advisory range was 40–120 months.

Both J-Boy and the judge in his case are white.

And, finally, I noted that Matt, himself was a repeat offender—a recidivist—convicted now in a case that involved nine offenses, whose cumulative impact totaled $780,000. Yet he was sentenced to forty months, of which, with the R-DAP, he will only serve sixteen.

Matt's response? **Yeah, it helps to be white!**

Ya think? The real travesty lies in the likelihood that the disparities and injustices that favor white offenders exist and *per*sist because, as I said before, to the taxpaying public believes prisoners "...get what they deserve" and that the so-called "face" of crime remains black and brown.

Complicating the issue is the fact that many federal prisons, like Cumberland, are built in non-urban communities and staffed by those communities' usually white, often culturally insensitive denizens. (Note to reader: go to www.realcostofprisons.org)

Many of Cumberland's staff members are, like my case manager, narrow-minded, sadistic rednecks, who seem to be of the opinion that they are somehow better people than are the inmates and that inmates are sent to Cumberland *for* punishment, rather than *as* punishment. They deem it their duty to pile their convoluted, cowboy brand of justice on top of the sentences imposed by the courts. Staff would rather chastise or sanction an inmate for walking on grass or for smoking a cigarette than to give him a straight answer to a legitimate question or to provide him with anything akin to a helping hand.

They bully, badger, and berate inmates at will—especially at the camp. Their blatant, unfettered abuse of authority appears to be fueled by their personal disdain for prisoners in general—and for minority prisoners in particular.

Add to the equation that staffs are largely under- or poorly trained to begin with and receive, on average, three weeks of what purports to be orientation before they are placed at the facility. As a consequence, their interpretation and implementation of BoP policies, in all areas of prison administration, is subjective and, therefore, uneven and inconsistent.

It is a potentially caustic mix, giving unregulated authority and control to a horde of ill-trained, mean-spirited, self-righteous, racist personnel—who are themselves little more than unethical bullies and buffoons—over a prison population that is predominated by people for whom those staff members have, at best, little cultural sensitivity...and, at worst, utter disdain. It's like pouring water on acid.

So what will it take for real change to occur? What will it take to dispel the tax-paying public's misconceptions that the only perpetrators of federal crimes—and, therefore, the only populations that are adversely affected by the dysfunctional system—are black and brown? I suspect that, as was true of America's drug, or AIDS, or poverty problems, the problems of a corrupt, inefficient, nonproductive, wasteful penal system will likely *not* be addressed until White America realizes the extent to which it is being directly impacted, woefully underserved…and egregiously duped. Which is to say, there will likely be no real prison reform until there are *more white people in federal prison*!

Anyway, back to Matt's impressions of the FPC. **I really haven't had many interactions with the counselor, but I've found him to be accommodating. He's accommodating but judgmental…and very condescending. Same with the case manager. She's not very nice at all, but I guess she does what she's supposed to do. I guess.**

But many of the Correctional Officers (CO) are ridiculous. They look at you and treat you like you are scum! And we're not talking about geniuses here, either. One idiot has wanded me five times in the past month. Every time, it goes off. And every time, I tell him that I've had a hip replacement. There's a difference between doing your job and just enjoying demeaning people… especially when many of them are more corrupt than we are.

As he related earlier, Matt had recently undergone total hip replacement. So I asked, "What about health services?"

Well, as I said, I had a total hip replacement surgery in July. I came here just four weeks post-op. I tried to postpone my reporting date, but the judge denied my request, saying that there were doctors and physical therapists at the camp, and that if they weren't able to do a suitable job, they'd refer me to an outside provider.

When I got here, the doctor, to whom inmates refer as "Dr. Death", "Dr. Kevorkian", "Dr. Do Little", or "The Grim Reaper", **says to me, 'You don't need physical therapy. Just walk.'** *Just walk*, **he tells me!**

Then a few days later, noticing my abnormal walk and fresh scar during an examination, the physician's assistant gawks at me and says, 'Whoa! You need physical therapy! Yeah, but they're not going to spend any money on you.

On the street, I am prescribed Nexium, for serious acid reflux. But they told me that Nexium is too expensive, plus I don't have a problem anyway. They told me to buy some Tums at the commissary. For pain, I should buy Ibuprofen. To her credit, one sweetheart of a nurse actually apologized to me. She said, 'I'm

sorry that we don't give you guys the care that you deserve.' We're inmates. Scum of the earth.

I couldn't help but to laugh a little on the inside, recalling the nightmare that had been my quest to get either attention for my chronic podiatric needs, or an exemption from the requirement to wear steel-toed boots that further exacerbate my foot problems. Or my thrice-tendered requests to be seen regarding a bladder leakage problem. Or the time I requested attention for an unexplained spot of blood on my underwear. Or the eye floaters, or the occasionally blurred peripheral vision. Or any of the range of maladies by which a fifty-seven-year-old black male can be beset…that in thirteen months of asking for help through the institution's formal processes were never addressed. For good measure, throw in my twice submitted requests for my medical records, which the department finally assured me that they would provide me upon my release…but did not.

Here sat Matt relaying to me that he needed something as specialized—and as expensive—as physical therapy for a recently replaced hip. Right! And here's a physician's assistant and a nurse in effect admitting their perceptions of how inmates are denied the quality health-related services they deserve—and which, I might add, the institution is budgeted to provide.

"What is a typical day for Matt Baum?"

Well, I go to a job where I do nothing all day but read. Maybe two days a month, I do something. Otherwise, I sit in a trailer all day and read. Which is actually a good thing, because I never read before. Now I read all the time.

Matt paused for a brief moment. Disquiet seemed to grip his face as he said, **This place—the first thing I noticed is that they offer no programs to teach you how to get a job. To me, there are no people beyond saving, no people who are not worth saving. But there's nothing here.**

They collect $27,000 a year to house and feed us. They get $27,000 a year more for us who are in R-DAP. That's $54,000 they get for us being here. Common sense says that some of that money has to be for teaching us something, something useable

in the job market. But there is nothing here, so they must spend little to nothing on anything that helps you when you get out. Gangsters remain gangsters. Drug dealers remain drug dealers. It's as if they're being prepared for nothing but failure. Like they're being prepared to come back.

The white-collar guys may not come back, but it's only because they came in better prepared for reentry. My third day here, I decided to teach a class on auto sales. I did it for twenty months before I came here. I'm good at it, and it's something anybody can do. I said, 'Wow! This is great! I'm gonna teach people how to sell cars. I look forward to it.

Then looking coyly at me, Matt added, **I want to give something back, for a change.**

Like the others with whom I spoke for this book, Matt was a joy to interview. He was forthcoming and open, hiding absolutely nothing. He shared his life in all of its sordid detail. And like the others, Matt confessed to getting a sort of relief from doing it.

It was difficult to do, at times, but in the end, I felt compassion, sympathy—almost pity—for Matt. Here's a guy who's a loving husband and father but who preyed on vacationing families' hotel rooms. A man with a keen sense of justice and right and wrong, who repeatedly betrayed friend and foe alike. He's a paradox. He is contradiction personified.

"So, Matt, if you could be anywhere in the world, doing anything you wanted, where would you be?"

I'd be sitting on the sofa, with my wife, Heidi, and my daughter, Eileen, eating ice cream and watching TV. That's it.

Realizing the risk at which I admit it, I say that I believe him. I really do.

Postlogue

Matt Baum was released in August 2013. He and his family still resides in metropolitan Philadelphia. He is employed as car salesman.

Gregory Bottoms

I met Gregory Bottoms—or G—in the camp gym, where he spent most of his days. I worked out in the gym six days a week—I did five hundred push-ups, walked five miles, and did five hundred ab crunches daily. My actual schedule was three days on, one day off. And until I saw G work out, I thought I was really doing something.

G was one half of a tandem—the other being a guy from Pittsburgh (I forgive him for that) whom I called L-Train—who met mornings to observe their own exercise regimen that, flatly, made mine look like resting. They worked every muscle, every day, in every way imaginable.

They did all the "ups": push-ups, sit-ups, chin-ups, pull-ups. And they did countless reps. They did wind sprints. They did miles. They did jumping jacks and toe touches. They jumped rope. They did an assortment of abdominal crunches. They dead-lifted—each other! In all, about three hours of a grueling, back-breaking fitness grind—and that was just their morning routine.

So needless to say, G was in tremendous shape for a mid-thirties-looking guy. Five foot eight, 180 pounds or so; bridge-broad shoulders; thick, heavily tattooed arms that seemed to extend from his shoulders down to his knees, thus earning him the nickname he got, courtesy of another of the gym regulars—King Kong! He had a thirty-six-inch waist with a fittingly thin face. His complexion was pale. Under his ever-present skull cap, the only hair that one could see was the reddish-brown goatee that he kept immaculately pruned.

More importantly, G was a genuinely nice guy. A true helper. See, not only was he a gym rat but he also worked there. G kept the place spotless! Mopping the floor, wiping down the machines, keeping everything in good working order, managing inventory, giving tutorials on the appropriate use of the equipment. He would help other guys establish their regimens. A true helper.

Apart from the gym, I'd encounter G at most of my usual haunts—in the library or the Education Center, at the Saturday inspirational movie shown in the Chapel, at Christian church service on Sunday evenings, and in the visiting room, where I first encountered his beautiful wife, Sarah—a sleek, smooth brown-complex-ioned beauty queen of a woman, whose comportment and carriage were so majestic, so stately that they almost made you not notice the cane she used to assist her severely impaired gait.

"So give me the 'quick and dirty' on the G Man. Tell me about your background. Where'd you grow up? What was your family like—as a kid? That kind of stuff."

I was born in 1970. I grew up in the metropolitan [Washington] DC area, within fifteen miles of the City. Me and my friends hung out uptown, in the area where all the upscale shops and clubs were. I went to school in Montgomery County [MD]—Germantown, Gaithersburg. My family finally settled in a community called White Oaks in Silver Springs. I was the youngest of three kids. It was me, one sister, and one brother. My brother and I are my dad's, biologically. My sister was my mom's from a previous relationship, but my dad adopted her and raised her as his own.

My father drank—a lot! And when he got drunk, he got violent. I vividly remember sometimes being in my bedroom during one of his drunken tirades and hearing the arguing—and sometimes the bumping around. I remember waking up and finding fist holes in doors and seeing a lot of beer bottles.

He was not really violent toward [the kids], except for one time I remember him putting his hands on me. One day, I came home from the pool. I was only wearing swim trunks. My dad was outside, just getting home. He handed me a big twenty-pound watermelon and told me to hold it. But it was ice cold against my wet, naked chest...and I dropped it. It splattered, and the next thing I knew, he hit me upside the head—hard!

But the thing I remember most about my dad is that I played a lot of sports when I was a kid, and he never came to see me play. Never. I guess it was the alcohol...and all that came with it.

Meanwhile, I was getting more and more into music. The song that got me hooked was 'Rappers Delight' by the Sugar Hill Gang. Man, I loved that song! I loved the culture. Break dancing. The dress. Graffiti. We spray-painted a few bridges, you know.

The whole nine. I was really into it. I wanted to rap, and I wanted to break dance. I was about ten or eleven, and I embraced everything about hip-hop culture. You might say that was the birth of 'G.'

The exuberance in and on his face was unmistakable. G and I had in common a love of music. We'd talked exhaustively about everything from the evolution of hip-hop, to our respective aspirations, to my own debacle with Sugar Hill Records. So I not only appreciated his passion but his disappointment, as he further related, **My father used to call me Tyrone, just to mess with me. It was supposed to be, like, a put-down. It didn't matter, though, because when I was about eleven, he woke up one morning and just left. The fighting between him and my mom had become too much for him, so he left. He and my mom broke up.**

"Tell me about your school days, especially in the years after your mom and dad split up."

Yeah, I was a so-so student, Bs and Cs, mostly. Socially, I was very popular except for a couple of rednecks, who didn't like me. One day, one of them sucker-punched me for no reason. But other than that, I was pretty popular. I had a crew of about six or seven guys I hung out with—two white guys and the rest black.

This was during my late junior high school years. I was thirteen or fourteen. My parents were separated. I had a lot of freedom. We would go down to Congressional Plaza, set up our cardboard and a hat for tips, and we'd break dance. We did it at the Holiday Inn Crowne Plaza, at a place called Bull Shooters, in Bethesda. We made about twenty dollars a week, man. That was pretty good for some thirteen- and fourteen-year-old knuckleheads...

G lit up with the kind of smile only the fondest memories can evoke. **We even had a manager! Johnny Ray. He had a big ol' Jheri Curl and drove this huge Lincoln.** He was laughing unabashedly now. **We used to battle other crews. A group called Radio Wave. Another one called the Mighty Pop-a-Lots. Man, we got it on!**

"Did you have a name?"

We were ECC—East Coast Connection... Predicting my next question, he added, **I was King Swift!**

We both had to take a "chuckle pause" on that one—G, at the memory, I was sure; me, at trying to imagine G in some big-ass MC Hammer pants.

G continued, **We used to catch buses to the city and sometimes stay out 'til past the time the busses stopped running. I remember one time in particular that we missed the time for the last bus and had to walk all the way from Georgetown to White Flint, in the Bethesda/Rockville area. I'm not sure of the actual distance, but it seemed like about twenty miles. I know we didn't get home 'til dawn.**

"Sounds like pretty garden variety teenager stuff."

Yeah, that's about right. But at some point between age fifteen and sixteen, my life took a turn for the worse, you might say. I started smoking weed and drinking beer—and experimenting with PCP.

"Did you all call it Angel Dust?"

No, we called it Love Boat. And it was fluent. It was no problem to get. I mean, our buddies' mom was selling five-dollar sacks.

"So you and your old crew were still hanging tough?"

Yeah, but we started getting into different stuff. Break dancing was phasing out. This was around '84, '85, and I was getting into 'go-go.' I'd go to places like the Black Hole, WUST Music Hall, and Cheriy's. *Every* weekend! Staying out 'til two or three in the morning. Still getting there on the bus, mind you. But I hung out. I hung tough. I got used to being not only the only white person in the club but the only one in sight!

The clubs on V Street and Georgia Avenue in the late eighties and early nineties were my spots. It was a big party. Fights. Drugs were literally in the air. I was fascinated. I still love that old go-go music.

G sat back in the classroom desk we had commandeered, still fondly reminiscing, only silently now. I got the distinct impression that we'd reached a turning point in the interview.

When I was sixteen, I got my driver's license. My mom cosigned for me to get a car—a Hyundai. From there, it was on! I

was still doing the clubs, but I was also doing the North Carolina college scene. When I was sixteen or seventeen, I met a guy named Squirrel. He was on the run, hiding from some drug dealers. He came to stay with his mom, who lived in my neighborhood. Squirrel introduced me to the 'business' of drugs, showed me how to sell 'em, how to make a profit from 'em.

I'm sixteen years old, and my mom thinks I'm in school. And I'm in the Bronx, New York, buying crack with Squirrel. We did it all the time—sometimes by car, sometimes by train. We were making money. But as quick as I made it, I spent it—or, I should say, I wore it. I was a clothes fanatic. Always sharp. Gucci sweat suits. In fact, I was voted 'Best Dressed' in my high school senior class. And they used to hate on me. I remember one time I came home and our front door was kicked in. Whoever did it took nothing but my clothes. Not the TVs. Not the VCRs. They just stole my clothes.

At any rate, as a result of my extra-curricular activities, I slipped in school. I got put on something called the WOC. I think it stood for Work-Oriented Curriculum. Which meant that I went to school from 7:30 to 10:30 then went to work. I worked at Jiffy Lube, and from that time to this, I have not stopped working. I've had no gaps in employment, up to one year prior to my incarceration.

"Talk about your current family. Take me to your adult years."

Okay, when I was twenty, I was working doing landscaping. One day, while I was at work, a guy pulled up in a pickup truck and, without getting out, yelled to me, 'Do you like what you're doing?'

I said, 'No.'

He said, 'Do you want a new job?'

I said 'Yes.' He told me to come to a certain Exxon station the next morning, which I did.

"Wait a minute. A strange guy pulls up, out of the clear blue sky, and offers you a job. Come on, G. Why you?"

He was laughing *at* me now, as though he had predicted—indeed, induced—my response. **Yeah, I thought the same thing.**

But I went anyway. It turned out that he was for real. He owned the Exxon station. And he put me to work. Then after my first or second day on the job, he told me that a mutual 'friend' had told him that I could get all the good drugs...because I hung with black people! He was interested in getting cocaine.

Sure enough, I always knew a guy who had the good powder. So I snorted a line or two of coke with him. Next thing you know, I was hooking him up. At first, about a quarter ounce a week.

That evolved into me selling ounces...at the station. I mean, I had people who literally came to the station and got a soda and a fifty-cent piece. I did it for years. Eventually, I added weed to the menu—all twenty-cent sacks. I was also doing the drugs myself. And through it all, I was still functioning at a high level. Still holding down the Exxon gig and working landscaping some evenings.

"Were you married while any of this was going on?"

Well, I met Sarah in 1990...she was a friend of mine's cousin. She had a four-year-old son named Eli when I met her. Eli's father had been murdered by his mother.

"By Eli's mother?! By Sarah?"

No. By his own mother. In the meantime, Sarah and me had our first child together in '92—a girl who was born prematurely. We moved in together in '91, and I started raising Eli as my own. The thing is, Eli is like *blue*-black. He is very dark-skinned. So you can imagine the reactions we get when I'm introduced as Eli's dad. It's like, 'Whoa!'

I had to chuckle at that one too...thinking about how people are. I could see them, especially the adults, Black or White—seeing this dark, darker, darkest black child, with his pale, white father and wondering, "Damn! If this boy is a hybrid, then his mama must be invisible!"

At any rate, Sarah and I got married in '97. We had another child together in '98—a son, also born prematurely. So yeah, I was doing my thing at the Exxon station and landscaping...and doing more and more cocaine...on Sarah's watch. I truly don't think she knew what was going on. She was a schoolteacher and worked a second job at a day care center. Her day care center job actually helped us in another way. The girlfriend of the guy I worked for at the Exxon station worked at the day care center, and she finagled it so that we didn't have to pay. That saved us something like $210 a week.

"How about your mom? Did she know about the drugs? Also, how was she with the idea of your having a black significant other? How about your siblings?"

First of all, my mom had no idea about the drugs. And she certainly never cared about my preference for a black woman. You see, she'd allowed a black friend of mine named Tre' to live with us for a while. My mom was my best friend. My siblings, not so much. Don't get me wrong. There's no animosity. Certainly, no hate. We are congenial, but not particularly close.

After my dad left, my mom went back to school. She got a master's degree at age fifty and eventually retired from the National Institutes of Health (NIH).

In the spring of '98, my mother retired from NIH...and broke the news to me that she had been diagnosed with lung cancer—Stage 4. The prognosis was not good. The whole thing weighed heavily on her, emotionally and physically. She had a townhouse in Germantown that she sold me for just under market value. Then after retiring from NIH in the spring, and after selling me her townhouse in the summer, my mom passed away, on October 17. Sarah's and my son was born on November 24 of that year. They just missed each other.

"Sorry to hear that, G."

Thanks, big man. Anyway, Mom left a one-hundred-thousand-dollar life insurance policy that my siblings and I split. I put most of my share into the house...and up my nose. I did more and more coke. And drinking. But like I say, I don't think my wife knew, 'cause I was highly functional. I worked hard. I was always responsible. I had excellent credit, a new car, was a good husband and family man. All while doing cocaine every day.

And I was doing music. I recorded some stuff in '94. A local producer—named Horse—ran an ad in the city paper, looking for hip-hop acts for his studio in northwest DC. That's how I first hooked up with Horse. We've been best friends ever since. The man's a beast!

So I was working from six in the morning to three in the afternoon, cutting grass in the evenings, then in the studio most nights. Cocaine is a *hell* of a drug!

We both laughed out loud at his interjection of the side-splitting line uttered by the late Rick James on comedian Dave Chappelle's raucous, self-titled late-night variety show.

Then G continued, **Then in '04, my daughter was molested on a school bus by some kids in the neighborhood. She was twelve. I didn't know anything about it. Neither did my wife. The way I found out about it was when this Asian lady pulled up in front of our house. I was sitting out front. She came up to me and asked, 'Would you want to talk about the incident?'**

I was like, 'What incident?' It turned out that the school knew, the bus company knew. The Asian lady was a reporter, so the press knew. Everybody knew but us! But when Sarah and I found out, we didn't know how to handle it. We thought about taking legal action against the school and the bus company, but we couldn't afford a good lawyer. Plus, we didn't want to subject our daughter to any more embarrassment. So we concluded that, before there was any more trouble, we'd leave the neighborhood. But where would we go?

We looked around and looked around, but everything in the DC area was too expensive. It offered no bang for the buck. Then somebody suggested that we look in Frederick County [MD]. I'm like, 'Frederick County? I'm white, with a black wife, and that's Klan country. Yeah, that's a good fit.'

But we looked in Frederick County anyway, and found a beautiful house—for $300,000. Two thousand five hundred square feet, two decks, hardwood flooring. It was in a court. It was perfect. Definitely worth the price.

So we sold our townhouse—that we'd bought from my mother in '98, for about $100,000. We sold it for $300,000! We put $90,000 down on the house in Frederick County. Plus, we

made some improvements. We did it up. Lighting, new fixtures, a bar, all new leather furniture. I mean, we laid it out...and then came move-in day.

Whenever we were shown the house, it was on weekdays—when none of the neighbors was home. But moving day was a sunny Saturday in April of '05. We pull up in our Ryder truck—I'm driving. And all the way down both sides of the street were all of our new neighbors. All White. And here we come—me the only White face, with an arm full of tattoos, my brother-in-laws, my wife, and my kids—all Black. One of the neighbors was bold enough to ask my brother-in-law if he was the new owner. He said no and pointed me out. I'm sure that was little consolation for the guy.

Throughout the summer, we had cookouts. Of course, we invited our friends—mostly black folks with good jobs, which meant they had nice cars. Sometimes, it was Sarah's family—older but still black folks in nice cars—coming to visit this white guy and his black wife and black kids. In Frederick County, Maryland.

One Friday evening, me and the kids were leaving the house to go pick up Sarah. It was around 5:30. I look over and I see about fifteen helmets and shields at the corner of my yard. Then, I hear, 'Freeze! Police! We've got a search warrant! Get on the ground!' My six-year-old son was terrified. One of my worst memories in life was lying on the ground next to my daughter—face-to-face with her—looking into her teary eyes, all of us lying there, with guns drawn and pointed at us.

"Was it the Feds?"

No, it was the Frederick Drug Investigation Unit, or something like that. Now, one of the things I never, ever did was do any drug business at my house or around my family. The only drugs I ever had in my possession at home was for my personal consumption. So when the officer barked, 'Tell me what drugs you got, or we'll tear your house up!' I told him I had nine grams of cocaine and twenty grams of weed upstairs, in my jacket pocket.

'Any guns?'

I said, 'Yes, I have a registered handgun,' and I told him exactly where it was.

Despite the small amount of drugs, the Frederick cops still threw six or eight charges at me: possession of cocaine with intent to distribute, possession of a handgun for use in connection with a drug crime, and a couple of paraphernalia charges. It was all in the local paper and everything.

One of the cops said to me that the reason they were there was because one of my neighbors had called them and said that they thought I was selling drugs because we had a lot of traffic in and out of our house. Still, like I said, I never sold drugs out of the house. But that neighbor's call gave them the idea to come by my house one night and go through my trash. In their search of my garbage, they found one marijuana stem. One stem!

That raid was on November 18 of '05. I immediately said, 'Fuck this! I'm through.' And I stopped everything. I still had my job, even though while all of this was going on, my boss sold his Exxon station. But the new owners kept me on. The new company had about forty stations around DC. My station became a Chevron station, instead of Exxon.

I went to court on January 6 of '06. It was snowing. I was there with my suit on, ready to get started with this case. But the judge said that court was cancelled due to bad weather and that we should check our mail for notices about the rescheduled date. Upon hearing this, my attorney said, 'I'll get these felonies dropped to misdemeanors.'

"So did he?"

Wait a minute. Check this out. While all of this is going on, [my wife] Sarah is diagnosed with cancer of the spine...which turns everything topsy-turvy. And on January 15 of '06, she undergoes surgery.

Then at about 5:30 on the morning of February 2, we are all woken from our sleep by our front door being kicked off the hinges. This time, the jackets say D-E-A [the Drug Enforcement Agency]. They're picking up the state case because one of my best friends was under investigation on a drug conspiracy case—and he had called me frequently on his cell phone. And vice versa. We were best friends, so we talked all the time…but not about drugs. At least not about any drug deal.

"So that's where the feds came in. Because you had a state drug case and talked on a cell phone with somebody they were investigating, they connected you to his federal case…that you had nothing to do with."

Exactly.

"So what's next?"

The arresting officers said we were going to Green Belt. My wife asked, why Green Belt

The officer replied, 'Because Green Belt is federal.'

But at that point, I still didn't know why, because I hadn't done shit! Then I heard over a walkie-talkie somebody mention my friend's address, which I recognized.

After we got to the Green Belt station, I saw my friend…and about eight or ten other guys that I didn't know. That's when they told us what we were there for. They split us all up. I briefly met with a lawyer. After they interrogated us, me and my buddy were taken to Baltimore. We spent five nights in the DOC [Department of Corrections] and one night in the super max, which was a trip in itself. Then they took us back to Green Belt for arraignment. We were let out on pretrial release. I went home on house arrest that ended up being nine months. In the meantime, I tried to get leniency from the court in the sentencing because of my wife's condition and my need to take care of her.

I didn't actually get sentenced until '08, when the judge said that she didn't have the authority to go below the sentencing guidelines. I was sentenced to thirty-seven months.

My court-appointed lawyer—whom I was very happy with, he was really good—he told me that we would fight the case, that we'd appeal the sentence on the basis of my wife's health…which we did. We lost the appeal because a guy in the same circuit, in the same situation, had lost his case, so they rendered my decision on the basis on that outcome rather than on the basis of my particular case.

So the whole process—from bust to sentencing to appeal to prison—was three-and-a-half years. I had to report here on August 4, 2009.

"On what charge?"

They tried to throw me into the five-kilogram conspiracy case. In fact, they came at me with a plea. I still remember the last sentence of the plea that read, 'I brokered several thirty-one-gram crack deals.'

I told my attorney, 'No way!' They couldn't convict me on *any* crack charge because I wasn't involved. So we went back to the US attorney, and they took all the crack charges off. They offered me a plea to a Class B Felony charge of possession with the intent to distribute. They had me on the phone talking to my friend about prices...which, they said, showed intent. I didn't know what else they had, but one thing you don't do—you don't take the government to trial. I knew I couldn't fight them, and I damn sure didn't want no ten years. So when they offered three, I took it.

"So is prison pretty much what you expected?"

Well, first of all, I had no concept of the difference between state and federal—I mean about how cases are handled. I knew a lot of people. I've literally seen a lot of people get probation or have had to go to classes or get fines, but no jail time for nonviolent offenses at the state level...especially first offenses. So I never thought that I would have to go to jail.

I never fathomed the thought of me doing any time on a first offense. Matter of fact, I remember the US attorney saying to the judge, 'Your Honor, we normally would not pursue jail time on a case like this...but the handgun bothers us.' And the handgun is why I'm still here.

I took the Camp's R-DAP [Residential Drug and Alcohol Program], and graduated in July of 2010. Which means I should have been out in August or September of that year. But because I had a handgun on my case, I was not eligible for early release. The people who run the program claimed they didn't realize that the gun was on my case. So they let me sit through the whole nine-month R-DAP, they got their $25 thousand for my being in it, and then they denied my release.

I'm doing an extra year for a handgun that was registered in my name, that I owned since I was twenty-one, that was in my house, in my drawer, not in my waistband or in my car. And although the [sentencing] enhancement [for the gun] was right there on my jacket [criminal history], this place claims they didn't realize it was there. They literally pimped me for twenty-five grand and then let me sit here for a whole 'nother year.

So, no, prison is not what I expected. Not the process, anyway. It's inhumane, and it has one purpose. Making sure that you come here. Definitely not justice. And not what they do when they get you here. It's all a farce."

"What about Sarah through all this? Healthwise, and otherwise."

Because of the toll this has taken on her, physically and emotionally, I decided that I was going to spend my bit fighting to get out, for just that reason. During all of this, Sarah has undergone a total of three surgeries—and radiation and chemo[therapy]. She has to get epidural treatments in her back every three weeks to manage pain. She feeds through a tube in her—she eats baby food and soft stuff like that. She weighed about 160 when I met her. You've seen her. She's probably in the teens right now. She's definitely not 120.

So I wrote my congressman and asked if they could assist me. That went nowhere. In here, I filed for what's called 'compassionate release' so I could be on home confinement and be there to care for her. I first filed in April of 2010. I applied first to my unit team—my [correctional] counselor and case manager—and was denied. So I appealed to the warden and the regional director. I was denied by them both. The warden's letter back to me stated I was denied, "although your wife's plight is tragic. Your unit team, the camp chaplain, and I are available for your support.'

I also filed for release under the Second Chance Act. I was denied at every level of that remedy process. They told me that 'if the judge had knowledge of the mitigating condition upon sentencing and rendered the sentence anyway,' then the Second

Chance Act would not apply. Plus, the Second Chance Act was to help with transitional needs like housing, not family.

I didn't want to give up, so I wrote the sentencing judge and informed her of my wife's further decline. The letter I got back was from a clerk in the judge's office, saying, 'The judge does not alter the terms of a sentence due to this kind of circumstance.'"

"Damn, G. I appreciate your determination. This must have been a hell of an emotional ride for you. And for Sarah."

Yeah, it was. Ultimately, I decided to just do my time. Concentrate on my physical, read books, try to not let my mind go crazy—and stay out of the way. Because there's really nothing here that offers any real self-improvement. I've been here twenty-one months and have twenty-two ACE [adult continuing education] class certificates—which will serve no purpose once I'm released...other than as paper airplanes or something.

Cool! G made the segue for me. His last observation had taken me right to the next topic I wanted to discuss. "What's your impression of the Camp?"

When I heard I was coming to a federal prison, I thought, 'Cool. I can learn something.' Man, was I ever wrong. Now, I'm not judgmental, but 75 percent of these folks are idiots. They prove that if you sit in a room, don't ever read, and don't try to learn something—if your biggest concern is about what you're wearing or eating—your brain turns to mush. It turns into mashed potatoes, man." Looking up from the piece of paper he's fondling, G says, matter-of-factly, "You know what? That goes for the staff and administration too! They warehouse these guys. Give them nothing. They collect all that money for the inmates being here and give 'em nothing. Then they put 'em out on the streets...and just wait for them to come back. Where's all the money go that the BoP gets for running prisons? While recidivism increases.

Meanwhile, staff members skulk around the compound, harassing you about tucking in your shirt or to stay off the grass then get into their [brand-new] luxury cars and speed off. That's where all the money's going! All while there are no staff-led..."

G hemmed and hawed through a procession of "Uh, uh," then emphatically concluded, **"*Nothing!* GED. ACE classes. All that shit is led by inmates. The education director is cool, but he's too cool. He just wants to collect his money and go home."**

G paused for a moment, as if pondering all he'd said. He was as emotional in his almost sermonic rant as he was profound. **The only beneficial thing to me about this whole experience is that it helped me realize what's important in life, the little things that we overlook every day. In my eyes, the three most important things are—apart from God—in this order: number 1, health; number 2, freedom; and number 3, love. Everything you do affects somebody else.**

I lost *everything!* My job of fifteen years. My house was foreclosed on. My cars were repossessed. I lost my good credit. My wife has to go through the most draining physical and emotional ordeal of her life without her husband around to help. I have to start all over again, like I'm fucking seventeen. Just so I can come in here and do *nothing* for twenty-six months at a prison with no fences that's two hours from my home. And for what? Who got helped?!"

Damn! G's words struck a chord with that one. *"Who got helped?!"* he posed, the words cutting to the very core of my own sentiments. *"And for what?!"*

Like G, I had been put in the position of having to start over. With nothing. But unlike G, having to do it at age fifty-seven. *"Who got helped?!"* Society and the economy lost a contributing member and a taxpayer. Another home defaults into foreclosure. *"And, for what?!"*

My wife is punished for something not of her own creation. Two nonprofit organizations suffer—one, because it 'won' a $500-per-month order of restitution that does not come close to sustaining it; the other, because it lost the opportunity to ensconce its much-needed youth violence prevention services into the after-school programming of two inner city schools. *"Who got helped?!"*

Like G, I was literally strong-armed by the prosecution into a plea agreement that asserted an amount of misappropriation that the prosecution knew and *admitted* it could not prove—because it did not happen! An amount contrived by the prosecution solely because sentencing guidelines for the amount they could prove—for a first-time offender of sterling repute—called for zero to six months!

So in the one-count wire fraud plea offer for my case, the prosecution contrived an offense amount, for which the sentencing guidelines advised a higher minimum jail time: twenty-seven to thirty-three months. The alternative was for me to go to trial and defend myself against multiple charges—one for each of the more than thirty times I made unauthorized use of the organization's credit card, each count carrying its own mandatory minimum sentence, and to which I had already admitted guilt, in the form of an unsolicited statement of apology to the organization.

"And for what?!" All for the judge to send me off, with his magnanimous permission to "come back and be the outstanding man I [was]."

"Who got helped?!" Like G, in the scenario that played out, no one was helped but the Bureau of Prisons (BoP) and the US attorney who prosecuted the case. The BoP was enriched by the nearly $30,000 per inmate per year that it received for our imprisonment—and the up to $27,500 more per year they did receive for G and would've gotten if they could have finagled my eligibility for the R-DAP—which they *did* try. The prosecutor benefited by both the financial incentive and the career boost he got for obtaining a conviction that lead to incarceration. *"And for what?"*

As the meaning of his words continued to resonate throughout my very soul, G went on, **Look it up on Google. They said I made two million dollars in six months. Hell, I couldn't afford a lawyer! Mine was court-appointed. I had a quarter-million-dollar mortgage, another fifty thousand dollars in credit card debt and bills. I had two thirty-thousand-dollar cars repo-ed. If I had made two million dollars in six months, don't you think I would have paid some of those bills?**

G's cynical half-smile was fading. This was tension I saw...and sheer exasperation. I could sense that the interview had taken its toll, when G offered, **Vic, man, I can see what you mean about the** other guys you interviewed…about how talking to you this way was therapeutic for them. I feel that way too. Plus, saying it out loud makes me feel like I'm not that bad after all, despite what the staff here try to make you feel *every* damned day.

"No question, G. Same here. I know you're like me. You know a whole lot of people who have done much, much worse things than you and I. Real bad guys, who just haven't been caught. But let me turn the page now a bit and ask you what programs and/or services you think should be available for inmates."

Shit, anything would be a step up. Definitely, CDL [commercial driver's license] classes for me. It would be easy for them to do, with all the vehicles they have at the garage. Or computer class…just basic operations, let alone the Internet. We asked for a computer with no cord. Strictly for learning purposes. It was denied. I guess they thought we'd rig it up or something. But you can't learn the computer without a computer or HVAC without… *no nothing!*

"Or Voice and Songwriting without the necessary equipment."

Exactly. Although if you teach a songwriting class, I'm going to take it, he said with a wry smile.

"You need another paper airplane?" We laughed. "What do you miss most about life on the outside?"

Being 'Dad'…and 'provider.' I miss bringing up my children. That's why I'm grateful that it's only two years. Because the real victims are my children, my family." He winked. "The second thing I miss is X-rated.

"What are your plans for when you get out?"

That's a tough one, Vic. Just call it TBA—to be announced. With what I'm hearing, getting a job may be tough. But I'm gonna get one. I'll do anything. Anything *legal*, that is. Shovel horse shit. Clean wheels with a toothbrush. I will not come back to this motherfucker. This ain't living, Vic. *It's dying with your eyes open.* Every day is painful.

The only thing left to ask? "If you could snap your fingers and be anyplace, doing absolutely anything, where would you be?"

Sitting at home, watching a DVD with my kids, eating some real food, with the remote in *my* hand—with my wife sitting right next to me.

My man! See you at the Grammys.

Greg Bottoms was released from Federal Prison Camp, Cumberland in April 2012. Residing in the metropolitan Washington, DC area, he is a loving, active father to his children. He is employed in the field of plumbing and heating, and still actively pursues his passion—music. As for the break-dancing? Not so much.

"What did we do?"

"So you were executive director of what seemed like a successful community-based organization that was rendering health services to a population that definitely needed it, and by my understanding, much of the success of the organization was due to your planning, persuasion, and foresight, is that right?"

Yeah, but let me not be so vainglorious. A good bit of the groundwork of establishing the organization's presence in the community had been done by my predecessor. She had orchestrated a deal with another existing community-based group in which to get a grant from the [Centers for Disease Control and Prevention] that put us on the map. It was an HIV-AIDS education and prevention project—a five-year demonstration grant. She'd set it up where the existing organization was the funded—or 'lead'—organization and our group was the partner. The up side of that arrangement was that it gave our group a platform from which to become visible in the community; in the realm of public health. The down side was that our organization still didn't have its own status as a corporation in the state of Maryland. It did not have articles of incorporation or bylaws or its state or federal tax exemptions. It did not have a viable corporate structure. That's why she set up the demonstration project the way she did, because our organization couldn't receive grant funds. Technically—*literally*—it still didn't exist!

In the meantime, a rift developed between my predecessor and certain members of the board. Next thing you know, she was out. And that's where I came in. My friend the board president called me and encouraged me to apply for the job. I did, and I was hired. Within the first six to nine months of my tenure, I did all of the legwork to get the organization formally established, drafted its bylaws and articles of incorporation, got its state and federal tax exemptions. Put it on the map, formally.

"Cool…"

After that, I buckled down and started trying to raise funds for the organization—both for programs *and* for the purpose of constructing the building that they envisioned as a base of operations. Like I said, before I came aboard, the organization was really little more than a concept—a collection of passions and ideas without direction. Hell, I had no particular skill for it, for organization-building. But I was, if nothing else, diligent, hard-working, hopefully smart…and *definitely* lucky.

I put in request after request for money; to the city, to the state, to foundations. Once, on a walking tour of the area with the mayor, I orchestrated the partnership between the city and a large, local law firm to acquire and then bundle the forty-two abandoned properties that blighted the 2.3-acre lot that was ultimately sold to us for six thousand dollars, and on which we eventually built a community health center. I secured a commitment from the city to excavate and prepare the lot for construction. I got other grants that ranged from $100,000 to $2.6 million—grants totaling about $4.5 million altogether—for construction. I engaged a developer, and in November 2006, the building was opened. Well, the grand opening was actually in March of 2007. And the beauty of it was that we didn't have a mortgage. It was completely paid for. I even recruited and negotiated the deals by which the building became fully occupied by other providers.

But here's the thing. The thing I was best at? Let me put it this way. A couple of years after the building was up, I met with the then deputy mayor of the city. I wanted to inquire about potential funds that may have been available through the city that the organization could possibly go after. After treating me with complete indignity—making me wait alone for half an hour before deciding to come into her office where we were to meet, taking phone call after phone call, interrupting my discourse, then literally looking at a television that was on and just to the left of me while I was talking—the deputy mayor finally asked me a question that stopped me in my tracks. She asked, 'What does [your organization] do?

Wow, I thought. That's a hell of a question. What the hell do we do? And that was when it occurred to me what my real 'gift' to the organization was.

"What's that?"

Well, my immediate response to the deputy mayor's arrogance was that the organization did exactly the same things we did a few years earlier, when as a state delegate she wanted to take credit for our growth and success. But the real relevance of her question stuck with me.

You know how a not-so-good-looking person hangs out with good-looking people because they think it makes them look better? You know, 'If they look good, then I must look good too.

"Okay, go ahead."

It's the same idea. I partnered the organization with other viable groups, which, in turn, lent an air of viability to us. I did it often and I did it well. My 'gift' was that I could create the illusion that the organization actually *did* something.

The other groups needed us but usually for only one purpose: to create for potential funders the illusion that the projects we were partnering on were 'community-based.' They all did it, including the hospitals. They recruited us to be the 'face' of the proposed project, but they were always the fund recipients. And when they no longer needed us, they shitted on us, if not dumped us altogether. One by one, when they realized that we were almost completely smoke and mirrors, those partners kicked us to the curb.

What did we do? The truth is, we really did *nothing!* We had no product, nothing that made us indispensable.

"Come on, Mr. Vic, that's a bit of an overstatement, isn't it?"

Well, maybe not. What I mean is this. We didn't treat anyone, we didn't examine anyone, we didn't medicate anyone. The most we did was advocate on behalf of what we perceived—or contrived as being—the community's health interests. We educated community folks on an array of issues, health-related and otherwise. We were brokers, sort of bringing together all of these real service providers, like the hospital, the clinic, legal services, housing and community development services. But what we actually *did*…what we really *made* was nothing. I could write grants. I could approach and persuade potential partners and potential funders. I could articulate the need in this physically blighted and otherwise challenged community for this service or that one. And I could paint a smiley face on what we did, make us seem vital to the community's public health and other needs. But at the end of the day, after we got the building built and occupied—which was, itself, a laudable accomplishment—our real, functional usefulness had been served. That's what made us—and, by extension, made *me*—expendable.

Hell, at the grand opening of our building the president of [the conglomerate under which our hospital partner operated] stood before a roomful of people and said that he never thought I'd actually get the building project done, which, for me, was a dead giveaway that neither he nor his cronies at the hospital were ever really committed to the idea of genuine community service. Oh, they had an objective, all right. Their objective—and their *only* objective—was to reduce the cost incurred by the hospital for providing medical care to uninsured men, care that they had to provide but couldn't be paid for.

But his comment said to me that the notion that they were even remotely interested in genuinely engaging with the community was disingenuous. It was pure bullshit. They only wanted it to *look* like they did. The board president and I talked about it all the time. How else could you justify the fact that the hospital would often compete with us for certain grants, those that didn't require either a partner or the perception of community involvement?

Anyway, it was from that very moment that I stopped deluding myself about the notion of the hospital's so-called commitment to us…and that I started trying to make that point to the organization's board. I started trying to impress upon them the importance of self-sufficiency, that once the clinic we helped start was operational and once the hospital could feel the financial effects it envisioned, our usefulness to them would have been served. But as I said before, my board's ineptitude was, all at the same time, the thing that I liked most about my job, as well as my biggest challenge. So they just didn't see the gravity of the situation. They couldn't be made to see it. They couldn't be made to see our irrelevance, not even the board president. Hell, she was straight. Her ass was covered. As far as anything else related to the organization was concerned, 'Vic'll handle it!'

"Sounds like this would be a good time to talk about the hospital. How'd they get you out?

Yeah, cool. But like I said before, the story has nothing to do with why I went to jail or with the reason I wrote this book. More than anything, it's a story about how some corporations—in this case, the hospital—exploit unsavvy community groups. They're certainly not the only ones who do it—hospitals or otherwise. They're probably not even among the most egregious offenders. But it's a story worth telling, I think, and it's certainly one that I'm intimately familiar with. So here goes.

The story begins on October 23, 2008, almost two years after our building was up and running. That's when the board president and I were asked to a meeting with the hospital president—a short, scrawny, bespectacled guy with thick, medium-length, curly, almost kinky, dark-brown hair. He wore this irksome but ever-present disingenuous smile on his long, narrow face. He always put me in the mind of that comic actor, Eugene Levy. He played in *Bringing Down the House* with Queen Latifah and Steve Martin. Anyway, it was to be just us and him, in his office. We—or, in retrospect, let me say *I*—had no idea what we were there to discuss, because us meeting with him was not at all unusual. We did so a few times a year, if for no other reason than to bring him up to speed on the organization's progress… especially while the building was under construction. After all, my salary and [my assistant]'s salary were both paid out of their budget.

By the way, while it was certainly not insignificant—and I definitely appreciated it—that was really the only contribution they made to the organization. I say this because a lot of people, in and out of the community, think that the hospital contributed to our building's construction cost. They did not. Not one dime, despite the fact that they stood to be the biggest beneficiaries from its successful operation. A lot of people also think that the hospital had administrative authority over the organization, which they also did not. In fact, they were very careful to put into effect a [memorandum-of-understanding] that specified that my position was leased to the organization for the cost of one dollar per year. They didn't want people to get the impression that they were riding shepherd of these 'po'ass colored folks.' Of course, that's *exactly* what they were doing, as was evidenced by the vice-president they dispatched to serve on the organization's board...who did little more than drive-thru our board meetings and whose input and observations at those meetings were always, *always* imbued of the hospitals best interest, not the organization's. And like I said, it was evidenced by the couple times a year that we met with the president. And to top it all off, the hospital trotted me out once a year to make presentations to their board about what great work 'dey was doin' wit' dey coloreds.'

See, the hospital was established back in the 1800s to serve the predominantly Jewish population in that part of Baltimore, who couldn't get treated at other hospitals. But through the years, more and more blacks moved into the neighborhood, as more and more Jews moved out. And despite retaining its adherence to ethnic Jewish traditions, in time, the hospital found itself ensconced within a neighborhood that was predominantly black. And as a consequence, as the neighborhood's profile changed, so did the demographics of the hospital's patient population. More and more of them were black.

Anyway, the hospital president opened the meeting by assuring us of how thankful they were for the wonderful relationship the hospital had enjoyed with us for all these years. He remarked to the effect that he was so-o-o proud of us for getting the building done...despite the fact that it had not, as yet, brought about a noticeable reduction in the number of men that were showing up at the hospital for care. Uh-oh...

I saw it coming, man. He went on to say that the hospital was experiencing some fiscal challenges, by virtue of the nation's economic recession, and that it had taken a toll on the hospital's budget. So according to the president, the hospital had no choice but to consider an exit strategy—the time had come for the community organization to stand on its own two feet. Oh, they weren't going to withdraw their support immediately, he said. They would continue to underwrite [my assistant]'s salary through June of 2009 and mine through June 2010. The way I looked at it was that I had until June 2009 to find money to replace [my assistant]'s salary and another year beyond that to replace my own. That was on October 23, 2008. I immediately relayed the timetable to [my assistant].

In January 2009, the hospital president sent me an email (which I still have) in which he asked me to write up and send him a list of my duties and responsibilities as ED—basically a job description. He wanted every infinitesimal detail. What was my role in all of our programs? What boards was I on? How much of the daily operations did I manage? He wanted me to outline every detail. I thought nothing of it and complied right away (which correspondence I also still have).

I really didn't start to smell a rat until around February—a little before [my assistant] left to take a job elsewhere. That's about the time that the Weasel started coming around more often. He was already on payroll at the hospital, working as a quasi-lobbyist, supposedly representing the hospital's interests down in the state capitol. But it was a clearly duplicative position because the hospital had a vice-president who had worked in that exact capacity for years. When the hospital first hired the Weasel, my board president and I theorized that they'd made up the position...perhaps, we thought, to appease the Weasel's father-in-law—a former superintendent of schools and a current hospital board member.

Anyway, like I said, the Weasel usually just came by to flirt with [my assistant]. But now he was beginning to check-in more with *me*—inquiring about organization business, in which he had previously shown little to no interest. His ruse was that he intended to 'look out' for us, regarding funding opportunities in Annapolis. [My assistant] found it odd too that he was coming around so much.

In March, [my assistant] left to take another job—a full calendar quarter before funding for her position was scheduled to stop. Because the hospital president had assured us that the hospital would continue to pay [my assistant] through June, I emailed him to ask whether the hospital would underwrite the cost of us hiring a temp for the remaining quarter. His response was no. I then asked if he would assign someone from the hospital's secretarial pool to assist me. Again, his reply was no, adding that the hospital would be making no further investment in the organization. So now I was charged with managing literally every aspect of the organization's operation—administrative and clerical. I had to open and close the building, I was attending meetings all around town, managing a never-ending stream of building-related issues, researching and writing grant proposals, managing programs that were under our auspices, answering the phones, sorting mail, paying bills. You name it, I did it. And this is how it was going to be for the next fifteen months or until I could find the money to pay for an assistant.

Then in April, my now *former* assistant called me at the office to say that she'd just received a call from the Weasel—asking her how much money it would take to get her to come back. I'm like, 'What the...?' But again, giving the slimy Weasel benefit of the doubt, I thought he was maybe on to something down in Naptown. Maybe he had sniffed out a funding opportunity. Plus, I was way-y-y too busy to deliberate on it. So I just let it ride.

Then in early May, I got a call from my board president. She was in a panic, talking 'bout, 'You got something you can do? You got any prospects for another job?' I just left from meeting with [the vice president who represented the hospital in Annapolis]. I should have known something was up when she asked to meet me up at the Quarry and it was all hush-hush and shit…"

The significance was that their clandestine meeting was convened at a location far removed from the hospital campus. Of course, now I'm curious to know what the hell is up.

"The first thing she asked me was what was my impression of [the Weasel]. Did I think I could work with him?"

"I'm like, 'What's up?'

"Vic, they gon' drop your salary from the budget—*this* year, and they gon' try to pawn [the Weasel] off on us as a replacement. Oh, they know he doesn't have executive experience, but they're saying that maybe I can groom him."

The hospital knew that there would be an uproar from the community if the organization failed, and they knew that having no one serving as ED would practically assure the organization's failure. So why not 'offer' the Weasel to the organization's board…as an alternative? Sure, he was inexperienced, but wasn't he better than having no one at all?

So on May 15, 2009, I was summoned to a meeting at the hospital—this time, alone. I met, not with the president but with a vice president. At that meeting, I was informed of what I already knew—that my salary was being eliminated from the hospital's budget, effective June 26—in just five weeks, a full twelve months sooner than the date that the president had assured me of.

It was perfect! It was good community relations, because by magnanimously offering an albeit flawed replacement, the hospital could avert incurring the community's ire. It was good, regarding the hospital's desire to control the organization, because they could control the Weasel in ways that they could never control me. It was good financially, because they could save my $80,000 salary, and the Weasel was already on the hospital payroll. It was good in-house politics, because the Weasel was a board member's son-in-law. Plus, the Weasel could learn the job on the fly, under the board president's tutelage, a board president whom (I guess) had no knowledge of the Weasel's frequent visits to the office...or of his prying into the organization's business and operations...or of his overtures to lure [my assistant] back to the organization's employ...or that, at the hospital president's request, I had written the damned blueprint for the job...

Cecile "Doc" Dwele

"The objective…is profit, not outcomes" (C. Dwele).

I've always thought there to be some merit to psychology's allusion to the so-called *Napoleonic Complex.* Loosely, it purports that some people seek to overcompensate for being small in physical stature by exerting extra effort to be leaders in their chosen disciplines. At its core, it is the simple premise that good (or *big*) things come in small packages. Or that "I will not be outdone solely on the basis of my small size."

When I was in college, I pledged to join a fraternity. It was 1976, so be clear—there *was* hazing, plenty of it! But for the most part, the violence and diminution to which I was subjected was no more than I expected. Frankly, by comparison to the punishment I knew was typically meted out on historically black college (HBC) campuses, the hazing that took place at my University of Louisville (U of L) chapter was modest. Plus, there were only five big brothers on the yard to pledge what started out as eight prospects.

I was at the tail end of my line—number 4, as it were, by the time my line (the 4 Disciples) was initiated. I was lean, handsome, confident, smart, could sing, and was popular. And I was tall…a fact which led to my worst night as a pledge.

Of the brothers on the U of L campus, one was Big Brother Peak—a 5'7" dynamo who was an overachiever in every way imaginable. He was an outstanding athlete—a running back on the football team, who was among the nation's rushing and all-purpose yardage leaders during his senior campaign. He was a straight-A student, majoring in computer science. He was an exemplary fraternity man, having earned the organization's first-ever national award for outstanding undergraduate achievement. And he, like the rest of the chapter members, was a superb, committed community servant… evincing a service ethic that inspired me to join in the first place.

While Peak certainly exhibited his share of Napoleonic tendencies, his antics were more playful than physically abusive. He'd do silly shit that was, at times, over the top but never dangerous. He asserted his "power" in ways that made you want to slap his little ass but never to hurt him because he was never trying to hurt as much as to humiliate you.

Jose was different. He too was short—5'8" tops. He was light-skinned, with a thick, neat Afro hairdo, classic "pretty-boy" good looks, and—as was Peak—very muscular. But unlike Peak, Jose was mean, downright ornery. He had a very violent nature that he put on and took off, like a hat.

I knew and ran with Jose before I pledged. He did not attend U of L, or any other school at that time but had pledged into the frat at a nearby HBC. In 1976, it was not uncommon for brothers from outside the chapter—or, as was the case with Jose, from no chapter at all—to participate in pledge programs. Even, at times, to be permitted to have access to pledges—sometimes unfettered access and sometimes off campus.

On this particular night, my fellow pledges and I (still totaling six, at the time) caravanned to Big Brother Jose's off-campus house. I'd been there many times before, so I thought little of it.

What I didn't know was that Jose held the opinion that my line's pledgeship was not "hard" enough, that we were "walking-in," to use frat parlance. So Jose had assembled ten or so of, ostensibly, his former chapter brothers together, for the stated purpose of "whipping us into shape."

In retrospect, it now seems plausible that, had we been more deferent, had our demeanor been more subjugate, then we might have spared ourselves what was about to happen. But we weren't. Jose certainly knew that I wouldn't be. Neither would the one of my fellow pledges whose twin brother was vice president of the entire region. We were, in a word, arrogant. Frankly, we thought they were bullshitting…

Until we felt the first lashes. These motherfuckers flogged us mercilessly for the better part of an hour, with a homemade article called "Silent Sam." It was a coat hanger, shaped and taped in such a way that all you could hear of it was the whir it made as it cut through the air on its way to its destination—your arm, your leg, your ass, your back. Whatever. And the lead assailant was Jose.

Long after the others had stopped, Jose—now, to his stated delight, towering over my huddled frame—was beating me, *just* me, without mercy, shouting in an almost insane rant, "Say who's the biggest now, nigger. Let me hear you say it. Who's the biggest now?"

I never forgot that—neither the night nor the lesson. After that night, I could never see Jose the same. Certainly, there was no way I could afford him the dignity of either my dropping line—quitting—or embracing him as my so-called "brother." Neither could happen, and neither did. But, from that day to this, I have never taken lightly the extreme(s) to which a short man might go to "cut me down to size."

And that scenario has played out many times throughout the course of my life. Even throughout the year-long episode that led to my incarceration, during which my Munchkin-sized successor at the nonprofit organization I ran used every tool at his disposal to annihilate and humiliate me. I could almost hear him saying, "Who's the biggest now, nigger? Let me hear you say it."

So when I met Doc, my guard was up. Cecile "Doc" Dwele, PhD, was a small man—in physical size *only*! At 5'7", 150 pounds, with a dark brown frame that clearly was at one time athletic, Doc puts one—or, at least, those of us old enough to remember—in the mind of Dick Tiger, a prominent Nigerian welterweight boxer from the 1960s. Like Tiger, Doc's distinctly West African features—deep chocolate complexion, close set eyes, ample nose, thick lips, perfectly round head, and high cheekbones—made him handsome but in the non-European sense...and distinctly masculine.

I spent portions of most every evening playing gin rummy with Doc. Sometimes, we'd have a "third," but Doc really preferred head-to-head showdowns. He took no greater pride than in beating an opponent by the most lopsided of scores. But he couldn't stand to lose, even if only by the smallest of margins.

And Doc was an absolute slave to "order," constantly straightening the deck or the discard pile, or insisting that one's cards not cross the imaginary boundary that only he could see, that marked each player's "space." He believed that all things had a proper place—and to Doc, that place was wherever Doc said it was. Doc was so committed to process that he kept score, no matter what. For example, the way we counted in gin rummy, there was a total of 380 points available in the deck. So if after a round in a head-to-head game, I amassed a score of 180, that meant that Doc's score was 200.

But Doc had to count, anyway. Even if it was clear that a game had been decided, Doc had to count. Y'all don't understand. Doc kept score, no matter what! Literally. On sheets of paper, in a file kept in his cube, Doc kept tally sheets of almost every game he'd played. The guy was lovable, I swear. But he was the every personification of "anal retentive." If I wanted to drive him bonkers, occasionally, when I knew the outcome of a game was assured, I'd not only refuse to count my cards but I'd also scramble the deck, so as to deprive him of the opportunity to do so. For Doc, this was akin to someone clawing their fingers down a damned chalkboard.

But as I got to know Doc better, I became increasingly impressed by his intelligence. He is among the smartest people I've ever met. Just ask him...

Speaking with an impeccable English vocabulary, Doc starts in his thick African accent. "**I was born in a small town called Asaba, in 1954. Asaba is the capitol of Nigeria's Delta State. Delta State produces 80 percent of Nigeria's oil. I was the older of two children—both boys. My brother died in 2008, of unknown causes. He passed away in his sleep. My mother is now seventy-eight years old. My father died in 1997, at the age of eight. So of my family, there is only my mother and me left. This is not typical for a Nigerian family. Nigerian families are usually big. For example, my mother is one of seven children. My father was one of five. And even they are from small families, by Nigerian standards.**"

"Tell me about your education, as a young boy in Nigeria."

I was raised Catholic, so I attended private schools: St. John's for primary education and St. Anthony's for secondary. St. Anthony's was all boys. In Nigeria, boys and girls attend school together until they are eleven or twelve years old. Then they are separated—boys with boys, and girls with girls. St. Anthony's was a premier school for boys. Graduating from St. Anthony's almost assured that a boy would go to college.

"Is it still that way?"

Yes, it is still that way. You must pass the West African Examination Council (WAEC) test to go to college. One's aggregate score determined where you went to school. The lower the aggregate score, the better. The best possible aggregate score is 6. You would have universities fighting to get you, with full scholarships. The cutoff point for university entry was aggregate 15. Scoring between 6 and 12 pretty much assured that you would get a scholarship. The only question was, to what school?

"So kids in Nigeria value education? They actually want to do well in school?"

Yes, that is true. Especially students who attend private schools.

"So what about the problems teens face in this country—like teen pregnancy, for instance?"

This is very rare. It happens, but it is rare. You see, in Nigeria, it brings considerable shame and dishonor to the family. So even if it does happen, the girl is withdrawn from school. The pregnancy plays out in virtual isolation.

"So okay, back to you, Doc. To whom or what do you attribute your values? Your thirst for success, your drive, your work ethic?"

I would have to say to St. Anthony's. Getting into that school was very important. Because all the reverend fathers and nuns were white, this was perceived, at that time, as an assurance of a solid foundation. It was a selling point, used to get parents to send their children. Better foundation, brighter future. So I made the best of it. I was a very good student...probably a nerd, by American standards. So were my classmates.

"You're still in touch?"

Oh, yes! Each class at St. Anthony's forms a club, through which we keep in touch with the school and with each other. They are called Old Boys Associations. By the way, of my graduating class of 1974, ninety students: forty are medical doctors; ten have PhDs, including me; ten are bank financing managers—the equivalent of a CEO in America; and ten are lawyers, including a law professor at Oxford, who is also a visiting professor at the University of Virginia each year. The rest are engineers.

"Wow, Doc. That's an impressive record of accomplishments—individual and collective."

Thank you.

"No doubt. So what was next? By the way, you and I are the same age. My high school class graduated in 1972. You said that you were in the class of '74. To what can you attribute the two-year difference?"

Oh, yes, I forgot. For the two years between 1966 and 1968, I did not go to school. My family—as were many families, at that time—was hiding. That was during the time of the Biafran War, the Nigerian Civil War. In that war, the East wanted to secede. Like your St. Louis, Asaba was the proverbial 'gateway' to the West, because one of its boundaries is the Niger River. We were in the middle.

As a consequence, many families were destroyed—many men were killed by forces opposed to the sitting government. They killed only men—few, if any, women or children. Ultimately, the opposition forces were defeated, and in 1969, I resumed attending school.

"So had your family been captured, your father would likely have been killed. And yours might be a much different story. But as it is…"

Yes, as it is, I'd say things turned out well. Three top universities in Nigeria offered me scholarships on the basis of my WAEC scores, including the University of Nigeria. I scored an aggregate 8. However, I told my father that I did not want to go to the University of Nigeria nor to any school in Nigeria. He said, "So you want to go to London?" I said no.

I told him I was intrigued by the Watergate scandal and by President Nixon, so I wanted to go to school in the United States. I thought this would disappoint my father. But if my father was disappointed, he did not let me know it. Instead, he said, "Tell you what. If you can get admitted to an American school, I'll take care of the rest."

I applied at the University of Oklahoma (Norman), Stanford, and the University of Arizona. Arizona accepted me first, so that's where I chose to go. True to his word, my father saw to the processing of the necessary visa papers, and I enrolled at the University of AZ.

In 1982, I earned a bachelor of arts degree in psychology. I went back to school in '82, to study both economics and psychology as a graduate student. In 1985, I obtained a double master's degree, in Economics and Psychology. From 1985 to 1990, I worked for the Arizona Department of Corrections as a treatment specialist. The Bureau of Prisons (BoP) does not know this.

"Okay-y-y. So, that explains why you're such an ardent critic of the system. You have an informed view of how counseling at a prison should work."

Yes, but let's come back to that. Let me finish telling you how I got here—to Maryland.

"Fair enough. Let me hear it."

Very simple, really. I worked very hard in Arizona to help get the Martin Luther King, Jr. federal holiday observed. It finally came up for referendum in 1990. It was defeated. I was very disappointed and disillusioned and said I'd had enough of Arizona. I decided to leave at the first opportunity.

I had met my wife, Patricia, at the University of Arizona. We met in 1980 and were married in '81. In 1983, we had our first child. Meanwhile, Patricia graduated in '83 as well. I still have a picture of her on her graduation day, pregnant and in her cap and gown.

Patricia was originally from North Carolina, but she had family in Baltimore, Maryland. So when I decided in 1990 that I had had enough of Arizona, we decided that we would try to catch on in Baltimore. I got a job offer in Upper Marlboro, Maryland, an hour's commute from Baltimore. So I accepted the job, and we moved in to an apartment in Baltimore. The job was a program director of a residential treatment center for youths, called Edgemeade. Patricia got a job working in the courts in Arlington

County, Virginia. When our apartment lease in Baltimore expired in 1991, we bought a house in Upper Marlboro.

"When did you go back to school?"

I worked at Edgemeade from 1990 to 1999. In the meantime, in 1995, I enrolled at the University of Maryland at Baltimore (UMAB) to pursue a PhD in psychology. I finished in 1999.

"So Patricia and you still live in the same house in Upper Marlboro?"

Well, I do. Patricia and I were married for twenty years. We had three kids—two girls and a boy. However, in '99, Patricia asked for a divorce because she found out that I had fathered a child outside of our marriage. That child—a boy—was with an African woman I had met who lived in Lanham, Maryland.

For a few years, Patricia and I tried to save the marriage. We tried counseling. But ultimately, we could not save it. We were divorced in 2002.

"Did you get together with the woman from Lanham? The mother of your second son?"

No. Nothing ever came of that. In 2003, I met another African lady, this one from Adelphi, Maryland. Her name is Marian. She became pregnant with my third son, who was born later that same year. We moved in together and were married while she was pregnant. We are still married.

I asked Doc to pause for a moment so I could both organize the information he'd given me and set up my impending redirection. As with all the interviews, gathering this information was a tedious undertaking. Because federal prisons prohibit the use by inmates of any kind of recording device(s), I had to conduct the interviews the ol' fashioned way—with a paper and pen(cil). Also, because I wanted to attribute quotes both accurately and in the precise vernacular of the subject, it required me to stop the speaker intermittently. But now, while I was keenly interested in hearing all that Doc was willing to share, I wanted to make sure that we got to all of the most critical topics and points.

"So, Doc, why are you here with me today, resplendent in Kelly green, courtesy of the US government?"

Doc smiled his huge effervescent smile and laughed from his belly. **That is a good question. Let me answer it. Throughout my career, I had set up all sorts of agencies: youth services organizations, day care centers, foster care programs, group homes. I trained staffs and administrators alike. But I did it as an employee of other agencies.**

Finally, it dawned on me that if I can do this for other companies, why not do it for myself, as a consultant? So that's exactly what I did. I sat up shop and began to contract with other agencies. And if they could afford me, I could make magic!

The sparkle in his eyes was blinding, as he continued, **I would help them get the appropriate licensing. I would help them write proposals. I would help them get government contracts, get 501(c)3 tax exempt status, conduct board member training, staff training, help develop policies and procedures, design and implement strategic plans. If they could afford me, I could make it happen.**

In 2002, I designed a program for the [Washington] DC Child and Family Services Agency. One of their directors asked me to come and run the program. I said okay. I sat up my own operation, which housed as many as thirty kids, some seriously emotionally disturbed, which required a large staff. Over sixty employees. It was an around-the-clock, 24/7 operation.

In the meantime, I did not give up my private practice and consulting. Eventually, it all became more than I could manage alone. The day-to-day operation of the program took care of itself. But the administrative function became somewhat overwhelming. So in 2004, I hired a new woman to administer the program. She was a very talented administrator.

But from 2004 to 2007, she did not pay the employer's match for payroll taxes. As the founder and CEO, I was responsible—solely responsible.

The IRS began investigating in 2007. Their investigation determined that we owed $550 thousand in back taxes, including interest and penalties. The actual taxes amounted to roughly $350 thousand. So I pleaded guilty to one count of Failure to

Collect and Pay Taxes. I was sentenced to twenty-four months plus $500 per month restitution, but no interest or penalties.

As had become typical of my interview style, I paused at this juncture. One of the things you learn early on is that inmates don't readily talk about their offenses. There's sort of an implied "Don't ask, don't tell" policy, as it were. My take on it is that it brings one face-to-face with his guilt. And with his shame. What it must have taken for this proud, intelligent, accomplished African man—father of five—to bare his soul to me, a relative stranger, and to the world, was something I did not take lightly. It could not have been easy. So I was compelled to let the moment linger, to keep him disarmed. I needed for Doc to understand that I, of all people, would not judge him.

I also recall the cathartic relief that interviewing with me had given my previous subjects. It seemed almost therapeutic for them; perhaps it was as much for Doc as well. Finally, after a minute or two of light banter, I asked, "Is prison different from what you imagined? If so, how?"

Yes! It's ve-e-r-r-y different, he said, using the rare contraction. **Even though we are incarcerated, we are not really behind bars. We have more physical freedom.**

The major shortcoming is the attitude and behavior of the officers and staff. To me, behavior is everything, and everything is a behavior. To excuse my language, the officers and staff have an 'I don't give a rat's ass' attitude toward inmates and their needs.

For example, I am diabetic. I have had diabetes for twenty-five years. When I first got here, I asked my correctional counselor for a diabetic menu. His reply was, "Oh yeah, I'm the one that brought you to prison."

"What did he mean by that?"

He meant that my being here is my own fault, not his. So I should just shut up and eat whatever I am served. What you see is what you get! To hell with your diabetes.

Doc and I had the same counselor. He had shown similar nonchalance to me and was, in fact, notorious for it among the inmates under his counsel. I should note at this point, what the counselor's role is defined in the official *Admissions and Orientation Handbook*, issued by the institution: "The counselor provides counseling and guidance for inmates in their assigned unit regarding institutional adjustment, [and] personal difficulties…"

At any rate, to Doc's observation, I merely added, "Yeah, that's him, all right. Any more to add?"

Yes. Health services. When I arrived, I went to the doctor, who is the camp clinical director. I told him that I needed medical clearance to get a lower bunk assignment—because of my age and diabetes. His reply to me was, 'If you can walk to this office, you can climb to an upper bunk.' So I went back to my correctional counselor and said that I cannot sleep on a top bunk.

He said, "Since you did not get medical clearance, you have to wait your turn, like everybody else.' Those are examples of what I mean by attitude and behavior.

"I contend that the portion of the total federal prison population that is housed in camps—approximately twenty-three thousand people—is underserved. I contend that regardless of their—whether drug use or drug sales or embezzlement or wire fraud or failure to collect and pay taxes, the prison system's best hope for achieving sustainable rehabilitation is among the Camp population. If for no other reason than the fact that they'll be released sooner than most others, the need for meaningful counseling and case management is essential to assuring campers' successful matriculation back into society, into their communities and homes.

"Therefore, my personal lament is not about such irrelevances as bad food, bad movies, TV room rules, or hard beds. I don't care whether the institution removes washers and dryers from the units, as a supposed energy conservation effort. Or if a handful of asshole guards (usually, little ones…I had to say it), living out their convoluted notion of power, choose to demonstrate the measure of their authority by, without notice and against Handbook regulations, requiring inmates to wear work boots to chow. It's a stupid-ass, redneck nuisance, the memory and effects of which won't last a week.

"But because I am adamant that there is a wealth of untapped and/or uncultivated potential among camp residents—even among the young, sometimes rowdy guys, who purport to be—I do care deeply about the glaring paucity of programs, services and support available to them. To me, it is nothing short of shameful…whether it's system-wide or indigenous to this facility. Especially, since the general public is purposely left with the misconception that reha-bilitation takes place, or even that opportunities for rehabilitation actually exist."

So, I eagerly awaited Doc's response when I asked, "Doc, what programs and services do you think should be available that aren't?"

Wow. They don't have any programs here. None. We are being warehoused. Quite simply, the programs that should be here are those that meet the inmates' needs. And I mean individual needs. We are not all at the same place—intellectually or behaviorally. We have different career and educational needs. Programs should be designed to meet each individual's needs.

You going to stop young people from doing what they are doing, and send them here, I feel that the role of government becomes to teach them new career pathways. As a person that ini-tiates treatment models from scratch, I feel that the government should rehabilitate inmates in their respective career choices.

"Uh-h-h, Doc," I mused. "What if their career choice is to sell drugs?"

Selling drugs is not a career choice—unless one is a pharma-cist. It should be things they wish to be or do when they get out. Vocations. They certainly have time to acquire new skills. They are not doing much of anything else. Playing dominos or cards. Sleeping all day. Doing push-ups. Working an hour here or there. This does not prepare them for the world; certainly not for the workplace.

Doc's comments brought to mind a story I'd been told recently by the guy who styled my locks. Tom was a thirty-six-year-old from Ohio. At the time, he'd been imprisoned for twelve years. He was scheduled for release in a couple of months. And he had such high hopes.

Tom had the laudable idea that he was going to start a mobile food service business. He'd travel to fairs, festivals, markets, et cetera, throughout his home state, setting up booths from which to sell his products. The problem, as I saw it, lay in the fact that Tom had no practical idea of the extent to which technology had evolved during his time away. Nor any idea of the implications that that evolution had on his prospects for starting and running a successful business.

In 1999, when he entered the prison system, email was still evolving. There was no Facebook or Twitter. You Tube and My Space were fledgling. No Craig's List, no Google, no Bing, or any of the myriad other social networking, marketing, and research tools that by 2011 were useful, if not *essential* tools for sharing and obtaining information about everything from marketing to research to business accounting to word processing.

But more fundamentally, Tom's misconception was that his was strictly a "cash" business. He'd never even heard of the EBT terminals that enable credit card transactions nor realized the extent to which people—consumers—transact business through noncash means anymore.

I couldn't help but to ponder how much Tom would have benefited from the availability of classes on such topics as basic computer operations, small business startup, food service/preparation, or how to use the Internet, just to name a few. Classes could be counselor-led. Or with a college just twelve miles west on I-68, curricula could be coordinated using teachers and/or students as instructors.

Admittedly, it would require some initiative, innovation, and perhaps, minimal investment on the administration's part. But so be it. Anything is better than sending a man, twelve years removed from society, back into that society without an iota of preparation. That is, preparation to do something other than recidivate...which an astounding five releasees had already done in the three months I'd been down, to that point!

Doc continued, **In early times, US prisons were for the sole purpose of punishment. But in 1971, there was a paradigm shift. The purpose became to rehabilitate, or to 'correct.' Thus, their names were changed from 'prisons' to 'correctional institutions.'**

But you know what? If I did not come here to see it with my own eyes, I, like most of the general public, would have thought that they were doing their job. You see, America loves to boast to the world that they are the most humane, civilized developed country in the world, and that that applies to its prison system. While there is no data to prove that [released prisoners recidivate] because they are 'bad people,' there is much data to support the premise that recidivism occurs, in part, because there is no meaningful rehab going on at all.

Doc was right. I was ordered by my sentencing judge to continue in both the mental health treatment and the Gamblers' Anonymous programs I was in before I got to prison as a part of my sentence. For the duration of the thirteen months I served, I got neither...despite the existence at the facility of what purported to be a psychology department. Doc will discuss that further shortly. But for now...

There are no counselor-led programs or classes here at Cumberland," Doc continued. "Any class offered is inmate-led. Which, given the caliber of some of the inmates, is not all bad. But let me speak about that.

I taught a ten-week ACE (adult continuing education) class on proposal writing. I asked the facility's education director for a marker—a simple marker—to use on the classroom board. It was bad enough that he did not have one, but he showed no inclination to provide any resources at all. Were he remotely interested in supporting the class, he might have gone to any dollar store and bought a handful of markers. Instead, his attitude was, "Do the best you can with what you have" which was nothing!

For the first two weeks, I borrowed a marker from another teacher. Later, when that teacher got sent to him a couple of markers, he was kind enough to give me one. The Education Department never gave me anything. Not even thanks for doing the class.

"So what inference do you draw from that experience?"

That there is no genuine interest in rehabilitating inmates at this camp. Doc paused. He leaned back in his chair but actually tightened the grip of his stare. I have been in this country for nearly thirty-five years. I came here because like so many others around the world at the time, I bought in to the notion that America is the greatest country in the world. In many ways, it is. Opportunity abounds, for many. But there are also far too many for whom real opportunities to succeed do not exist. It's a sham, like in this instance. They purport to their constituents and to the world that they are facilitating true rehabilitation. Yet they offer no counselor- or staff-led programs. They permit inmates to teach ACE classes but provide them with no resources. They even require a curriculum so they and their contractors can go back to their respective stakeholders and say, 'Look at all the great classes we're offering. Look at what we're offering the inmates at no cost to them,' while all the while, they are providing no real effort and utterly no resources.

Doc was certainly right. I'd proposed to the Education Department that I would teach separate ACE classes on voice and songwriting. I proposed to donate the electric piano, drum machine, and four-track studio that I'd require. All I needed from the institution was the books from which to teach (two books, at a cost of fifteen dollars each) and class space. After about three weeks during which my proposal languished on his desk, I met with the education director for the Camp, whom, it so happened, was accompanied by the young, purposely tough-looking forty-ish black woman who headed the Education Department for the entire institution, who did all the talking.

She said that they'd love for me to teach the classes and then summarily disallowed *all* of the equipment and said I'd have to pay for the books myself. I declined her generous offer, Doc's words echoing in my head, "Look at the great classes we're offering. Look at what we're offering the inmates."

Knowing full well the fireworks it would ignite, I asked Doc his impression(s) of the Camp's Residential Drug and Alcohol Treatment Program (R-DAP). Then I sat back to watch the show.

R-DAP is a joke. It is a laugh. I was director of Second Genesis—a [metropolitan Washington DC-based] residential treatment facility, from 1998 to 2002—so I can tell you what a residential treatment program should look like. I designed their program that operated seven facilities, including their program for women and children in Upper Marlboro.

The treatment model we used is the same as they claim to use here. It's called therapeutic community, or TC.

I was familiar with the TC model because, as executive director of a community-based men's health program, I participated intimately in the selection process by which a Pennsylvania-based program was chosen to implement a TC program in Baltimore—subsequently serving as both an advisor and referral source to the program.

TC is very intensive. It starts with an assessment that is done within the first thirty days. That assessment is used by the clinician as the basis for developing an individualized treatment plan for each resident. The plan takes from nine to twelve months to implement. One's plan is dictated by one's needs. If, for instance, a resident has multiple issues, his treatment plan will be designed to address each of those issues.

"Okay, Doc. I'm your patient. In addition to an addiction to heroin, I present with symptoms of depression. What might my TC treatment plan look like?"

Well, the first thing we would need to determine is your commitment to quitting. None of this works without that. But that is particularly true with TC, because it is a very highly structured environment. And it's one step at a time. You would be required to enter a twelve-step program—like Narcotics Anonymous—that you will attend daily. You will be assigned to a group of residents with similar issues; your cohort. Your cohort is your first line of support. You hold each other accountable for doing what you're supposed to do, for being where you're supposed to be. Actually, because of this, TC requires minimal staffing because an individual resident's success is interdependent upon that of the other members. Your recovery in TC becomes your life. A daily ritual. And as you are ready, your treatment counselor will facilitate your movement through each phase of your treatment plan. The NA.

The mental health services. Education. Job readiness. Whatever has been determined by your plan.

That's the nine-to-twelve-month residential component. After that, you are still required to go to NA for the next three years. You are still in TC, only on an outpatient basis. You still report and visit periodically, per schedule, a record of which is maintained and provided to your probation officer. In these ways, TC is comprehensive. It is thorough. And assuming that the resident is committed to his recovery, the information and services he receives while in TC—including mental health services, housing counseling, job readiness and placement, continuing outpatient aftercare—greatly increase the chances that he will be successful.

By comparison, men in the R-DAP program here are referred in to the program if they have any history of drugs or alcohol in their presentencing information, and have thirty-six months or less left on their sentences. It is a five-hundred-hour program—approximately nine months. The inmate's incentive for entering is that when they complete the nine months, they are eligible to get a year knocked off of their sentence. R-DAP purports to employ the TC model.

Participants in R-DAP are required to move in to the same housing unit. No one resides there but them. Residents of other units are not permitted to even set foot on the premises. In the morning, all participants attend what is supposed to be drug education—for as little as fifteen minutes. It is rarely more than an hour. Then they meet with their cohorts for an hour. That is it. There is no real assessment and, therefore, no real treatment plan. There is a treatment professional, but she is that in name only. Her real objective is to make sure that prospective participants become eligible, that they stay eligible, and that enrollment stays full. You want to know why?

"You bet I do."

They keep the program at full enrollment because the institution receives twenty-five thousand dollars for each participant...money that comes from an entirely different source than does its general operating budget. This money is not from the BoP. In that way, it is a fraud.

"Well, what's the alternative?"

The best alternative, if the BoP's intent is to engender real recovery, would be—one year short of his release date—remand the inmate to home confinement at one of the successful private facilities, where he would get the intense, comprehensive treatment he needs. Which is not going to happen, because of BoP's financial incentive that I just discussed, to keep herding people through the program, while not being held accountable for outcomes.

"So, does R-DAP compete with private programs like Second Genesis and Gaudenzia for funding? And aren't they accountable for results?"

Well, no, they are not competing with programs like Second Genesis. And because of that, they are not held to the same standard of quality. Second Genesis, Gaudenzia, and other private programs rely on Medicaid, for the most part. As a result, their continued funding is based on the quality of the service they provide; the outcomes they produce. It is outcomes-based.

On the other hand, R-DAP's funding is program-based. All they have to do to keep getting funded is to keep enrolling participants. They simply must demonstrate that they enrolled x-number of participants, of which x percent graduate. Private programs are monitored regularly—as frequently as twice a year—for new programs. If their performance is poor, then their funding is threatened. R-DAP's funding is never threatened. They just ship residents in, get paid, and then ship them out.

"I know of an R-DAP graduate who took copious notes of his experience. He is a very wealthy white-collar offender, who on his attorney's advisement, finagled his eligibility for the program in the first place. He shared, with unmitigated delight, that in the nine months he was in R-DAP—supposedly, a five-hundred-hour program—he was in class for a total of—seriously, I mean this—twenty-seven hours! Twenty-seven. That's 2-7."

Doc went on, **Let's say a guy comes here. Let's say he's been in jail for six years. Remember, doing nothing. At twenty-four months, he is enrolled in R-DAP's TC program. He completes the program and goes to a halfway house. There, he has no support that matters to him because he's not been exposed to any real treatment. He thinks that they are just being hard on him, unnecessarily. There is no continuity. It is as if he went to college without finishing first grade. BoP has accomplished its objective of getting twenty-five thousand dollars for his participation in the program. And he has accomplished his objective of getting out up to a year early.**

The participant's objective is to get out early and live happily ever after. The system's objective is to keep him and others like him coming back to prison. Which outcome do you think R-DAP makes most likely?

"I'm hearing you say that R-DAP is ineffective. But it also sounds like if they tried to, they could be an effective program. So to what single factor do you attribute R-DAP's ineffectualness?"

Privatization. In fact, I believe that many of the weaknesses throughout BoP are attributable to the fact that prison services— many of them—are privatized. The services are performed by private outside companies under government contracts. So the objective of the contractors is *profit*, not outcomes. It is certainly not rehabilitation.

Right now, as we speak, there are four contract officers housed down-the-hill, in the administrative offices. Their role is to serve as liaisons between their companies and the BoP. They manage their respective companies' contracts. That includes reporting, and it includes billing. In fact, you know the head counts that we do several times a day? Their biggest usefulness is for purposes of billing.

It is what I call the 'Hilton Hotel' scenario. Hilton has hotels all around the world that bear its name. But they do not build them. Or better yet, take Boeing or Lockheed. They build aircraft carriers. Those aircraft carriers bear the name and insignia

of the United States Air Force (USAF). But the USAF did not build them.

Similarly, BoP contracts its services to companies. Those companies agree to deliver services, in exchange for fees or other consideration. Those companies hire, train, and deploy staff, who don the name and insignia of the BoP. But they are not federal agencies, any more than Lockheed or Boeing. At most, they are what's called a 'quasi-federal government agency.' Sometimes their employees are qualified. Sometimes, they are not.

"As you know, Doc, the bane of most of our existence here at Cumberland—even bigger, in my mind, than the lack of programs—is the case manager and correctional counselors—at least ours. In addition to Cumberland's *Admissions and Orientation Manual*, all of the documentation I read prior to coming here was that these two staff members are our first line of support. It falls to them to help us navigate our way through the system. To help us adjust upon entry, to facilitate our further development while we're here, to assist us with the array of problems that might arise—with everything from getting a job here to getting education to managing our personal finances to problems that might arise with other inmates. They are our advocates. Here, they are anything but that. Indeed, they are more adversaries than advocates. Can you talk about that?"

Sure. And you are correct. They are supposed to be our advocates. But at the very heart of their ability to perform that function is that they *must* establish a relationship with the inmate. That relationship is most important in any counseling or case management scenario. You certainly cannot case manage without it—not effectively, anyway. They should know the inmates by name, know something about them, know something of their cases, yes. But as importantly, know something about, for example, their family. Or how does he get along with the other inmates? Does he need to contact his lawyer, his judge? How's his job? How's he sleeping at night? Find out his preferences.

It certainly requires more than looking away from you when they encounter you on the compound or slamming the door in your face or trying to mess up an inmate's release date or try-

IN THE COMPANY OF A KNOWN FELON

ing to, in any way possible, worsen the inmate's experience. They will break their necks to catch you with a cigarette but won't say 'Good morning.' It is pure intimidation, intended to demean you; to dehumanize you. It is also intended to keep you from asking anything of them. I don't know what that is, but it is not counseling, and it is not case management.

I requested to interview Doc because I felt he'd be insightful. He did not disappoint. He enlightened me about the system in ways that I hadn't imagined. Regarding his personal life, he was honest and forthcoming. For the better part of three hours, over the course of two days, he had indulged my prodding and probing. I wondered if, like the others, the forced introspection had caused him more anguish or more relief. I didn't ask, opting to stick to my script.

"What are your plans after you're released, Doc?"

The first thing I will do is to go to Nigeria. I want to visit my mother.

"Has she ever been here? To the United States?"

No. She will not fly on an airplane, so I am going to visit her for a while. While I am there, I will look further into a business option I have previously explored. I am thinking of opening a micro finance bank.

Before I could ask, he said, **That is a bank that works with small- and medium-sized businesses and gives them access to financing and works with them to make them successful. I have already submitted my application to the Central Bank of Nigeria that issues the authorizations.**

"What about your current practice? Does your conviction affect your licensure?"

No, it does not directly affect my licensing. My business is still running for now. But the problem is that the current contracts I am in—the government contracts—come up for renewal in 2012, and they may not be renewed because of this.

Lightening up, now, becoming more perfunctory than probing, I asked, "You had any visits lately?"

Yes. My [current] wife, Marian, comes about once a month. Of course, my eight-year-old boy comes with her. The other chil-

dren are grown, so they come too—either by themselves or with Patricia, who also comes occasionally.

"When you were a kid, what did you want to be when you grew up?"

I really did not think about much, other than being a businessman. I was a very bright student. I knew that I could have been anything I wanted to. I chose business. That is why I studied economics. But my experience at the Arizona Department of Corrections led to my desire to specialize in psychology.

"Who or what do you miss most while you're in here?"

Of course, I miss Marian and my young son, Nathaniel. I have been with him since he was born. I miss all my kids. This is the first time that I am not there for them. It is hard.

I also miss my various social activities. I am very active in several American and Nigerian organizations. I am very active in Nigerian politics.

And finally, "If you could snap your fingers and be anyplace, doing anything right now, where would you be?"

"I would be with my wife and son, in Nigeria, visiting my mother."

"Thank you, Little Big Man."

"You are welcome."

Postlogue

Cecile Dwele's mom passed away in August 2011, in Nigeria. Of course, he was not permitted to attend her memorials. Doc subsequently wheedled his way into the Residential Drug and Alcohol Program (RDAP). Early in his tenure, he voiced an observation about the program's poor implementation and lack of efficacy. He was admonished by the program's director and flatly threatened with expulsion, if he did not desist. He did. And he was released without further incident in November 2012. I have had no further contact with him.

Case Management
(The Overview)

The purpose of this chapter is to explore the concept of *case management* in general—and its function within the prison system in particular. To some readers, it may seem that I do so to an extreme. At first, I too struggled to find the context in which such elaboration was germane to a book of this nature. "Perhaps, it is a topic best addressed in another forum," I mused, "and by professionals, rather than by a layperson, such as I surely am." So I apologize in advance to any reader that finds this subject matter, presented by this writer, in this book, extraneous.

However, I ultimately decided that it is not only appropriate but also *imperative* that even the most casual reader be aware of what effective case management entails and thus of its importance to the accomplishment of the supposed core purpose of prisons. Namely, the purpose of rehabilitating offenders, rather than merely punishing them.

I can only surmise that the powers-that-be within the United States justice system agree with me, or (1) they would never have adopted the phrase *correctional facility* in lieu of the word *prison*; (2) they would not insist to the whole world that a prime objective of corrections in the United States is the rehabilitation of prisoners; and (3) the case management function within the correctional system would not exist. Add to that the tremendous and ever burgeoning expense of operating prisons that is borne by the taxpaying public, and you have all the reasons I feel that the public has not only the right, but the *duty* to know whether its funds are being used in a manner that is both efficient and efficacious. Or not.

In its National Standards of Practice for Case Management document, the Case Management Society of America (CMSA)[1], defines "case management" as "a *collaborative* process of assessment, planning, *facilitation*, and *advocacy* for options and services to meet an individual's *holistic* needs through *communication* and available resources…"

As I've highlighted with italics what are, to me, the key words in CMSA's definition are

- *collaborative*—suggesting a partnership, in which the client is actively and meaningfully engaged in the process; that the effort is joint, two-way, mutual, shared;
- *facilitation*—which is the process of making something easy or easier;
- *advocacy*—implying support, encouragement, backing;
- *holistic*—meaning to take into account one's physical, mental, and social conditions in formulating and/or implementing a plan of treatment; and
- *"communication"*—the exchange of ideas; interaction; consultation.

Why is all this explanation important? Consider that an article in the April 2012 issue of *Prison Legal News*[2] asserts the following:

---

[1] "The Case Management Society of America [is] the leading non-profit association dedicated to the support and development of the profession of case management." www.cmsa.org

[2] "*Prison Legal News* is an independent…monthly magazine that provides a cutting-edge review and analysis of prisoner rights, court rulings and news about prison issues." www.prisonlegalnews.org

The 'Public Safety Performance Project of the Pew Center on the States'[3] issued a report concerning recidivism rates for released offenders. The report...concludes that recidivism rates remained relatively unchanged at around 40 percent between 1994 and 2007, despite a quadrupling of spending on corrections.

The report continues, concluding,

The system designed to deter offenders from continuing their criminal behavior is thus failing miserably.

And costing more and more. So again, why is all this important? It's important because *recidivism*, by its very definition, means that offenders are repeating their offenses, thereby compromising the safety of American communities.

It's also important because it contradicts the common misconception held by many taxpayers in those American communities that serious, meaningful efforts at rehabilitation take place in America's prisons, the notion that prisoners receive services and treatment while in custody that prepare them to lead law-abiding lives upon release.

It's important because according to the Pew Center report as of 2009, total annual spending on corrections at the state level was estimated at about $52 billion. The report says that prison now accounts for one out of every fourteen general fund dollars at the state level and that one out of every eight state employees now works for a corrections-related agency.

---

[3] The Pew Center on the States provides nonpartisan reporting and research, advocacy, and technical assistance to help states deliver better results and achieve long-term fiscal health by investing in programs that provide the strongest returns.[They] bring policy makers and experts together to develop solutions that are driven by facts, and conduct reporting and in-depth research across the 50 states and the District of Columbia, using evidence to determine which policies work and which do not." www.pewstates.org

It's also important because when one visits the FPC Cumberland, among the items on prominent display in the lobby—on a wall directly across from the one on which hangs pictures of the US president, the US attorney general, the director of the Bureau of Prisons (BoP), and the FPC Cumberland warden—is a statement of the institution's core values that includes the assurance that staff will "demonstrate uncompromising, ethical conduct…in all our actions."

And finally, this level of detail is important because it points to the penal system's long and consistent failure to effect meaningful rehabilitation of any kind. Thus, to me, all this is important because any extent to which that failure of the penal system is attributable to incompetence, institutional deception, and/or willful neglect should be exposed and corrected. It cannot merely be tolerated. Not by the American public that underwrites—and is deliberately deceived about—that system. I contend that there is entirely too much at stake.

Consider this. The aforementioned Pew Center report recommends strategies for reducing recidivism. The strategies they propose have the dual objective of (1) holding offenders accountable for their transgressions *and* (2) controlling the amount of money spent in the corrections process. They include:

- beginning reentry preparation at the time offenders enter prison;
- using evidence-based programs specifically tailored to each prisoner's criminal risk factors; and
- matching…treatment and supervision with an offender's risk and needs assessment.

Now consider this. Most of the Pew Center report's proposed strategies are functions that fall directly or indirectly within the realm of CMSA's definition of case management. Therefore, it is not a stretch to hypothesize that most of the ability to increase the efficiency and effectiveness of the correctional system lies within the scope of its case managers. And theoretically, it wouldn't cost an additional dime! That's because the money is already allocated in institutions' current budgets, in the form of salaries and other line items earmarked for case management staff and services.

I believe that case management is *the* realm in which there exists the greatest opportunities to make and sustain positive impact in the lives of inmates, especially at the camps, which for most inmates represents the last stop before they return to society and, especially, for *younger* inmates. Young inmates arrive, for the most part, un- or undereducated, un- or underskilled, and otherwise largely unprepared to do anything upon their release except return to their former criminal lifestyles. It's a missed opportunity to provide meaningful intervention that can change not only the life of a young man, but—if it prevents recidivism—the family, community and society from which he emanates.

In other words, *if case managers do their jobs better, then recidivism will decrease.* I'm just saying…

My Case Manager

Despite my exhaustive efforts to do so, I could not find either a job description or an overview that spelled out the skills, knowledge, education, or experience required to fill the job of case manager in the federal prison system. Likewise, I have been unable to find any document that specifically sets forth the duties, expectations, responsibilities, or desired outcomes of the position.

Therefore, I cannot definitively claim to know the extent to which the prevailing paradigms and best practices within the field of case management apply, as relate to federal prisons—if at all. All I am privy to is my limited research reflected herein and the notions gleaned from my experiences with and observation of the case manager to whom I was assigned during my thirteen-month stay at the FPC Cumberland. Beyond that, all I can do is speculate.

Clearly, though, if one accepts CMSA's definition of case management, then one must also embrace the premise that at the heart of successful, effective case management is building a solid case manager/client *relationship*. A productive relationship between the case manager and the client is an essential component of formulating and implementing a successful treatment plan. In fact, I will take the further leap of speculation—without benefit of research or investigation—and hypothesize that among individual, similarly-situated correctional facilities, recidivism is lowest at the institutions at which competent, caring case management occurs.

Now let's see. My case manager, while I was in the General Housing (or "G") Unit at the FPC Cumberland. How can I put this, to best convey my point? How can I leave no uncertainty about what I'm trying to say so that the reader perceives not so much as a scintilla of ambivalence about my feelings and impressions of my case manager? Hmm. What to say, what to say?

Oh, I know. *I hate this bitch!* With every fiber of my being, I deplore her and everything that she represents. I not only despise each breath that she takes but the fact that she takes them. Simply put, I wish that she was *not!* Is that clear enough?

I know, I know. That's pretty strong language and even stronger sentiment. After all, she's somebody's mom, somebody's wife, daughter, sister. She's a human being, one of God's creations.

I don't care. *Fuck* her! Judging by her every action and interaction that I was privy to, she never gave one iota of consideration to my (or any other inmate) being someone's husband, father, son, brother, or pop-pop. It seemed to me that all my case manager ever saw me as was an "inmate," for whatever negative connotation the word entails. She treated me as though I was not even a person, but a thing. Inanimate. Inhuman. Unworthy of even the simplest shred of dignity or respect. So all I recall my case manager as is the hateful, spiteful, soulless bully that her actions suggested she was.

Be clear. My sustained hatred of my case manager says more about me than it does about her. I can honestly say that prior to this experience I had never truly hated anyone before. I never knew what it felt like, how all-consuming hate can be. And feeling that my hatred was justifiable or was somehow righteous was of no consolation. No matter how justified I felt or how entitled I felt to harbor such animus, at the end of the day, it diminished me. It took way-y-y too much effort and energy. And it was something that I literally prayed to God for the capacity to overcome.

That point established, my disdain for my case manager—as deep as it is—is as much for her ineptitude as it is for her insensitivity. It bothers me as much that she actively facilitated nothing during my time at FPC Cumberland that was remotely rehabilitative, instructive, educational, or useful to my reentry, as it does that she ineptly (and, I suspect, maliciously) mishandled my release or that she willfully and repeatedly made sport of mispronouncing my name.

Prior to my surrender, everything I read about prison suggested that the one thing I needed to do was to establish a positive relationship with my so-called unit team: my counselor, my unit secretary and my case manager. As the name suggests, each member of the unit team had offices in the inmates' housing units, although they were not live-in staff.

In my reading, I learned that the unit team would be the staff members who would manage my stay at the camp. I read that they were the staff members through whom I should seek assistance for any problems that arose. They would help me with everything from my social adjustment, to my rehabilitation, to my physical and emotional well-being, to my release and reentry, to facilitating the written plan by which to further develop my personal skill(s)—called an Individual Skills Development Plan (ISDP). The unit team would be my advocates, especially my case manager. According to the literature.

So I deemed it, at worst, to be in my best interest to forge an amicable relationship with my unit team. Moreover, not only was it a sensible posture for me to adopt, but it was entirely consistent with the kind of man I am. Generally speaking, I am compliant and respectful of authority. But I *abhor* bullies!

It's one thing to not help someone, to willfully deprive someone of needed assistance. Like, for example, if a medical professional were to refuse to administer first-aid to a patient who presented with an open wound.

It's one thing to not help, but it's something else altogether, to actively seek to *harm* someone. Like, if the aforementioned medical professional not only refused to treat the open wound but instead poured salt into it. Such scenario would be especially egregious if providing first-aid is precisely what that medical professional is paid to do.

In the estimation of not just me but every single one of my fellow inmates with whom I ever conversed on the matter, that's what my case manager did. She sought to harm people. Figuratively speaking, she poured salt into the open wounds that were incarcerated men's circumstances and she seemed to take sadistic delight in doing it. She bullied, she intimidated, and she brazenly disrespected inmates, without evincing so much as a shred of conscience. As a consequence, inmates—her clients—sought, at all costs, to avoid interactions with her. That's the antithesis of the attitude that I read one should harbor about his case manager or that the case manager should seek to foster. So much for the case manager/client relationship.

But while it would have been my preference to have an amiable relationship with my case manager, I realize that it was not an imperative. Congeniality was not what she was paid to provide. Like it or not, I got that. I understood it, cognitively, at least. Plus, I fully realized the ways in which her failure to maintain *professional detachment* could potentially mitigate her effectiveness. After all, she was a woman working with an all-male population.

As well, case managers, among other unit team members at FPC Cumberland, were not only therapists but also bore correctional responsibilities. Therefore, it is reasonable to me that a modicum of detachment was required by my case manager, so as not to compromise those occasions on which she might need to mete out discipline, say, if she discovered that an inmate had cigarettes or a cell phone or other contraband. All of which is to say that one might theorize that my case manager's gender and her "police" responsibilities—real or perceived—were factors that justified her extreme callousness.

That said, my unit secretary was a woman. As well, she had the same dual roles of administrative and correctional authority as did my case manager. The unit secretary's demeanor was always professional, even at times terse. She could certainly never be accused of failing to maintain the appropriate detachment. However, she was decidedly more cordial. Not buddy-buddy, not even remotely. Cordial. And respectful. She replied in kind when greeted. She thanked inmates for holding a door for her or for making the offer to assist her with a load. As well, she was accommodating, always willing to provide requested assistance or information yet always appropriately mannered. She certainly was never mean or loud or rude or brash or never adopted any of the demeaning tactics employed by the case manager. She never lorded over us the authority that we all knew—and respected—that she had.

Furthermore, consider the case manager in FPC Cumberland's other housing unit, the program (or "P") unit—a man, who was anything but friendly. He was a soft-spoken white fellow—a tight-assed, forty-ish, balding, bespectacled, albeit physically fit geek, who spoke in an absolute monotone. Like my unit secretary, his comportment with the inmate population was decidedly detached. But he maintained a respectful relationship with the men on his case load. More importantly, he advocated on their behalves. Like in the case of one inmate who was initially placed in my unit—and, thus, was initially under the purview of my case manager.

Like me, a nonviolent first-offender, Kyle was told by my case manager that he would not be recommended for halfway house placement. She coldly informed him that he was not eligible—and that therefore she was not going to submit the necessary paperwork by which to process him for halfway house placement. Because of her, Kyle was resigned that he would not get his rightful early reentry release. Kyle was a large, jolly, but gentle man and completely unknowledgeable about prison procedure. He took the case manager at her word, having no reason to do otherwise.

Kyle was eventually transferred to the P Unit—and, thus, fell under the purview of the P Unit case manager. Within the first days of his stay there, the P Unit case manager learned of my case manager's failure to submit the aforementioned paperwork by which to effect Kyle's early release. Immediately, the new case manager rectified the situation. Turns out that there was absolutely no basis for denying Kyle's halfway house eligibility and *voila*—just like *that*—his eligibility for early release was restored. The only thing about Kyle's case that changed—the only difference impacting the appropriate handling of something as important and life-affecting as his timely release—was the person who managed it, his case manager.

Sadly, Kyle's was but one among many instances wherein my case manager undermined an inmate's best interest. There was the time she told an unknowing, language-impaired African inmate that he would not be released in April, as his court sentence stipulated, but would, instead, have to remain incarcerated until September. Five more months. Only through the intervention of the inmate's eventual probation officer on the outside—which the inmate was advised by a fellow inmate to seek—was the case manager compelled to process his rightful release. In April, not September. Then there was the Far East Indian fellow, on whom she attempted to perpetrate the exact same ruse—this time, though, debunked by virtue of my advisement. I'm just saying...

My first inkling that my case manager would be less than helpful occurred during my very first encounter with her. It was the morning of my second day at FPC Cumberland. Because it is such an essential part of who I am, among the skills I looked forward to honing while I was incarcerated was my songwriting. I anticipated nothing short of a deluge of inspiration from my new experiences and acquaintances and could hardly wait to get to it.

I write best with the aid of a recording device. Naively emboldened by what I'd read about her role, I saw my case manager in an office that I later came to know as belonging to the unit secretary. I tapped on the door and politely asked for a minute of her time.

She was short—about 5'1" or 2"—and obviously physically fit. Not buxom in that Hollywood starlet kind of way but fit, like a gymnast or a swimmer. However, any asset she earned by virtue of her fitness was immediately negated by her ever-present angry, stern, tight-lipped expression. She appeared rankled by my temerity, having the gall to actually approach rather than avoid her. On this occasion, her coarse, just-short-of-shoulder-length auburn hair was pulled back into a wannabe ponytail so that her face was fully exposed. Bad idea.

Her complexion was ashen, almost ghostly. Her jaws were sunken, and her unadorned face seemed, from the frontal view, triangular; with the forehead being its widest part, descending down to two bugged, wide-set eyes, then tapering down past her Scandinavian high but uneven cheekbones and those tight, sunken jaws, and drawn lips, ending in a point at her chin; triangular, and stood on a point, like a "yield" sign. Her chin and nose were both decidedly pointy and, minus warts, made her look, in profile, grotesque and witch-like. To me, there was nothing vaguely appealing about her aesthetically. Indeed, the combination of her mean, unwelcoming disposition, her shrill voice, and her unsightly face made her, in a word, ugly. That was my first and lasting impression of her—ugly, inside and out. I used to joke that she probably strapped on a pair of bat wings at night and moonlighted as a stone gargoyle, perched atop some old relic office building. I'm just saying...

On this my first encounter with her, I sought to endear myself to my case manager, as I'd read was advisable. So when invited into the room, I politely but genuinely introduced myself and handed her a piece of paper on which I had written the address to my website—www.BigVix.com. After tendering an expressionless retort that could best be described as perfunctory, she tersely asked what I wanted. Alluding to the slip of paper I had just handed her, I told her that I was a songwriter and offered that she could check the veracity of my claim by visiting the website. Then I asked if she could advise me of how/where on the compound I could obtain access to a recording device, to facilitate my songwriting endeavors. She took the paper from my hand and dismissed me from the room, never dignifying me with a reply.

Later that day, in my quest to find a recorder I learned about something called the Zimmerman Act—legislation by which the use by inmates of electronic devices is prohibited. Okay, so I got that. But what I didn't get was why my case manager didn't simply tell me that. She just put me out of the office and never said another word, regarding my inquiry, not from that day to this. Not exactly the most effective relationship building technique.

What she did do, a few days later, was summon me to her office over the compound's intercom. As others have inadvertently done from time to time throughout my life, she mispronounced my name as "Free-erson," rather than "Fry-erson." So when I reported to her office, I politely corrected her on the pronunciation. Her response was a succinct, cavalier "Whatever." She did it several times after that. Every time, I'd correct her, even once assertively saying, "No, it's Fryerson. It's not Freerson, and it's not 'whatever.' It's Fryerson."

Still, she persisted. Until the time when I was in Special Housing, a.k.a., "the Hole"—twenty-eight days, during which time she visited my cell but twice.

The first time she visited me in the Hole was on June 7, 2011. She called me Freerson and slid through the slot in my cell door a piece of paper for my signature. When I leaned over to retrieve the document, I corrected her yet again. Only this time, I peered up at her and saw her, in turn, peering up at the guard who had escorted her to my cell. Not realizing that I could see her, she was looking up at the guard, impishly shrugging her shoulders—and *snickering!* That's when I realized that mispronouncing my name was some kind of game to her. That's also when I decided that I would never again give her the dignity of thinking that it got under my skin.

By the way, the only other time she visited my cell while I was in the Hole was to take from my door a letter that I'd written and left for delivery. It was a letter I wrote to my congressman, Elijah Cummings, to thank him for his intervention, on my behalf. Inmates in the Hole were required to slide their stamped, outgoing mail through the door sill, unsealed so it could be inspected prior to delivery. Before I could stop her, she snatched my letter from my cell door. I don't know what became of the letter, but Congressman Cummings, who is a personal friend of my family, inquired of his office staff. I told him that my letter would have stood out, not only because it was from me but because both the letter and the envelope were written in pencil! Congressman Cummings and his staff insist that they never received my letter. The reader may feel free to infer what you will. I'm just saying…

Of course, later on there was the matter of how she either maliciously or ineptly screwed up my own early release as well as the time in February 2011, when I was referred for transfer to another facility.

My transfer had been deemed necessary by the medical director at FPC Cumberland, because I regularly took a blood-thinning medication to treat a condition called atrial fibrillation, or A-fib. The main symptom of A-fib is an irregular heartbeat. While the condition itself is non-life threatening, when one has an episode, one's irregular heartbeat can cause blood clotting to occur. The greater risk, then, is that a clot can make its way to one's brain and trigger a stroke.

Because of one's heightened stroke risk from A-fib, patients on blood-thinning therapy must have access to a certain minimum level of health care, in the event that an adverse episode occurs. In the federal prison system, that minimum level of health care is available at what are known as Care Level 3 facilities. The FPC Cumberland is rated as a Care Level 2 institution.

The fact that I was on the medication was clearly and repeatedly disclosed in all of my pre-sentencing interviews. It is documented in all of my presentencing reports. That clear and repeated disclosure and documentation begs the obvious question why I was not placed at a Care Level 3 facility in the first place. But for whatever reason(s), I was not.

At any rate, the standards for every phase of operations and procedures throughout the BoP are contained in documents called *program statements.* That includes the standards for determining one's eligibility for furlough, defined as "temporary release from custody under carefully prescribed conditions."

When I learned of my impending transfer, I went to my counselor to inquire about receiving a furlough—pursuant to guidance found in the applicable program statement. Statute 570.33 of that program statement says, "The Warden or a designee may authorize a furlough...for an inmate to transfer directly to another [BoP] institution..." Generally, for transfers to another institution, furloughs of up to twelve hours may be granted. The length of the furlough is calculated on the basis of the distance between institutions. This was fine with me, especially considering the alternative.

The alternative to transferring via furlough is being placed in transit, being transported via the BoP system. As relates to being transferred, furlough is the preferred mode; certainly, preferred by inmates, and one would think, by the institution, given that the inmate bears all related cost(s). Inmates' preference for furlough is based on the amount of time involved in effecting the actual transfer and, to a lesser degree, the physical comfort in which one travels.

Lest the reader be misconceived, an inmate's preference for furlough has nothing to do with his desire to take part in extracurricular behavior (i.e., shopping, carnal knowledge, escape, etc.)—or at least it need not. The amount of leave time allotted is rarely enough for doing anything other than driving to the new designation. In my case, the calculated driving distance between FPC Cumberland and the institution to which I was newly designated—in Butner, North Carolina—is 365 miles; estimated driving time, six hours. I probably would have warranted a seven-hour furlough; eight, on the outside.

As it turned out, the terms and recommendations for my transfer had already been foregone before I ever learned of the proposed move. Nevertheless, I asked my counselor about getting a furlough, who correctly referred me to my case manager. According to the document authorizing my transfer, the warden and case manager had made the arrangements.

Before going to the case manager's office, better judgment inspired me to go to the law library to get a copy of the pertinent program statement. Then armed with the document, I made my way to her small, sparely appointed office, where the following conversation ensued:

"I just learned that I'm scheduled for transfer."

From behind her desk, my case manager replied, "That's right. So?"

"May I use your phone? I need to call my wife. She's on her way up here to visit me tomorrow." It was Thursday, and my wife was driving to visit me the next day. Not knowing when I would be transferred, I wanted to stop her from coming, if I weren't going to be there.

"No. You can call her on your own. You don't need to use my phone."

I suppose I should have been relieved to, at least, now know that I wasn't scheduled for transfer the next day. After learning only hours earlier of the impending move—by being summoned to the message center and told (by my counselor and the guard on-duty) to pack all my belongings and take them to the shipment station *immediately*— no one had seen fit to dignify me with any details. What, why, when or how. I was, prior to this minor revelation, being kept in absolute darkness.

Pulling the program statement from behind my back, where I had been holding it, already folded to the page where the eligibility guidelines were, I said, "I want to know if I can get a furlough. According to this, I'm eligible."

"No, you can't. That doesn't apply to you."

"Why not?" Pointing to the relevant paragraph, I observed, "This part seems to apply to me."

"Well, it doesn't," she snapped. "This is a medical transfer."

I listed ever so slightly closer. Admittedly perturbed by her detachment but still appropriately measured, I pointed to the part of the program statement that is entitled "Transfer to a Medical Center"—*the very next paragraph!*

"Oh, you mean this section," I said. "I meet every one of these criteria."

Clearly irritated by my persistence, she said more emphatically, "Well, you're not getting one. It's too late."

At that point, I relented. Later, I did, indeed call my wife. I suggested that she call our Congressman's office, to enlist their involvement. I didn't mind the transfer, especially if it were better for me, health wise. Plus, by that time, I had already begun writing this book and I thought that the opportunity to compare conditions—and to garner interviews—at a different facility could be interesting, toward that effort.

By the time my wife visited the next day, she had contacted the Congressman's office, whose representatives had, in turn, begun to intervene on my behalf—not with personnel at the FPC Cumberland but directly with the BoP. Those conversations transpired throughout the weekend, with nothing being resolved by the time that my wife's weekend visits ended on Sunday afternoon. I bade her farewell, and we both resigned ourselves to the likelihood that the next time we saw each other, it would be in North Carolina.

At about six thirty on the following Monday morning, I was summoned to the institution's main administrative center—to be processed for transfer. There, I was strip-searched, issued paper attire and thin, cloth shoes, handcuffed, and shackled at the ankles and waist. From there, along with twelve inmates from the medium-security facility, I was herded onto a forty-seven-passenger bus. As we boarded, there was a handful of heavily armed US marshalls standing behind the opened doors of three marked sport utility vehicles, guns drawn and pointed.

We were transported to the Harrisburg (PA) Airport. During the 2.5-hour, 150-mile trek to Harrisburg, I remained manacled— handcuffed as well as shackled. My handcuffs were attached to a chain around my waist in such a way that I was scarcely able to reach my mouth with the two slices of stale, ice-cold white bread and the sliver of yellow cheese that was tossed to me in a brown paper bag. It was demeaning in every aspect, especially for a fifty-six-year-old, disabled, nonviolent first offender, who met each and every criterion for furlough—medical or otherwise.

Harrisburg was the location where inter-institutional transfers were carried out. There were probably thirty-five to forty transport vehicles present—buses, vans, cars...and a white, unmarked jet airplane. There were conveyors from institutions throughout the Eastern region; from Pennsylvania, New Jersey, Ohio, West Virginia. I sat on the Cumberland bus for the two hours it took officers to exchange inmates between institutions. It was February, so it was cold outside, with a mixture of snow and rain falling, as prisoners were transferred from one carrier to another—each inmate donning nothing but their paper clothes and thin, cloth shoes, while the guards wore heavy coats, boots, and gloves. I must admit that I was both appalled by their unconcern for the prisoners' well-being and, at the same time, strangely embarrassed by my naiveté for expecting anything different.

Meanwhile, I had learned my transfer itinerary. I was to be boarded onto the jet and flown to the BoP's holdover facility in Oklahoma. I was to be housed in Oklahoma for an indefinite period until a bed was available at Butner. Then I would be flown to the dilapidated facility in Atlanta (Georgia), from where I would be transported by bus to North Carolina. My transit could have taken a week or more, with my family having neither access to me nor knowledge of my whereabouts. I would travel more than 2,500 miles, on a trip that would take more than a week, and see me spend time in at least two higher security jails, all at government expense, rather than simply be permitted to make a 365-mile, six-hour drive, at my own expense, and self-surrender, as I had at FPC Cumberland just two months earlier. I'm just saying…

Of course, I was seething as I pondered, *Why wouldn't the FPC Cumberland recommend me for furlough?* It simply made all the sense in the world. And at a minimum, why wouldn't they have waited until they knew that a bed was available at Butner before putting me in transit? I suspected that I knew the answers to both questions.

I deduced that they didn't put me in for furlough because the ones at FPC Cumberland with the wherewithal to do so—"The Warden [and] designee," according to the program statement—were sadistic, mean-spirited abusers of authority, who seemed to deem it their duty to heap insult onto injury at every opportunity.

Putting someone into such circuitous transit is known, in institutional parlance, as *diesel therapy.* The inconvenience it engenders for the inmate is deemed by the administrator(s) as a form of punishment. I've heard staff members threaten inmates with it, like the FPC Cumberland administrator, who burst unto one of the wings in my unit and proclaimed, "If I find out that anyone here calls himself going on a hunger strike, I will personally put your ass in diesel therapy for so long that your family won't recognize you when you come out." In my case, the In-Transit form that I found in my central file indicates that it was the case manager who set up my transfer, with the warden signing off on it.

I also deduced that the same reasoning applied to the question of why FPC Cumberland wouldn't defer my transfer until a bed was available at Butner. But I also suspected that another likely reason—the more subtle reason—was liability.

I was in the health services center on Tuesday of the previous week, for something entirely unrelated to my A-fib. Being hard-to-forget is one residual effect of being 6'8" in such a closed community. The medical director just happened to walk into the room where I was being treated. He recognized me as "the big guy who takes [the blood thinner]. We probably should get you transferred." As I wrote earlier, two days later, I was summoned and told to pack my things.

So sitting shackled like an animal aboard that dank bus on a tarmac at the Harrisburg Airport, I suspected that seeing me again reminded the medical director that I was on blood-thinning therapy at his Care Level 2 facility, and it raised in his mind the question, not of my health care but of his and the institution's liability. And, I suspected that, with likely no regard for my health care, the medical—himself, a quack of questionable competency, who was known to, presumably on the basis of cost, regularly maltreat, undertreat, or refuse treatment altogether to inmates presenting with treatable ailments and injuries—decided that I needed to go…and I needed to go *now!* It seemed to me most likely that in his bean counter's mentality, the medical director concluded that both he and the institution could be held liable in the event that an adverse episode occurred while I was still in their custody. Just an educated guess, but if it walks like a duck and quacks like a duck…

Anyway, as the last of the inmate transfers were completed, one of the marshals came to me on the bus and said that he'd received a phone call. He said that my transfer had been "scratched." I asked him why, but he claimed to not know. My—thought—indeed, my hope—was that the Congressman's office had prevailed upon the BoP to allow me to transfer via furlough.

I returned to the Cumberland processing center at about 5:30 that afternoon, where I was again strip-searched. This also happened to be the day that I met the P-Unit's then new counselor—a man who, unbeknownst to me, would eventually become *my* counselor. He watched as I was given two duffle bags loaded with my property and dismissed to make the slippery, half-mile trip up the snow-covered hill to the camp on foot, with the cane that I required to walk. The counselor must have thought it was some kind of joke or something, because all he did was make light of my impending difficulty. I knew he wouldn't offer me a ride, as well he shouldn't. But amid his poking fun at me, it never occurred to him to offer to take my property up to the camp, where he was heading in his car. Apparently, his idea of "demonstrat[ing] uncompromising, ethical conduct…in all [his] actions" was to push his glasses back off his ample nose and yuck it up at the expense of a struggling man. Hell, after all, to him, I wasn't even a man. To him, I was only a filthy inmate!

By the time I got back up to the camp, my case manager had gone for the day. No one, from the processing center staff to the night guards, could tell me why my transfer had been scratched. All anyone knew was that I was no longer scheduled to leave. The next morning, I asked my case manager, who claimed that she didn't know either. "I'm surprised to see you myself" was all she said. In fact, I didn't learn until later that day—from my wife, whom Congressman Cumming's office had contacted—that the BoP had been persuaded to let me stay at FPC Cumberland, for the duration of my sentence. I had eight months remaining on my sentence at that time.

The crazy thing was that nothing had been done to abate or in any way mitigate either the health risk at which I was, by virtue of the blood-thinning therapy, or the institution's liability risk that my continued presence at the camp represented. I'm just sayin'…

But here's the thing. In an episode as important as this, my case manager was ineffectual, either by lack of will or lack of ability—or both. In the only role she played—processing the actual transfer papers—the only thing my case manager did was to make things worse for me. She authorized diesel therapy, rather than a furlough, for a fifty-six-year-old, disabled, nonviolent first-offender, who had self-surrendered and who had never been anything but cooperative, compliant, and even cordial with her. Rather than better, she chose to make the situation worse in a life that was already disheveled by its circumstances. She poured salt into my open wound.

Rather than to make any effort to provide the help and assistance by which inmates' lives might be restored to functionality, my case manager did everything in her power to make their situations worse, to steepen their inclines. All while taking a paycheck for, at best, under-performing—if not forsaking altogether—the all-important, life-changing task for which she was responsible. That is, the task of trying to return to society men who have been amply prepared for successful reentry. She allegedly even told one inmate, at his first unit team meeting that if she had her way, inmates would serve every second of their sentences; that there would be no such thing as early release or good time. As I said repeatedly during my time at the FPC Cumberland, *she has no business with people's lives in her hands…*

In the rehabilitation process—*any* rehabilitation process—no one is more critical than the case manager. As best as I can discern, in the best-case management scenarios, the case manager coordinates the process, consulting the client—in this case, the inmate. The case manager advises and instructs the second-tier caregivers—in this case, the warden, the camp administrator and staff. And s/he coordinates other key service providers—in this case, the unit manager, counselors, drug rehab and health services teams, halfway houses, and probation officers. All of this is toward the goal of ensuring that the inmate's development plan is clearly defined and has the greatest likelihood of facilitating the desired outcomes. In an effective rehabilitation scenario, the case manager and the organization are expected to strive for and maintain *quality* in service provision.

Quality. Excellence. Having value, worth. My observation and experience at the FPC Cumberland is that the case manager to whom I was assigned pays little to no attention to the quality of service she provides, neither in terms of her interactions with inmates nor of the outcomes her case management engenders. Rather, it seemed clear to me that her—and, by extension, the institution's—emphasis was on *quantity.*

They make sure to convene quarterly "team meetings," meetings convened with the unit team, chaired by the case manager and attended by the inmate. Ostensibly, they are meetings at which to engage the inmate in the effort to formulate, implement, and monitor his individual skills development plan—ISDP. New, first-time inmates look forward to their initial team meeting, especially those who, like me, did their diligence prior to arriving and were of the notion that the case manager was someone who gave a damn. That delusion was summarily dispelled the moment one sat through one meeting.

This farcical, abject waste of time was only redeemed by the fact that it rarely took more than five minutes. My meetings were rarely attended by anyone but my case manager and a counselor. I don't recall the unit secretary ever attending one. The following exchange occurred during my final team meeting, on December 22, 2011, and is typical of all the team meetings I attended during my stay:

In her usual loud, harsh voice that was clearly intended to intimidate, my case manager yelled from inside the usually unoccupied room where sat a large copier machine, a simple gray metal office desk and one or two four-drawer file cabinets, "Next."

I walked in, saying nothing, and took my seat in the chair across the table from where sat my case manager and my counselor—the aforementioned Mr. Yuk-Yuk, from the tail end of my aborted transfer episode.

"Well, this is your last team meeting," the counselor said, snickering as he stated the obvious. Since our encounter at the processing center, he had become my counselor, by virtue of the reassignment of my previous one. During the time that he was my counselor, most of our encounters were typified by him making one crude attempt or another to either embarrass me, or to either assail my intelligence or assert his own. I said nothing.

The case manager, as per usual for these meetings, read to me from the prepared ISDP, "Looks like you've completed level three of the walking program. Looks like you took an ACE class, and let's see, looks like you taught one…"

"Two," I interrupted.

"Two. Okay," she allowed, while making no correction to the document from which she continued to recite. "You're scheduled for release on February 3. You've got twelve months of home detention after. Your wife is going to pick you up. You'll live with her at [your house] in Baltimore. Is that right?"

I was incensed at her arrogance. December 22 was the day after I would have—*should* have—been released, were it not for her. I might have alleged that she's simply motivated by the enmity with which she treated every inmate. Like I said, there is not one past or current inmate I know who would describe their experience with her as positive. Not one!

Or I might have alleged that her disfavor was racially motivated. That's because a short time after denying my request to transfer via furlough, she authorized another inmate—a white one—to transfer to a facility in Otisville, New York, by way of furlough. Or I might have contended she was racist because of the tactic she chose to use implementing my sentence, that she opted not to employ when implementing the sentence of another inmate. That other inmate and I surrendered on the same date, were both first-time, nonviolent white-collar offenders, had identically stellar personal and professional backgrounds, identically spotless institutional records and identical fifteen-month sentences that were to be followed by court-ordered home detention—except he was white.

But it seemed to me that, either way—regardless of whether she was hateful or bigoted—my case manager's actions clearly evinced incompetence. That conclusion was not only borne out in her mishandling of my release but in the warden's written response to a formal inquiry I submitted, requesting to know why I was going to be detained beyond my so-called 10 percent date.

In his reply, the warden wrote, "You are eligible for [residential reentry] placement," directly controverting my case manager's claim to the contrary. The warden's response continues, "[but] due to the amount of time remaining to be served on your sentence…there is insufficient time to process a referral for home detention placement."

The warden's response was dated December 12, 2011. It further stated that it takes more than sixty days to process someone for home detention. My release date was February 3, 2012, leaving me with about fifty days left to serve. Ostensibly, that meant that there wasn't enough time to rectify the error.

In other words, the person responsible for processing my release—none other than the pokerfaced troll now seated across from me, showing no hint of compunction—dropped the ball. She simply chose to not file the paperwork by which to effect my timely release, but she *did* file the paperwork for my aforementioned similarly-situated fellow inmate. And, apparently, she filed his paperwork sixty days or more prior to our shared 10 percent date, because he was released on that date. December 21.

I sat there pondering why, given that *everything* about our cases was the same, would the case manager process the cases differently? According to the warden's written response, it turns out that she shouldn't have. It turns out that I should have been released on December 21, not February 3. And it turns out that despite my inquiry, despite my attorney's inquiry, there was not one person within the entire BoP who had either the decency or the wherewithal to supersede my case manager's blunder and simply say, "Hey, we made a mistake. This guy should be out of here. Let him go…now!"

Translation: I was screwed! My right to early release was violated. As a result, the day of this, my last unit team meeting, was the first of the extra forty-five days I was incarcerated.

So yeah, in my mind, at that moment, I charitably chose to go with *incompetent*, and I said nothing in reply to her question regarding where I planned to live, except "Yes."

"Well, sign this," she said as she shoved the ISDP across the table to me and expressionlessly added. "Just keep doing what you're doing. Any questions?" Then before I could reply, she blurted out, "*Next!*"

Five minutes and an advisement to "just keep doing what [I'm] doing." That's it. That's all it ever was. Nothing meaningful. That's why the inmates hated it. It was a complete waste of time. But by perpetrating this ruse, the unit team—and the institution—got to report that they convened a meeting at which to discuss my "development plan." They got to pull off the absolute scam that they played *any* role in assisting me in any way.

According to the CMSA,

> The case management approach assumes that clients with complex and multiple needs will access services from a range of service providers, coordinated by a caring professional. The goal is to achieve seamless service delivery.

To me, that single statement embodies the essence of effective case management. It sets forth the essence of what would have been invaluable to—but was blatantly missing from—my correctional experience at the FPC Cumberland. Namely,

- a caring provider, who understands and is sensitive to the complexities of inmates' circumstances;
- an array of services, coordinated by that caring provider; and
- a development plan that is client- rather than institutionally-driven.

In most every area of social or human services delivery, client input is viewed as a critical component of the service planning process. Regardless of the issue, eliciting input from those directly affected is widely held as a best practice for service planning. As a former community organizer/planner, as a nonprofit executive, as a youth services provider, as a health educator, as a parent involvement coordinator, even as a singer, obtaining feedback from the target population has always proven to be a key component of successful strategic planning. *Quality* feedback.

During my thirteen-month stay at FPC Cumberland the activities in which I was involved included: a Black History Month planning committee; a singing group; a quilting circle; personal physical fitness; ACE classes I took; and ACE classes I taught (songwriting and voice). The sum total of any of these programs that were suggested, coordinated, or provided by my case manager is *zero*. Indeed, the only program she suggested me for…was GED. The FPC Cumberland receives a $2,500 incentive bonus for each inmate that obtains his GED while in its custody. The inmate gets nothing, except the diploma. One problem, though. As I noted in my pre-sentencing interviews, I earned my GED in 1974!

The compulsory quarterly unit team meetings would be excellent forums for obtaining quality feedback—if the case manager treated them as something other than perfunctory. If inmates felt that their problems and concerns would receive even a modicum of genuine consideration, they would, in turn, embrace their role in the process of their own rehabilitation. Instead, they often fail to see the usefulness. If inmates were engaged beyond merely being barked at, recited to, and then disingenuously asked, "Any questions?" there would be anticipation or eagerness among inmates to attend unit team meetings. Instead, they dread it. Indeed, inmates housed in my unit, to a person, do everything they can to avoid *any* interaction with the case manager. Their mind-set is to "stay out of her way."

Case management as it was dispensed by my case manager during my stay at the FPC Cumberland was a disgrace. To the meager and disingenuous extent that she even tried, my case manager was ineffectual. What's therapeutic about a case manager, first refusing an inmate's request to marry his long-time fiancé and the mother of his children, and then when he marries her anyway, removing the inmate's now *wife* from his visitor list—after the wife, as the inmate's fiancé, had been on his visitor list for *five years*? My case manager did that.

What is rehabilitative about trying to deny an inmate the use of the cane he needed for walking and that had been authorized by the health services department? My case manager did that.

I submit that my case manager's methods were antithetical in every way to the goal of achieving the "rehabilitation" or "corrections" that the BoP asserts are among its objectives. To whatever extent her methods are typical of the way case management is practiced throughout the federal prison system, they cannot be condoned. I'm just saying…

Donald Mudd

"Bringing down another man is a small man's way of making himself look big."

"Huh? I mean, I get it. But I didn't think this guy could even talk!" That's the thought that went through my mind when Donald "Don" Mudd interjected his unsolicited witticism into my and BC's conversation. My surprise by his interruption was eclipsed only by my amazement at not only his speaking but also at the cogency and depth of his quiet utterance.

The truth is, my friend BC and I—BC, twelve years Don's senior; I, a whopping twenty-five—were, albeit playfully, deriding another acquaintance. We didn't mean any harm, but Don was right to remind us of the immaturity of our behavior. Damn! You really can't judge a book by its cover! And Don's cover was entirely—perhaps, purposely—misleading.

Don was one 5'10", 175-pound muscle. I mean one solid muscle from head to toe. Not in the overblown, bodybuilder way but not slim either. He was muscular in the same way as is vaunted Ralph Lauren fashion model, Tyson—broad-shouldered, narrow-waisted. As if sculpted by Rodin—but out of caramel. Don would put Tyson to shame. His closely shorn but not bald head, his perfect teeth, his mannequin facial features, and his intense, golden-brown eyes gave Don the countenance of a god—or, at least, a statue of one.

Don's speech was a droning monotone. He meted out conversation as though it were his gift to you. One actually felt privileged when he decided to grace you with a few words. He had a quiet yet overall quite menacing look that belied the warmth conveyed in his rare but genuine smile…and that I came to know.

I was born in 1979, in the small southern New Jersey town of Bridgeton. I'm the oldest of four kids, raised by a single parent—my mom. My dad went into the military when he was seventeen or eighteen then got in some kind of trouble and never came back. I'll never know why he di'nt come back, because he died. But he never came back.

We were raised in a two-bedroom house, which, if I saw it today, would bring me shame. I couldn't probably stand up in it. That's how small it was. But my mother worked hard to feed five mouths on her one income—probably about $300 a week. She worked in housekeeping. That was in the eighties and early nineties. I guess you could say we were poor.

When I was a teenager, we moved to a three-bedroom house, still with one income; although my sister had a baby and had her own income from welfare. But I started running the streets, committing petty crimes—stealing, robbing, hurting people—when I was about thirteen. I was focused on things like my appearance—my hair, my looks, my clothes. I wanted to be accepted, so one way to do it was to be doing bad things. They made me seem "cool," he said, using two fingers on each hand to simulate quotation marks. I was also smoking weed and cigarettes and drinking alcohol. I di'nt necessarily like it, but I did it. By the time I was fifteen, I was going home just to change my clothes and get back out in the streets.

I dropped out of school when I was in the tenth grade. I was about sixteen. That's also when my oldest daughter was born. That's when I started selling real drugs. I say "real drugs" because before that we would beat people by selling them stuff that we packaged to look like drugs, but it really wasn't drugs. Now I'm selling actual drugs—to take care of my daughter and to support my new habits—cigarettes and weed. But I stayed pretty low level, until I was about eighteen or nineteen.

That's when I started observing and listening. I especially watched the one guy who was making good money. Finally, I asked him, "How come when you come out, we can't make no money?" He told me that it was all about the quality of his product. Now he was saying one thing, but I was hearing another. I would have—still have—these, what I call "conversations within," where I converse with my inner voice. And my inner voice was telling me I was putting too much of myself into it. That if I was putting so much of myself into the game, something wasn't right. What I heard my man say is that if the product is good enough, I di'nt have to work so hard to sell it. It would sell itself. That's what I heard…and that's what I did. I upgraded my product. Pretty soon, everybody was sayin', "D's got dat good. He got dat ready rock." Now I'm the one getting all the play when I step on the block. I went from having forty to fifty dollars in my pocket, to having thousands of dollars. Wasn't nothing for me to have thousands of dollars in my pocket…or in my safe. I was getting a name for myself and all that came with it. I was dressing, looking good, the whole nine. Ladies were shootin' at me, like, 'Who are you?'

And I'm like, 'I've known you my whole life. I'm from right here in this neighborhood.' Then acting as though he were pointing toward another imaginary girl, 'and I used to go to school with you!'

We both chuckled a bit. I was thinking of an episode from my favorite TV show, *The Andy Griffith Show*. On this particular episode, a reclusive farmer raised the curiosity of Deputy Barney Fife, who was determined to get to the bottom of why the guy was so mum, so mysterious. To Barney, the guy had to be up to no good. Later in the episode, Barney learned that the man was neither a miscreant nor a deviant. He was merely preoccupied by matters related to his wife's pregnancy and impending delivery. And to Barney's chagrin, he also found out that the guy could talk. And talk. Then talk some more.

While Don's oratory in no way chagrined me, his talkativeness was mildly amusing to me and certainly a surprise. Indeed, I took it as somewhat of a compliment that he felt comfortable enough to open up to me. But truthfully, I was starting to look for a fucking "Pause" button. Just kidding…

I was making a name for myself—making good money, doing bad things. At twenty-three, I came face to face with that. That's about the time—in, like, '03—I got my only real job. I was a security guard at a supermarket. I was trying to make a change. I had worked there for a minute, when the guy whose place I took—who was on crack—starting telling everybody I had that rock. As security guard, I was exposed to the monthly checkers, as well as the big money customers. Next thing you know, I'm

killin' 'em! I'm making more money at the store than I was in the hood.

"So how did you go down? How'd you end up here?"

First, let me say this. Before twenty-three, I di'nt see this coming—I mean, prison. I di'nt see that it was the only way that I would be purged. I di'n't see that I was depriving my children of a father; and their mothers of a responsible 'baby father.' At twenty-three, I did start to sense that this might be the likely outcome of my immaturity and wrong decision making. I tried to avoid it. That's why I got the supermarket job. But I think the truth is that I had no real guidance. I mean, I had people that would talk to me but no positive mentors. I don't blame that, though. I blame me. Because, as I said, I have these conversations within myself. And there's a good force and a negative force. And the negative force in this instance was...fear. I believe that's why I'm sitting here with you, Vic. Fear. Ignorance. Lack of feeling competent. I quit jobs because I felt incompetent. I can't take criticism. I couldn't take being fired. So I stayed on the wrong track, avoiding anything that challenged me. And I ignored what I believe were my senses—I want to think it was God—that told me the right things to do.

It was remarkable at times, Don's use of language. His was an amalgamation of street talk and eloquence, of thoughtfulness and of vacancy, of innocence and of sageness. Like the nugget he dropped on BC and me. It was as spiritual as it was matter-of-fact. He was, at once, mysterious—which was a desired affectation and transparent—which it would mortify him to know. So I eagerly awaited his take on his arrest and subsequent ordeal with the legal system, being not entirely ignorant of it.

I shared an apartment with my second daughter's mother. My daughter was two. Me and my girl, Tina, were kind of on the rocks, so I was in and out. For all practical purposes, I was homeless, living out of my car. All my clothes and stuff were in the trunk.

One night in '05, I went by to check in. Then looking at me with the innocence of a twelve-year-old, he confessed, **Actually, I**

went by for some sex. Anyway, Tina and me were sitting in the living room smoking weed and talking, when, for some reason, I decided to go check outside. I went into my little girl's room. At the time, it was empty, except for a computer. There was no bed in there. I peeked out the window and di'nt see nothing. I moved away, but something told me to check again.

I thought I was just being paranoid. But this time, I saw a van ease down the street then past the complex, then stop, then back up. Then I noticed two unmarked cars trailing the van. My first instinct was to run. I had taken off my shoes and had on some slippers. My thought was to go tell Tina what was happening and to make a run for it. But Tina was nowhere to be found. Then as I headed to get my shoes and go, I passed by our room—where my Booty-Boo was sleeping on our bed. And I said that there's no way I can leave my baby by herself. But still I had to go. Now!

So I decided to go toward the front door rather than out the back, where I think I definitely could have got away. It was a two-story building. As I get to the bottom of the stairs, I see a uniformed police officer and two in plain clothes, congesting the doorway, preparing to ram the door. I reached for the door to unlock it and surrender. When I unlocked the door, they hit it once. It startled me, and I yelled, 'Hold up!' and went to turn the knob when they hit it again. The door gave way and flung open.

Then there was a long pause. They looked at me, I looked at them perplexed, and said, 'I know you heard me say I'm gonna open the door.' Finally, one of the plainclothes guys tackled me. The way I was lying, I was face down on the steps. I looked up to the top of the stairs, and there was Tina and my daughter—both of them yelling and scared. They handcuffed me and sat me on the steps. Then they made Tina and the baby come outside while they searched the apartment. They found three grams of weed, and a digital scale. The scale was not a problem, though, because it had no residue and it was where it belonged—in a kitchen. Then one of the cops said they found two grams of crack inside a car speaker at the bottom of the steps.

Meanwhile, more cops come, a couple from behind the building. They found nothing except a car. They asked me about the plum-colored Chevy Cavalier, which they said I was allegedly dealing drugs from. They found the car, but I said it di'n't belong to me and that I don't got the keys. I said it was somebody else's car, who was incarcerated, who had asked me to watch it. One officer came with a Slim Jim and jimmied the door open. Then they put the K-9 in the car—the dog. He came out of the car, then went back in and came out again. The cops went into the car with a flashlight—one, DEA, one from the Cumberland County Drug Task Force. Under my car seat they found 106 grams of ready rock—which, I guess gave them the probable cause they needed to crowbar the trunk open.

As I said, I was living out of my car, so all of my clothes were there in bags. They took all the bags out and threw them on the ground. Then they dumped the clothes on the ground. When they searched the clothes, they found my gun—a chrome .380 that was hidden inside a white wool hat.

Realizing that there was no need for my scripted questions because he was answering them all, I just went into cruise control and let Don talk.

I guess I was under arrest because someone read me my rights. But what I heard most of all was the DEA cop telling me that I had a 'unique' situation. He said what they wanted me for was questioning in a homicide that I'd been implicated in…and that if I provided certain information, it could help alleviate my dilemma. The thing is, I di'nt know anything! I was prepared to take full responsibility for what I did, but I di'nt know anything about the homicide. I mean, I'd heard about it, but I di'nt know any details, and I certainly wasn't involved.

Don must have misread the expression on my face to be one of disbelief because he looked at me more intensely and insisted, **For real!** I di'nt have the information they wanted. So when one of the officers started threatening that he could involve Tina—and have my daughter taken from her—I made up a story so they would accept that I was solely responsible—for the drugs.

They finally locked me up—not on any charges for that night but for some old warrants, traffic stuff. I was given thirty days. They gave me a summons on the drugs and gun; they just held me. This is the state. The idea was to hold me long enough—to get me to work for them, to wear wires and stuff, to help them get kilos and guns. I said I di'nt know what they were talking about, that I was willing to cooperate for what I'd done but not to help [them].

"So you said no?"

I said no. They said, 'Well, in that case, we're turning your case over to the feds…and you'll get sixty years. If you cooperate with us, we'll make sure you only get two.'

Looking at me and doffing the white baseball cap he's wearing, Don says, So I thought about it. The conversation within. But here's the thing. If I did this thing, the type of people I would have to implicate are the type who would stop at nothing to get pay back. Nothing. I wasn't so concerned about me but about my family. So I asked them, 'What about my family?' They said they'd relocate me, Tina and my little girl, and give us protection. But I said, 'What about my mom and my grand mom and the rest of my family?' They said no, they can't do that. So I said no.

Two weeks later, the feds pick me up and put me under their custody. They took me to the federal detention center in Philly, which is where I began my stay in federal prison. I was under no indictment, mind you, but I was in federal custody. No money. No contact with my family. No clue of how serious this all was. And to be honest, no hope.

There is no federal holding facility in south Jersey, so I stayed in Philly. My court proceedings were in Camden [New Jersey]. At my arraignment, I pleaded not guilty and was assigned a public defender. I still di'nt fully understand how my case got passed on to the feds.

"I sat in Philly for ninety days—still under no indictment. But let me say this. I was not in touch with anybody, until I was able to get my address to my sister—who passed it along to Tina. Remember, we were not doing so hot when all this went down.

Well, she wrote me a letter and told me that she loves me and was gonna be there for me. That letter was a big deal to me. Right then and there, I made a vow to make her a part of me—a part of 'Don's world'—forever. Along with my daughters, Tina is a permanent part of my hopes and aspirations.

"This note to Tina: You had to be there. You had to see the look in Don's eyes when he made this declaration. In fact, most every time he spoke of you. He was sincere, no doubt about it. So if he's out now and the inevitable tough times arise, you just remind him of what he told Big Vic, while we were at FPC Cumberland. Tell him to get a grip, to go somewhere and have one of his 'conversations within' and then get back to loving you in the manner that you deserve...and that he avowed to me on May 1, 2011.

After some time, I finally got a visit from my public defender. He came to me with a plea offer from the feds: ten years. He said if I di'nt take it, I'd be facing fifteen years to life. Even though I'm still not indicted. My thought was that if I do this, I charge myself, I indict myself, and I find myself guilty. He also says I can possibly beat some of this—giving me at least some hope. But he also said that you have no rights with the feds if they find you guilty. I declined the plea offer.

My lawyer came back about thirty days later, but when he came back, he had a whole different attitude. Now he's saying he don't see how we can beat this; he sounds hopeless all of a sudden. I'm thinking they done got to him 'cause he's pushing hard to get me to plea out. In the meantime, other, more knowledgeable inmates are telling me things about seeing cases thrown out for due process and that they beg to differ with his opinion that I can't beat this. Don looks at me and says, 'I'm saying this to my lawyer and I'm saying that the fact that I'm still not indicted violates my speedy trial right, which you should know.' And, when I told him that I remember him telling me that with the feds, I have no rights, he looks up and says, 'I never told you that.' I stopped in my tracks and ended the interview right there. He gonna look me right in the eye and say he di'nt say that?

I wrote the judge a complaint alleging that I was being poorly represented. The court fired him and appointed me another lawyer.

I sat for five months before my new lawyer got my indictment, but he said I had a good chance to beat it. The indictment was for crack. I asked for a speedy trial, even though I di'nt fully understand how the feds do business. How they bend the laws to get their man because now, they supersede the drug charge with a gun *and* drug charge. The gun and drug charge carried a sentence of fifteen years to life and a $4 million fine. I'm twenty-five years old and ignorant to a lot—especially about federal law. I was shell-shocked, confused. I couldn't think straight. Fifteen years to life? Four million dollars?

I sat for thirteen months—from August '05 to September '06. Over that period, I consulted with my attorney for a total of one hour and fifteen minutes. In thirteen months.

So now it's two weeks before my trial was set to begin. The judge in my case had moved to Trenton, so that's where my case was tried. Two weeks before trial, I'm anxious, I'm desperate. Now my lawyer's talking about them threatening me with being tried as a 'career criminal,' because they found out about my priors. They're talking 'three strikes'! They're hitting me with scare tactics, hitting me with the 'life' thing. I'm mad as hell. At the feds. At my lawyers, who don't seem to want to help.

I hear the frustration in Don's voice. I see it in his face, as he relives his nightmare—or at least this part of it. He pauses, presumably for the sake of composure, then, **So the trial starts on September 25 of '06. It lasted four days. On September 29, I was found guilty on all charges. On March 2 of '07, I was sentenced to 211 months—17½ years. And because it's federal, no possibility of parole. My fine, though, was lowered from $4 million—to $300. I've been in prison ever since.**

Don and I were in a room in which band equipment was stored. In the interest of privacy, we had sequestered ourselves there but were still only a pane of glass removed from the din of about twelve or fifteen guys playing cards and dominos and shooting pool. We could

hear the cacophony of sounds: pool balls clacking; cards being shuf-
fled, cut, and dealt; dominos being slammed on unpadded tables;
and of course, the smack-talking requisite to each pursuit. Yet the
weight and girth of Don's words provided a sort of eerie insulation.

It seemed dead quiet for a moment. It was a familiar moment
for me, as I had seen and experienced it at a point in each interview
I'd conducted. But it seemed to me that it was a particularly poignant
moment for Don. As though he were thinking, "Wow, there it is!' Or
'All this shit really happened—and I was there for every second of it.
And now, here I am."

**Since my sentencing—even to this very day—I've been
appealing. I appealed the pretrial, the motion to suppress. I
appealed the sentence. All kinds of stuff. I was sent to a medium-security facility—Schuylkill—with about fifteen hundred
guys serving sentences from five years to life. With a life sentence
in the federal system the only way out is in a body bag. There is
no parole, not since the eighties.** Don was referring to the time
when the practice of mandatory minimum sentencing began, the
practice by which judges' sentencing authority—their ability to
exercise discretion—was effectively usurped...and from where the
most egregious of the disparities in the penal system emanate in my
observation.

**I was [at Schuykill] with other first offenders *and* with hard
core types. In 2007, Congressional amendment 706 was enacted.
706 reduced the sentencing disparity between crack and powder
cocaine convictions from 100 to 1 to 80 to 1. I was eligible for the
reduction, so my 17½-year sentence dropped to 15.**

Don was referring to the unequal standard within the federal sentencing system, by which convictions for one gram of crack
cocaine is similar to that for one hundred grams of powder cocaine.
In '07, the disparity was reduced to 80 to 1, and in 2010, to 18 to 1.
By the time of my release in February 2012, several individuals had
been granted their immediate releases on the premise that they had
served the time to which they were rightfully subject. When I left,
Don—who was among the guys that came out to bid me off—was
still awaiting disposition on his case.

Right now, I'm awaiting a decision on another appeal I've filed—this one, on the basis of the crack/powder disparity *and* technical errors in the court proceedings. See, pursuant to 3553(a), the judge had the right to sentence me to a lower sentence. She could have exercised leniency on the basis of several so-called 'correctional factors.' Positive factors and negative factors. For example, my impoverished, single-parent upbringing, my lack of parental guidance, my lack of education, my and my family's drug abuse. Because of these factors, she could have sentenced me with consideration of rehab, rather than for punishment. Instead, she concluded that she di'nt have the authority to exercise discretion, because it was unprecedented in the Third Circuit. I believe it was cowardice. That she was more concerned with her career than with exercising a just decision. She was scared to set a judicial precedent that might later be deemed not in favor with other magistrates in the circuit.

Right again. The judge in Don's trial could have could have 'exercised leniency on the basis of correctional factors.' I reference to him the case of my bunkmate. J-Boy was convicted, like me, of one count of wire fraud. In his case, he stole and then sold on *E*Bay about $480 thousand dollars' worth of *government property*. Almost half million bucks! Of US government property.

Notwithstanding a few differences between the cases—not the least of which, being that their cases were heard in different locations and by different judges—the sentencing threshold for $200,000 to $400,000 offenses is twenty-seven to thirty-three months. Above $400k, it's up to ten years.

Ostensibly, federal guidelines transcend jurisdiction. It's not supposed to matter whether the case is heard in New Jersey or in DC. It's certainly not supposed to matter if one defendant is black and from an inner city environment, and that another is white and from non-urban surroundings.

However, according to J-Boy, the judge in his case took into consideration, among other factors: the broken home in which he was raised; the fact that during his childhood he was in three foster homes; and his military and private service in Iraq and Afghanistan.

J-Boy was sentenced to eighteen months…*far below* the guidelines for his offense—or mine, for that matter, even though the value of his offense was more than twice mine.

As for Don, as of this interview, he is awaiting a decision on his appeal. He and his lawyer hope to get the appellate court to order the judge in his case to sentence him in accordance with the language and spirit of Don's first remand, when his sentence was reduced from 17½ to 15 years. To do that, they will have to deem the judge to have been errant in her execution of jurisprudence. If the appeal is granted, they would go back before [preferably, the same] judge to 'fix' the procedural error.

Since the original trial, Don has been a model inmate. He obtained his GED. He's amassed stellar work and inmate evaluations at every one of his four institutions. He's volunteered in several service initiatives, both organized and informal. And his behavior has been exemplary, as is evidenced by the fact that his risk level assessment has consistently decreased until he got designated to a camp.

"Sensing that we'd gone as far as we could with Don's legal dilemma, I felt it was time to get back on script. 'Is prison different from what you expected?'

Yes. We tend to think of prison as the worst environment to be in, but it's not…like, don't drop the soap. Like you might be harmed. I guess it can be like that, but it all depends on how you carry yourself. There are certain undesirable things that you can be pressured into. Especially if you carry yourself as weak or dependent. You'll find yourself as part of an organization…like a gang or a religious group. Or a workout 'car' [group].

You can conform to them, but if they're troublemakers, *you'll* become a troublemaker. If they wear certain things, then you wear those things. Tats [tattoos]. Hats. Sneakers. Colors. Hairstyles. Beards. You do it to be accepted, to fit in. And for real, it can be a little hard to just be yourself and not have harm done to you. Especially if being yourself means bucking up against somebody. And if the somebody you buck up against is in a group, it becomes all the more difficult for you. It's for security. For the protection afforded by groups, by numbers. The gangs can come at you, but

you get more pressure from religious groups. Depending on the group's objective, you can make them look good.

"Already knowing from a previous conversation that Don had never affiliated with a group, I asked, 'How did you manage to avoid joining a group?'

I never needed it. First of all, I never bothered anybody. I never tried to harm anybody. Like I said, the religious groups, they came at me, but I di'nt think it was for me. I worked out with some guys, but that was about it for me. It's different at different facilities...basically, depending on two factors: security level and the population. I've been in a medium [security facility, Schuylkill] that had 1,500 guys, and at a low [Fort Dix] that had five thousand. At those facilities, the group influence is pretty strong. You feel more inclined to join a group, and there's always some kind of confrontation. And typically, there are more guys with violent backgrounds and longer sentences—which can mean, with less to lose. But, at the camps where I've been [Fairton and Cumberland), the groups are barely even noticeable, except the religious groups.

"Talk about the staffs at the different facilities. Can you compare them?"

Sure. Understand that *all* staff has BoP rules to abide by, depending on the security level. Staff at the higher security facilities are generally advised to be more respectful—especially of inmates of higher sentences, like at the mediums and up. At lows and camps, the staff and administration look at you with more condescension. Because you're new, they feel like they've got to be your teacher, gotta teach you 'prison etiquette.' They think, like, because you never been to jail before, you can't really handle prison.

It depends on the COs [correctional officer] background. COs here at Cumberland rotate between facilities every quarter. So COs coming from the medium harbor a little bit of disdain for campers. To them, we have it easy. We enjoy more freedom of movement. At other levels, you have much less freedom. There are walls and cells and barbed wire. Like you might have ten-minute moves. 'Ten-minute moves' means you have ten minutes to get from one place to the next. If you're late, you can get a shot [sanction].

At the higher security spots, the COs don't really mess with you for nothing. Here, at the camps and lows, they mess with you for *anything*. They really try to exert their authority because they have the idea that you have to submit to them, for fear of being moved to a higher security spot.

"Hold up. My thought was that the threat they hold over campers is that if you buck, you may jeopardize your out date, that they'll add time to your sentence.

Yeah, that could be true. But the real threat is that they'll put you in higher security, with harder guys. They play on your own fears. And it's a myth…'cause it's the same guys!

"What do you mean?"

I mean, like me. I used to be in a higher-security jail. I worked myself down to a low, then to a camp. Lots of guys here have. It's the same guys. I got seven years left on my sentence. To a camper, that's like life! The only difference 'down the hill' [at the medium-security facility] is that you can't do some of the stuff that you do here. The inmates there don't stand for it. Cutting in line at chow? They ain't having it down there. Same way with keeping your cell or toilet dirty or playing loud music and stuff, when somebody's trying to sleep or just being disrespectful. The inmates at higher security spots don't go for none of that. But other than that for the most part, it's the same guys.

The fear that the COs play on is the uncertainty. I just said that they think the average camper is fearful of the other inmates. Campers buy into the stigma. But there's also the uncertainty of where you'll be transferred. You could go to a spot ten hours away, instead of two. That would mess with your family ties. So it's the threat of inconvenience that they play on too, the not knowing the outcome. You can get a shot that warrants a bump but doesn't add time to your sentence.

But for real? Some COs are just disrespectful and inconsiderate at all levels. They stereotype, and they are afraid of confrontation. They'll do stuff behind your back. Or they'll pick at you and nitpick. I think it's cowardice. They're taught not to communicate with inmates. In fact, to them, that's your name. Inmate. That's who you are, who you always have been, and who you always will be—inmate. You're an eight-digit number, not a person. So you, an inmate, have to worry about the other inmates *and* the COs. Staff makes it more difficult than it has to be.

"What programs and/or services should be available that aren't?"

I think young people—like, say, eight to forty (damn, Don! Thanks)—should have more education programs and more apprenticeship programs. Since I'm here, I should be able to pursue more education, or a career. Especially, since that's what they tell the general public they're doing.

"Don, did you know that the director of the BoP recently gave testimony to a congressional committee reviewing mandatory minimum sentences, in which he cited a litany of programs and educational opportunities that he says are available throughout the prison system?"

Well, he must have been talking about programs in the mediums and up. For example, they had a real horticulture program at Schuylkill. And a carpentry program. They were taught by either staff or someone from the outside certified in the fields. Where you actually earned real certification. It was hands-on. Ain't nothing like that here—or at any of the other low spots I've been in. Here, they get outside people to teach, like drug programs and parenting, but that's about it. They should add programs where you can earn some kind of certification. Like, in auto mechanics or CDL. With all the vehicles they have in their garage, they could easily arrange something like that. Programs like that really mean something. They have real value. I'll be here for seven more years. That's plenty of time for me to learn a skill—especially since I *want* to learn.

"Once, out on the compound, you said to me that they used to have more programs at camps. But you said, inmates didn't take advantage of them, so the BoP stopped them. Explain."

I really think what happened is this. I think the camps used to be populated by a higher percentage of older, white, white-collar types—guys who would take advantage of opportunities like that. It was, so to speak, a higher class of inmate. Before crack!

With crack, the whole prison system was flooded with, like, street guys...and in some instances, guys who couldn't read, guys who couldn't write...mocking now...but hey, I'm not gonna tell you I can't read and write. And I ain't tryin' nothing that will expose it. You want me to get a GED—and expose my intellectual shortcomings to others? You must be mad. Then turning back into Don, he continues, 'The programs are over their heads, Vic. And they're scared. They can't get out of their own way. They can't get out of the cell that's within them.'

"How do you spend your time here?"

Observing. Analyzing. Critiquing myself—my life. Building my physical self. I exercise. I watch what I eat. I *love* to study the human body, spirituality, psychology, people's behavior. I read, I go to movies. I love to inspire people through my words and actions. I like to work. You can't just not progress. I have friends, but I don't look for friends. I let God put them in my life. And I love thinking about life after this.

"Okay. That's a nice segue. What are your plans after you get out?"

This might sound abnormal, but I plan to remain the person that I am. I don't have dreams of wealth. I just want to be a hardworking, hard-loving, faithful, respectful, and respectable husband and father—perfect, in my own eyes. I'd like to remain the person that you see now. You, Vic. You cast discernment on me. You say, 'Don, you're a decent guy.' I like that. I can die with that. That can be my legacy. That I was decent to everyone in my universe. Prison don't teach you how to become who you are, Vic. You're gonna continue to fight yourself, and you're gonna continue to lose. Because nobody can beat you but you.

"Who do you miss the most?"

That's easy. Three people. My [fifteen-year-old] daughter, Renee, my Booty-Boop, Chante', and Tina. That's it.

"Fair enough. *What* do you miss most?"

I don't really miss anything. I'm just anxious about what it's gonna be like when I get out. I don't miss anything about my past life. Everything I could miss, I still have.

"You had any visits lately?"

No. Not for about six months. To be honest, I don't want any. My mom offered to come, but I said no. I don't want to hit the Reset button. I appreciated the gesture. She was gonna be traveling to Virginia and thought about shooting over here to see me, thinking that it was close…which it's really not. So I said no. And I really don't want my kids and my lady to drive all the way here and not be able to engage them as family. I'd have to engage them as a prisoner. Limited touching, sit this way, don't do that. I'll wait that one out.

Don was right to be concerned about how the quality of the 'visiting experience' can be diminished by how staff interprets and enforces the rules. They do so, in many instances, with a complete absence of not only compassion but also common sense. Take, for example, the previously referenced visit by Easy Lamb's family. Or like the time a visitor of mine made the 2.5-hour trip from Baltimore, only to be denied the chance to see me on the basis that she was not on my visitor list, in the computer, even after I produced the list that had been left me by my counselor, on which her name clearly was. I had no reason why the name wasn't in the computer, but certainly neither my friend nor I had anything to do with the snafu. Forget compassion—where's the common sense?

Or like when my family traveled from Kentucky (7 hours) and Virginia (2.5 hours) to visit but were denied the opportunity to visit me at the same time, because the form on which I had requested and obtained permission to entertain more than three adults at a time had, again, not made its way to the VRO. Again, after I'd done all that was required of me. Where's the common sense? So I wholly understood Don's desire to spare his family and himself the potential indignity.

"Last question. If you could snap your fingers and be any-place, doing absolutely anything right now, where would you be? What would you be doing?"

"I'd be in a home that we own with my little girls…and Tina, as my wife. Cooking on a grill, or watching a movie."

Postlogue

Don Mudd's appeal was reviewed by the judge in his case in January 2012. His appeal was denied. Don remained at FPC Cumberland until his release, in August 2018. I have had no subsequent contact with him.

Michael "Mike" Pentangelo

"I wish there were more people here who acted like you, but look like me."
Don Mudd, to the subject of my next interview.

Meet Mike. Michael Antonin Pentangelo. My first impression of Mike was arrived at hastily—which says more about me than it does about Mike. Before we'd ever shared so much as a hello, I'd lumped him in with the rest of the all-white, all middle-aged, all white-collar offenders, in whose company he seemed to constantly be. For the most part, these guys were okay—to me, anyway, among the other black inmates. I choose to believe that my treatment was afforded on the basis of my age and comportment, the way I carried myself. Of course, I also realize (given the frequent number of occasions on which it happens) that it may not have been so much about *how* I carried myself, as it was about the fact that I carried myself in an admittedly imposing 6'8", 290-pound, dreadlocked package.

Either way, all of them were cordial enough to, at least, speak; some, to even engage me in cursory conversations, albeit usually about the weather, or sports (of course), or some other innocuous topic that was not likely to inflame. And they condescended. Some unconsciously. Hell, some of them were condescending to others in their little pentagenarian, Aryan brotherhood, let alone to me. And why not? There were guys in their cadre who were billionaires, millionaires; some gonnabes and some wannabes…the latter, sort of forcing their way into the "club," their only congruence being their age, race and, in most cases, their politics. Indeed, under any other circumstances, some of the truly affluent guys were no more likely to embrace the gonnabes and wannabes, as they were to embrace…well, me. Of course, prison being the great equalizer of men, it took some longer than others to realize that behind the walls, they—we—were all the same. Inmates. And as Don and other previous interview subjects had relayed, inmates sometimes seek the cover and protection of numbers, of groups.

So they all spent entire days sometimes, in the safety of their lair—the library. It was their sanctuary from the black and brown men by whom the camp is overwhelmingly populated. And what better place than a library? It's got books! After all, as comic Chris Rock says, "Books are like Kryptonite to niggers." They hovered there, exuding their perceived superiority, lacking only T-shirts that proclaimed, "Don't get it twisted. I'm in here, but I'm *still* better than you!"

So by virtue of his affinity group, I prejudged that Mike was like many of the others—arrogant, condescending, and perhaps, bigoted. They sat in the library all day, watching *Fox News*, and brazenly espousing opinions like "Obama was not born in the United States." While supporting legislation that would permit a known non-native—Arnold Schwarzenegger—to run for the presidency.

They were the kind of guys who self-righteously labeled as *"idiots"* anyone who looked, acted, believed, or opined differently than them. They vehemently declared that chief among those *idiots* were any celebrities or athletes who dared to make public their opinions about politics or social issues...especially, those who conveyed viewpoints that were not of their own bent. For fun, I used to piss them off by asserting that I *agreed* with them, but only if that same standard applied to the likes of entertainers like Dennis Miller and Ted Nugent, or politicians like former senators Fred Thompson and the late Jack Kemp, and former congressmen Fred Grandy and Steve Largent. And of course, they declared that the election of a black man as president was proof-positive that there was no more racism in America!

But the first time I got a glimpse of who Mike really was, was in a current events circle in which we both participated. The circle convened weekly and was populated mostly by the crew above-described, with a much smaller smattering of mostly black, mostly younger, mostly Democrat guys, whose viewpoints were usually posited and championed by yours truly. Actually, it was billed as an adult continuing education (ACE) class, but no one taught anything. The class leader simply brought up topics for discussion and then laid back and let nature take its course.

The topic on which Mike spoke that day was "health care reform," or "Obamacare," as critics called it. I support(ed) it. Mike did not. Circle participants jousted a while. Then amid all of the vitriol and bombast, Mike—to my surprise, a lifelong Democrat—calmly relayed an analogy that, to me, was the most cogent, thoughtful and reasoned opposition view I'd heard in the two years of the plan's existence. And I told him as much. He certainly didn't change my opinion, but he changed my view about the opposition viewpoint.

Over the course of the next few days, we talked and talked. And we found, to neither of our surprise, that we had more in common than not. Although we had certainly come to those commonalities by way of decidedly different paths:

My family came to America from the Province of Palermo, on the island of Sicily. We lived in the small village of Ciaculi, a few miles east of the City of Palermo. It was a simple, happy life for the children, but for the adults, it was a constant struggle for survival and taking care of the family. I remember the village had one church, one bakery, one delicatessen, and several village fountains. One butcher, one shoemaker, and several people that dealt with contraband meat and wines. My grandmother helped with the contraband wine supply," Mike said with a wink and a smile.

Sicily had no middle class, to speak of. There was the rich, the poor, and the tradesmen. The expectation was that the male children in the family would all work. The ideal plan was to set up the oldest boy with a house so that he could get married and start his own family. Then the next boy and so on. Whether you were male or female, if you were not married, you lived with your parents.

There were four children in my family—three boys and one girl. I was the oldest. For reasons that I didn't discover until later, my father didn't wait to see if our future would be better. He decided to come to America. When he was asked why, his answer was always, 'So that my children could get an education.' As I grew older and learned about life in Sicily, I believe that there was another reason. An invisible force. A deadly virus. The Mafia.

Anyway, Dad worked the land. My family tenant-farmed tangerines, which means we did not own the land. We farmed it for the owner.

We moved to America in 1956. We arrived by boat. Coming here was an adventure. Not so much the ocean voyage, but I remember the changing scenery on the train ride from New York City to our eventual destination, Buffalo. The mountains. The lakes. But my first real impression of America was at night, after a slight snowfall. The city was wet and glistening from the reflection of the city lights. When I think of it, it reminds me of a phrase Ronald Reagan used—I can't recall the exact context of the quote, but he referred to a "shining city on a hill." That's how I now remember my first impression of Buffalo—a shining city on a hill.

Our biggest challenge was the language. I couldn't speak English. My parents couldn't either, but it was not as much of a problem for them because they had family and neighbors here that were Italian and spoke English. They could translate for them. Of course, by about the third year, me and my siblings could help too. It took about two and a half years for me to become fluent enough to not stumble with ideas and instructions so I could grasp the education that was being provided. I'd say we adjusted—we assimilated easily and well.

You know, kids can be hurtful, but they don't mean any harm—and we got through it okay, with no ill effects. In fact, in high school, I was active in student government. I was president of the Student Council when I was a senior; plus, I was in a lot of other activities in junior high too. But I think we all assimilated well, despite my parents' inability to speak English. My father used to say, 'The reason I have knives and forks is so I don't have to eat with my hands,' which was his way of saying that he didn't need to speak English, as long as he had us around.

At a diminutive 5'8" tall and weighing about a buck-fifty, soaking wet, Mike's appearance is anything but imposing. His face is lean but not gaunt; his complexion, olive. His hair—both that on his neatly coifed, widow's peaked head and his half-inch wide, tapered moustache—is mixed silver and black. He is stoic in demeanor, distinguished in carriage. His dialect, though definitely New York, didn't necessarily give a hint of his deep Italian heritage.

But the one attribute of Mike's that commands your attention is his eyes. They pierce right through you, to the core. His glare is neither grim nor menacing. It's—for lack of a better description—firm. Like a handshake, tacitly conveying the message that "I'm in control here!"

"So, Mike, talk about your current family. Your own family. Are you married now?"

Yes, I'm married to my second wife. We've been married for thirty years. I think she's gonna keep me! We have five kids altogether. I have a daughter from my first marriage, she has three children from a previous marriage, and we have one child together. I also have five grandkids, who are the apple of my eye. My first wife and me, we get along well with my first wife's family. We celebrate some holidays together.

I knew something of Mike's professional background...at least, his recent background. I knew that he was mayor of a small-to-medium-sized municipality in New York State. Everyone did. In fact, we all called him "Mr. Mayor." But I didn't know much of his other work history and background. So I asked, "Other than your time in public office, tell me of your background; your work history, your education."

Sure. I've had some odd job or another since I was fifteen. I earned a two-year degree in electronics from a community college. I've been a construction electrician for thirty-five years. Other than that, I had ten years in public service—six part-time, four full-time—in the higher echelons of local government.

"What were your aspirations as a kid?"

I had very simple goals, like my father before me. To get a job and raise a family, to serve government in some capacity, to give back to the country and the community that gave me so much. I was in the Army reserves for nine years. I've also done a lot of volunteer community service, for a number of community efforts, usually involving my skill as an electrician. But I had no lofty goals. My parents worked to raise a family. They struggled. To them, struggle was part of life. To them, they struggled so their children didn't have to struggle as hard—so they could

have a more comfortable life. And that's what I aspired to do for my family.

"How did you end up here, in prison? How long is your sentence?"

To the reader, I pause here, necessarily and almost apologetically—almost—to contemplate the balance between being responsible and being sensational. During our interview, Mike shared with me a great deal of details about his ordeal—direct quotes, which would, no doubt, be of interest to even the most objective reader.

However, I find myself with a bit of an ethical quandary. I have long held the opinion that too few journalists—even if, by including myself, I stretch the bounds of the definition—consider the ramifications to innocent parties, of the information they divulge. I feel that there is—or, certainly, should be—a line between what is responsible and irresponsible journalism. I believe that solely in the interest of sales and/or ratings, both print and broadcast media have abused the privilege afforded to them by a trusting—and sometimes gullible—public by being imprudent—hell, let's face it, sometimes blood-thirsty—in both their quest for and dissemination of information.

To me, it is no more responsible for a writer to report recklessly—and then simply deflect to the alleged perpetrator all of the responsibility for any fallout that ensues—than it is for a drive-by shooter to scatter-shoot into a crowd, sometimes cause irreparable harm to innocent bystanders, and then shrug-off blame to the intended target or, worse yet, which is sometimes true in both scenarios, simply not care who gets hurt—even when they don't "get their man." To me, there *is* such a thing as too much information.

With that in mind, I have chosen in this part of the interview to exercise what I hope the reader will appreciate as responsible judgment—by telling, rather than quoting, the story relayed in parts of Mike's interview. Thereby, I can omit certain details that might further impugn Mike's family, friends and associates—all of whom have endured embarrassment, ridicule, unfair scrutiny, and worse, since 2005—for something in which they had no hand. They were innocent bystanders in a scatter-shoot; a witch hunt. And that's what

Mike's case was—a witch hunt. As is true throughout the rest of the book, quotation marks (") indicate direct quotes from Mike.

Complicit in the effort to bring about Mike's demise were the media in his town—both broadcast and print—and the Federal Bureau of Investigation (FBI). In his defense, at no time during our interview did Mike ever allege that events in his case were politically motivated. The most he did was to admit the plausibility of it when I conjected it. Now, as then, he felt he had nothing to hide—politically or otherwise.

"In 2005, toward the end of the second year of my first term, the FBI had begun to investigate charges of public corruption. In the midst of a public corruption probe, a second term in office was impossible. So I decided not to run for reelection and I returned to private life and restarted my business as a self-employed electrical union contractor.

"Being retired from the union and collecting a pension, I was limited to working forty hours or less per month. The forty hours were restricted to hours that I would be 'working with tools.' All other work, including consulting and managing, were excluded. The informal understanding I had with the union was that for any month that I worked over forty hours, I would have to reimburse the pension fund for that month.

"I struggled to build up the business: the overhead, the cost of insurance, tools, maintaining a service van—it all required more money than the business was generating. Plus, the constant coverage of the alleged public corruption case by the local press and tabloid made it difficult to build a customer base. So I used my pension check to cover my operating expenses, as well as my living expenses.

"One month led to the next, until the union requested an audit. The audit began at my house, on my dining room table. I gave the auditor representing the union everything. I did not keep a 'second' set of books. By this time, I had had a conversation with the business manager and admitted to him that I had been working more than the forty hours per month allowed.

"Remember, the FBI had been trying to build a public corruption case all along. So upon learning that I had sometimes worked more than the forty hours, the FBI filed a complaint. They used my admission to the union's business manager as my admission that I had violated federal law. They used him as their star witness and my audit as the evidence...and charged me with embezzlement.

"In the plea deal, they dropped the public corruption charge, after what was now a five-year investigation. And now, I'm paying my debt to society."

The media and the FBI exhaustively "investigated" Mike in an attempt to either link his known offense to his public service or to find evidence of something—*anything*—incriminating that they could tie to his time in office. There was no such evidence. Because Mike neither said nor implied that the two entities colluded, I cannot responsibly make the assertion. Neither, as a person of some common sense, can I dismiss the notion.

Either way, both the FBI and the media harassed Mike's family, friends, and associates brutally and relentlessly. Both interviewed his neighbors, even questioning the veracity of their responses when they said that they could not say anything bad about him. They'd say, "You mean, you've known this guy for twenty years, and you can't think of a single thing he's ever done that you would consider as wrong?" Both the media and the FBI relentlessly and recklessly pursued finding anything incriminating—even if toward different ends.

The media wanted a salacious story of political corruption and scandal that it could use to sell papers or to boost ratings. Never mind that while he was in office, Mike kept near his desk a box filled with papers that he invited reporters to scour through. He said to them that the box contained "everything you ever need or want to know about my service." Not one media representative—in all the years of their so-called investigation—ever so much as opened the box.

Instead, they harassed him and his family for sound bites, virtually skulking in bushes and looking under rocks for the nothing that was there. Ultimately, the media chose to cobble together stories from either their own unverifiable conclusions or from court documents.

The feds, though, wanted to "get their man." In their futile attempts to prove their public corruption case, they brazenly told Mike's attorney that they were going to "get [him]" on something… either the public corruption case or the union embezzlement charge that eventually landed in their laps—either case carrying 2½–5 year sentences. It didn't matter to them. I reiterate that the union case—and the related investigation—not only had nothing to do with the public corruption case, but it was unearthed by virtue of *nothing* that and FBI actively did or initiated. All they did was become aware of it. And becoming aware of it, they seized upon the opportunity to bring charges.

And after a five-year investigation, Mike pleaded guilty to a one count falsifying charge. A devoted husband, father, and granddad. A sixty-five-year-old patriot, who proudly proclaims that this—the USA—is the greatest country in the world. A public servant. A kind, conscientious, and yes, *honest* man, Mike was made to serve thirteen months and a day, convicted of embezzling $51,000 of from his own pension funds, monies that *he* contributed—it was his own money. He was forced to accept a plea agreement. And the amount of pilferage the FBI reported to the media was $120,000, not the actual $51,000.

Back to script now: "Mike, who do you miss the most, now that you're in here?"

I think, generally, I miss my family. I miss my wife. I miss the activities we used to do with my grandkids. I have five. And I miss my kids—as I said, I have five altogether. Also, as you know, I turned sixty-five a few days ago. My daughter always has a special celebration of my birthday every five years. Needless to say, I missed that this time around."

"Is prison different from what you expected?"

It's not at all what I expected. In our case, there are no walls or fences. Three hundred twenty people, with usually less than four cops. But if their mission statement is to rehabilitate and to complete restitution to the wronged party, that's not accomplished. I see it more as a warehouse for people, to get them out

of circulation, so the government can say that they've done their job.

For example, I expected to improve my word processing skills. There are no programs to make that happen. They don't even have a computer that prisoners can use. I was even thinking about learning a musical instrument—I was shooting for the sax.

When I wanted to teach a class, I learned that I had no opportunity to do research, and I learned that we had limited resources. Unless information is in your head or in your pocket, you can't use it. For many of us, it would be more beneficial to society if we could be out there working, fulfilling our restitutions. We represent no security risk. That's why we're in a camp in the first place. Because we pose no risk to society.

So since we pose no risk to society and since we're going to be back in society sooner than later, why aren't we being prepared to go back into society? Mike's brow furrowed, and his face contorted to a decidedly stern, pinched eyebrow glare, as he continued, **They do not offer any courses that you'd get accreditation for. Not so much for me, but look at all these young men here, who will have spent an enormous amount of time doing nothing. Nothing to where the real world would hire them.**

"What kinds of programs and classes do you think the BoP should offer?"

Some of these guys are here three years, five years. Even more. They could learn to be plumbers, carpenters, electricians so they could become productive members of society. Leaning in, and running his fingers through his neatly trimmed salt-and-pepper mane, he says, **Anybody that's here, if they have the ability to get a GED** [as every non high school grad is required to do, as a condition of his release], **I'm convinced they have the ability to learn word processing or public speaking skills or definitely a trade…like HVAC, for instance. If they could have these types of opportunities at camps, inmates would be able to connect to somebody in the community. They could work at schools or businesses or for government entities like DPW [Departments of Public Works] or**

Parks [and Recreation], or any other activities you'd be expected to be familiar with when you go back home.

Mike paused thoughtfully for a moment and then offered, **One important thing, Vic. Many of us were rehabilitated the day we walked into the courthouse. For the government to impose a burden that is strictly punishment and strictly economic is a big waste of taxpayer dollars. It's a loss for inmates and a loss for society. The cost of our imprisonment—housing us, feeding us, clothing us—is a burden the taxpayers shouldn't have to subsidize, also, the cost of a frivolous investigation. The FBI dogged me for five years, harassed my family. The US attorney forced me into a plea agreement, with the threat of two trials, when my offense was $51,000. I mean, look at my restitution. It's $51,000!**

Society also loses because I could be working and paying taxes, contributing to the economy. All that time and all that waste. For me to plead guilty to *exactly* what I had agreed to with the union in the first place! Noticeably agitated by the recollection, Mike pondered aloud, **I admitted my guilt. I admitted my mistake. Why would they try to destroy me? Why try to define my whole life by this one incident?**

For what? Who got helped?

"What are your plans for when you're released? What's next?"

Well, first and foremost, I'm going to make up for the lost time with my family. I'll work, of course, and probably resume my volunteer work as well.

"Is your electrical business still running?"

No, I'll have to restart it.

"Last question, same as I've asked everyone else…although I have a sense that I could probably answer it for you. If you could snap your fingers and be any place, doing absolutely anything right now, where would you be?"

Home, with my wife…and my grandkids. That's it.

"Thanks, NoNo." I wanna be like Mike.

Postlogue

Mike was released from FPC Cumberland in December 2011 and returned to his home in upstate NY. His plan was to resume his electrical contracting business. He hosts a call-in talk radio program that broadcasts daily in his town's listening area.

The Conclusion

Here's the bottom line. There is but one way that the deliberate mal-feasance that is perpetrated at the FPC Cumberland and other insti-tutions can persist. That is, through the lack of real accountability. They do what they do because nobody's really watching—*and they have no honor.*

Institutions are held to standards of accreditation by groups like the American Correctional Association (ACA)[4]. According to the mission statement posted at its website, the ACA "provides a professional organization for all individuals and groups, both public and private, that share a common goal of improving the justice sys-tem." Toward that mission, the ACA regularly monitors institutions (usually semiannually) in every aspect of their operations, including administration, food service, health services, educational and cor-rectional programming, among others. The ACA monitors for the purpose of ensuring the practicality of and compliance with existing standards, as well as developing and disseminating new standards.

In the preamble of its Declaration of Principles, the ACA asserts,

> The treatment of criminals by society is for the protection of society. But since such treatment is directed to the criminal rather than the crime, its great object[ive] should be [the criminal's]... regeneration.

---

[4] Founded in 1870 as the National Prison Association, ACA is the oldest associa-tion developed specifically for practitioners in the correctional profession. www.aca.org

The preamble continues:

> We believe that [the] principles of HUMANITY,
> JUSTICE, PROTECTION, OPPORTUNITY,
> KNOWLEDGE, COMPETENCE and
> ACCOUNTABILITY are essential to the foun-
> dation of sound corrections policy and effective
> public protection.

The ACA Declaration of Principles goes on to list no fewer than seventeen principles, which, if genuinely adhered to, would bring about the qualitative improvements to the corrections experience to which I have alluded. Their principles include, among others, that

- corrections is responsible for providing programs and constructive activities that promote positive change for responsible citizenship;
- corrections must demonstrate integrity, respect, dignity,
  fairness, and pursue a balanced program of humaneness,
  restoration, rehabilitation; and
- the dignity of individuals, the rights of all people and the
  potential for human growth and development must be
  respected.

While it is not my intention to in any way impugn the ACA, the occasions when they made monitoring visits to the FPC Cumberland were little more than dog and pony shows. The administration would order inmates to clean up the compound, inside and out, and either relegate us to or banish us from certain areas, while they conducted "feel-good" guided tours orchestrated to perpetrate the ruse of compliance. Supplies that had been out of stock mysteriously appeared. Meals were prepared to the letter of the applicable menu. I recall during a health services review, being summoned by the FPC Cumberland staff and examined for an array of maladies for which I had for months been denied attention. When the outside reviewer just happened to interview *me* later the same day, the camp's health services staff had added a new prescription to my list of medications—one that had previously been denied me and that, thus, I had not begun taking.

These are *my* stories and observations. I don't present them for the purpose of whining or complaining, "Oh, woe is me." On the contrary, the message is, "Woe is *you*, America!" I present my experiences as examples of the opportunities that case managers and counselors in the federal prison system have to impact prisoner outcomes. My experiences are but a window through which the reader may ascertain a sense of the relevance and utter importance of rehabilitation, especially the role of effective case management.

The potential impact on me of my case manager's dereliction was only mitigated by my own efforts and my own preparation to reconstruct my life circumstances upon release. I have knowledge, skills, experience, abilities, and a support system that made my successful reentry more likely, notwithstanding the lack of meaningful case management.

However, far too many—perhaps, most—of the inmates under my case manager's stewardship are men who lack the formal education, skills, work experience, or support systems to successfully navigate the myriad challenges to successful reentry that await them upon release. Coincidingly, I can reasonably conjecture that the impact on their lives of her dereliction is potentially devastating; it increases exponentially the likelihood that their reentry will be difficult at best—or at worse, that they will recidivate.

It is my hope that this book enlightens readers, at least to the point of curiosity. I hope that that curiosity triggers the American public's insistence upon an independent investigation, preferably an investigation in which inmates' feedback is obtained—and for which feedback inmates are insulated from reprisal. Because I know the incompetence, the apathy, the corruption, the dereliction of duty, and the shameful waste of human and fiscal resources that an independent investigation will uncover. And when the American public becomes uniformly aware of the extent to which it is being duped by a federal prison system that is little more than a cash industry, I hope they turn their ire on their representatives in Congress, who, despite the overwhelming evidence many of them already have, do nothing to fix the dysfunction.

Please don't get me wrong. I am in no way suggesting that inmates are saints, least of all, me. I committed the offense to which I pleaded guilty. Notwithstanding the artificially inflated amount of the misappropriation or the prosecutorial bullying to which I was subjected, what I did—which is to say, the action that my offense entailed—by my own description, was egregious and it warranted punishment. I did it! Point blank. Even if the amount of money I took had only been one dollar, my transgression warranted punishment.

But it also warranted meaningful rehabilitation and reentry services. It warranted at least an attempt to mitigate the gambling addiction to which my misdeed was concomitant—and as was ordered by the judge in my case. And it warranted my receiving services that gave me the best shot at making a productive reentry to society.

Because of the judge's order, I spent thirteen months at the FPC Cumberland as punishment. *Despite* the judge's order, I spent *not one second* of those thirteen months receiving anything akin to meaningful rehabilitation, treatment, or reentry services.

And on top of everything, my case manager *did not* do to enable my successful reentry. The one thing she *did* do relative to my reentry was to deprive me of the 10 percent early release time to which I was statutorily entitled, time that is allotted *specifically for the purpose* of facilitating reentry. In other words, on the one hand, she did nothing to aid my reentry, and on the other hand, she delayed by forty-five days my ability to do so on my own. She poured salt into an open wound.

The FPC Cumberland touts the existence of a Career Resource Center. The center's mission statement reads as follows:

> The Career Resource Center was created to assist
> inmates as they approach release, in choosing a

career path, seeking and obtaining employment
and locating schools and training programs...

The mission statement also asserts that it provides services that assists [inmates] in other areas pertinent to their successful reintegration into society, including:

- Locating housing
- Obtaining health and auto insurance
- Understanding credit and the credit reporting system
- Banking and money management

The statement concludes by saying that a "career resource professional" is available to provide individual assistance. The career resource professional at FPC Cumberland was an inmate. His "resources" consisted of nothing more than a small assortment of brochures and pamphlets on the topics mentioned in the mission statement and who had no connections to any resource on the outside.

In my thirteen months on her active case load, my case manager made no effort to facilitate on my behalf—or even to refer—any of the services allegedly available in the Career Resource Center. Moreover, she made no effort to facilitate or refer any of the following services or accommodations; any and all of which were pertinent to my successful rehabilitation and reentry:

- addiction counseling
- twelve-step programming
- mental health counseling
- job readiness
- job search
- housing assistance
- financial counseling
- financial assistance
- family counseling
- obtaining my institutional health records
- connection to social services

- life skills training
- pre-release counseling
- post-release instructions

Whether due to incompetence or maliciousness, my case manager's actions are tantamount to neglect. While such neglect cannot persist in a vacuum—which is to say, it cannot persist without the knowledge and, perhaps, complicity of the entire administration—such malfeasance by a case manager in the prison system is potentially the most harmful.

Therefore, the extent to which my case manager's dereliction is exemplary of case management throughout the federal prison system should be a cause for concern...and action. A case manager is supposed to be an inmate's first tier of support and assistance. Case managers are charged with developing individualized plans to facilitate each inmate's educational, emotional, physical, and psychological improvement, as well as his transition back to society. Without that support and assistance, neither the inmate nor society has a caring advocate. Without a caring advocate (to under-gird and help guide his own efforts) the inmate has little chance of being rehabilitated, nor society of welcoming a rehabilitated citizen back into its midst upon his release.

Finally, I'm saying this:

If, on the *punishment* side of the corrections equation, there was no such thing as "good time" or early release and...

If an inmate's entire sentence entailed enduring conditions like those I experienced on my hellish bus ride to and from Harrisburg or during my month in "the Hole" and...

If inmates were assigned to hard labor and...

If the buffoonish louts that run the place beat me and called me "nigger" (to my face) and...

If they fed me gruel and slop...

If the system heaped upon inmates any form or amount of punishment they could conceive of...

I would be fine with it! *If!*

I would be fine with any form or amount of punishment meted out in the corrections equation:

If, on the *rehabilitation* side, institutions did their due diligence...

If they paid the issue of rehabilitation more than mere lip service.

That due diligence begins with delivering *meaningful* case management that incorporates the best practices and paradigms, such as have been referenced herein.

I know one thing. The proof is in the proverbial pudding. The pudding is the outcomes. The outcomes, in this instance, are the number of lives reconstructed, and reconstructed lives equates to decreased recidivism.

The consequences of not addressing the fixable failures of the federal corrections system are entirely too adverse to everyone's best interest to simply let languish. The most important step in addressing those fixable failures is to address the fixable failures of the case management component. According to everything I gleaned from my research, observations, and experiences, the American public, the inmates, their families, and their communities are all best served by fixing the flagrant incompetence and lack of engagement that sometimes masquerades as case management. As I said before, to the extent that my case manager's inept, indifferent attitude and methods reflect the federal prison system's so-called commitment to rehabilitating the men and women in its care, custody, and control, they cannot be condoned. In the effort to reform prisons and reduce recidivism, that's the best place to start. I'm just saying...

Author's Postlogue

I was released from FPC Cumberland in February 2012. Without delay, I began implementing the life action plan that I had formulated for myself during my thirteen month hiatus. That life plan included finding gainful employment, getting formal treatment for my gambling addiction, teaching freelance voice and songwriting classes, recording a follow-up CD, facilitating community workshops, making and marketing custom handmade quilted products; trying to get my songs published, obtaining more singing engagements (including developing and marketing a Luther Vandross tribute show), applying for an Open Society Institute (OSI) fellowship; and of course finishing the manuscript for this book.

Despite having ample formal education and a vast array of relatable work experience, finding a job was the one life plan item I was completely unable to fulfill. While I would be hard-pressed to prove it conclusively, my firm suspicion is that my status as a convicted felon was a strong deterrent to my obtaining employment.

In 2014, I reapplied for the OSI Baltimore Community Fellowship, having won but declined the award in 2010. In the renewed application, I proposed to develop and launch a specific prison reform initiative that targeted high school and college students. I was invited by OSI to submit a full proposal, but ultimately was not selected to receive the fellowship.

Nonetheless, owing to a patient and supportive wife and family, I have been fortunate to cobble together a living. I stay busy as a lead singer for two local jazz bands, as well as, for a Motown tribute group that performs throughout the Delaware-Maryland-Virginia region. Plus, I did write and coproduce a stage show in tribute to the life and music of R&B great Luther Vandross. The show debuted in 2016 in Baltimore, and has subsequently been performed twice before sell out audiences in Louisville (Kentucky). The show, entitled "A Song for You", is currently being marketed for presentations in cities throughout America. For updates the reader may visit BigVix.com/a-song-for-you. Stay tuned.

And now, I'm able to add publishing this book to my list of fulfilled objectives.

I owe an unrepayable debt of gratitude to my compatriots at FPC Cumberland, who permitted me to interview them for this book. Each man consented to being interviewed, knowing the reprisal that could befall them. Without their input my challenge of being perceived as something other than "just another whining ass convict" would be precipitously more difficult.

I'm also privileged to count former *Baltimore Sun* journalist, Lionel Foster (who interviewed me for this book) and Attorney Brandon Alexander (who pinned the book's prologue) among my truest friends. I met them both in December 1994, when they were fourteen-and-twelve-years-old, respectively, enrolled in the inaugural class of my performing arts-based violence prevention initiative called The PEACE Project.

With true journalistic cynicism, Lionel pushed back with such force against many of my postulations that he made me question the saliency of my own case. Brandon's unscripted and unedited words powerfully shed light on a truth that has been muted for far too long.

Each person, in his own way, confirmed the enormity of the challenge. But, at the same time, my interaction(s) with each man only steeled my resolve. So, to all who contributed to this book, thank you.

But, it's not just about me...or them, for that matter. Our country is bleeding young lives into a federal prison system, that is, for all intents and purposes, forsaking its responsibility to do anything more than warehouse them—while they (the prisons) take the money and run.

For most of my adult life, I have in one way or another taken an active role in efforts to improve the lives of the disaffected inner-city youths, single parents, uninsured men, the medically under-served, the homeless. Now, there are two more groups of disregarded Americans whom I hope to affect by writing this book—the incarcerated young able-bodied nimble-minded men and women for whom virtually no systemic effort at redemption is being made, and the American public that thinks every—hell, any—effort is being made toward that end.

I know of which I speak because I am both. I am a taxpayer, who for years was imbued of the misconception that the federal prison system provides inmates with at least a shot at meaningful rehabilitation. In that regard, I am you.

I am also a convicted felon, who sat wasting away for thirteen months, without benefit of a single institutional effort to facilitate my successful reintegration to society, and who witnessed firsthand the shameful, methodical, apathetic, and intentional disservice that practically relegates thousands of redeemable lives into the revolving door that is the federal prison system. And, as my young friend, Brandon admonishes in his prologue, "…there, but for the grace of God,"…go you.

—Vic Frierson

About the Author

Born in Louisville, Kentucky, Vic Frierson has amassed extensive and diverse experience in the fields of youth, family, and community service. He was principally responsible for the startup, management and administration of two successful community programs in Baltimore, Maryland: one, a unique coalition between a local hospital, a neighborhood health center and impassioned residents of a medically underserved community that resulted in the establishment of a community-based, community-managed health center for *under-* and *un*insured men; the other, an innovative performing arts-based program that targeted teens at high risk from violence and other risky behavior.

As a community organizer and advocate, Vic has a demonstrated track record of improving conditions for Baltimore's chronically underserved populations, including out-of-school and otherwise high-risk youths, un- or underinsured men, families of Head Start children, and homeless men. In 1996, he helped research and co-author *Prevention Tools: Building Strong Communities*, a book of strategies published by a quasi-government organization called the Baltimore City Partnership for Drug-Free Neighborhoods to aid communities in their efforts to prevent or reduce the impact of substance abuse.

In 2010, Vic was selected to receive the coveted Open Society Institute Baltimore Community Fellowship. Additionally, he completed the Greater Baltimore Committee's influential program called the Leadership, as well as was in the inaugural graduating class of the Harry and Jeanette Weinberg Foundation Fellows Program in 2006 and 2003, respectively...all for his outstanding civic accomplishments.

On January 3, 2011, as his punishment for having pleaded guilty to one count of wire fraud, Vic surrendered into the custody of the Federal Prison Camp in Cumberland, MD. Thus began the thirteen-month rude awakening, of which his book *In the Company of a Known Felon* is the result.

CPSIA information can be obtained
at www.ICGtesting.com
Printed in the USA
BVHW080754110220
572026BV00004B/319